The Graphics of COMMUNICATION

Exploring the Graphic Arts and Design

Ivan Bradley

ISBN 13-978-0-578-95745-6

The Graphics of Communication: Exploring the Graphic Arts and Design

This book is the result of nearly 20 years in the graphic arts field and 30 years of teaching the craft and art of creating design and layouts. The focus of this book is to provide a comprehensive overview of the technical and artistic skills and knowledge one uses in the profession to produce communication through whatever media or form it may take. I thank my wife Loretta for her continuing support, my good friend John for encouraging me to enter into teaching, and the special educators I've had the fortune to work with.

Table of Contents

History of Graphic Communications 1

In the Beginning 3
Materials and Methods 10
Into Mass Production 13
Industrialized Printing 16
Mass Communication 20

Printing Methods 25

What the Ancients Invented 27
To Print a Play 30
A Method to Make Currency 34
More Than Just a T-Shirt 39
Is That all There is? 41

Color 45

Color My World 46
Color Theory 49
Color Psychology 53
Color Description 58
Digital Color 65
Color Systems 67

Typography 71

Representational to Symbols to Characters 72
Font to Foundry to Photoshop 82
The Importance of Typography 86
The Anatomy of Type 88
Measuring Type 91
Type Categories 95
Typesetting Formats 100
Type Adjustments 103

Communication 105

Communication Model 106
Perception 109
Interferences 111

Design Process 123

Determining the Design Problem 124
Coming up with a Design 128
Principles/Elements of Design 135
Creating Layouts 142
Publication Design 153
Logo Design 166

Paper 173

The Importance of Paper 174
Papermaking 175
Specifying Paper 181

Finishing and Binding 191

Finishing 192
Binding 198

What's Next? 201

A Change in the Paradigm 202
Variable Data Printing 205
Functional Printing 207
Digital Publishing 209

Conclusion 213

Glossary 215

CHAPTER 1

History of Graphic Communications

Of all of our inventions for mass communications, pictures still speak the most universally understood language.
— *Walt Disney*

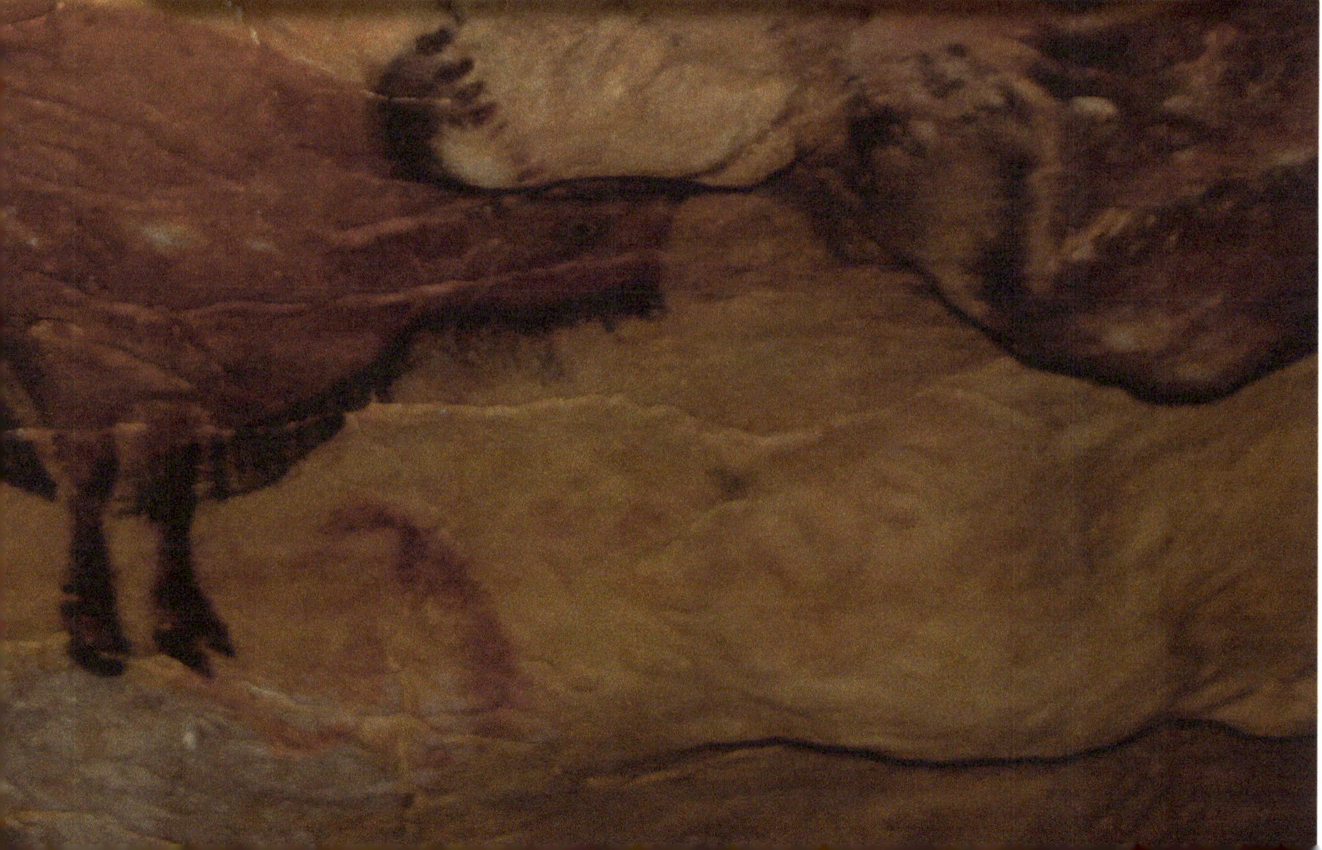

Communication has never been a static ability. From the day our species first learned to speak, communication between humans has provided the basic social glue of our existence, responsible for creating and maintaining cultural coherence. Ever since then, the message exchange process has never ceased to evolve and change: content creators have always had to adapt to existing channels, tools, styles, registers, or ritual processes that humankind has invented along the way. Throughout this evolution, we can identify critical moments when major changes have shifted the entire communications paradigm.

- Speaking: survival possibilities and sociocultural development
- Writing: expansion and cultural continuity
- Mass printing and universal reading skills: exponential growth of authors' influence
- The New Ubiquity: Connected computers and changed roles for authors and audiences.

— Changing Paradigms in Technology and Communication, Ray Gallon and Neus Lorenzo

In the Beginning

Section 1

30,000 BC – 1000 AD

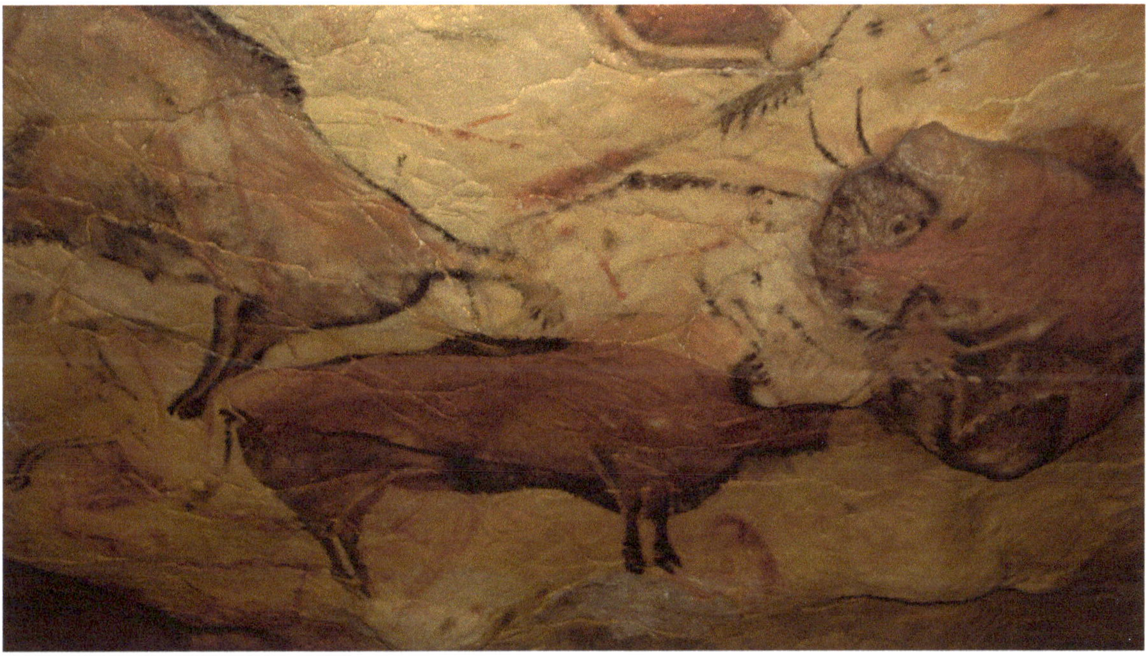

Early humans created cave art, from the Smithsonian National Museum of Natural History David H. Koch Hall of Human Origins, by Karen Carr.

Graphic Communications has a very storied history that has dramatically influenced all of us profoundly in the way we think, act, and communicate.

The graphic arts (graphic communication) is the art of communicating through visual images and has it's early beginning some 30,000 years ago. Early humans, particularly in Europe, began drawing on walls of caves (pictographs) and carving on stone (petroglyphs). The caves of Lascaux, France, and Alta Mira, Spain, have excellent examples of cave wall paintings created by early humans and are the earliest known attempt at a visual record of their life and communication. These drawings were created from the use of minerals and charcoal utilizing brushes, hands, and an "airbrush" made from hollowed

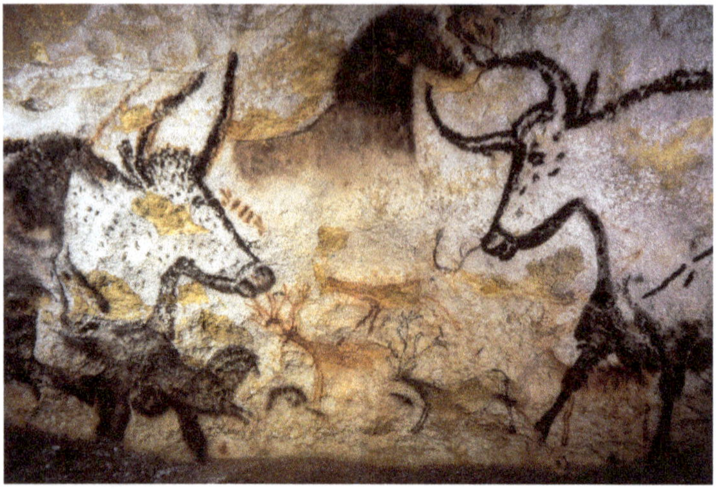

The Great Hall of the Bulls. © *CNP Ministry of Culture and Communication, France.*

reeds in which the painter would spray color from their mouth. They are beautiful and anatomically accurate. Scientists that have studied these and other cave paintings suggest that they may have been made for religious purposes, demonstrate hunting techniques, a record of events, or perhaps simply graffiti. Whatever the purpose, any or all of these certainly are a means of visual human communication. *http://www.culture.gouv.fr/culture/arcnat/lascaux/en/*

Writing Ink

Man began to develop other means of visual communication including first "writing" using symbols that eventually developed into formal style writing, as we know it today. A more in-depth study of writing and the development of type will be studied in *Chapter 4 - Typography* later in this book. To facilitate this means of writing, implements like a reed pen, and writing material such as parchment came into use. By 400 A.D. a stable form of

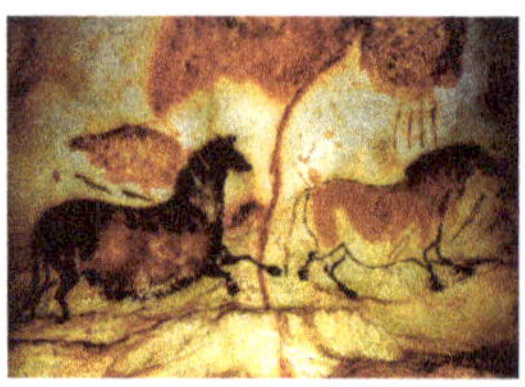

Earliest known visual record, cave wall paintings of horses, Lascaux, France, 30,000 BC.

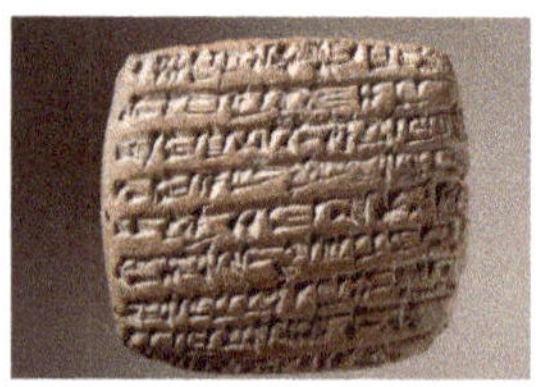

Cuneiform, "wedge-shaped writing" developed by the Sumerians, 3500 BC.

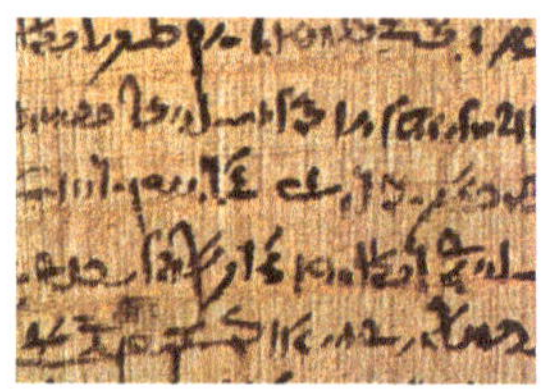

Papyrus, a writing material with Demotic Egyptian script 2600 BC, with writing using an early writing ink.

ink was made from a composite of Iron "salts," such as ferrous sulfate, was mixed with tannin from gall nuts (they grow on Oak trees) and a thickener. Its color when first applied to paper was a bluish-black, rapidly turning to the familiar dull brown color commonly seen in old documents. The basic formula would remain in use for centuries.

Papyrus is a tall, aquatic plant, Cyperus papyrus, of the sedge family, native to the Nile valley.

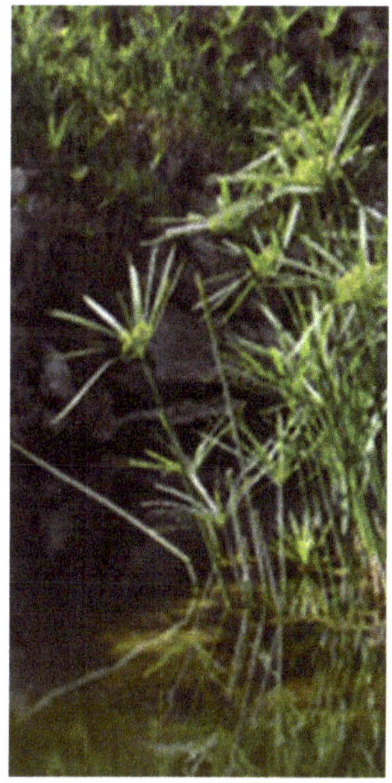

Papyrus

Long before paper was invented, other materials (also known as substrates) were used for writing. One of these was the use of papyrus, a tall reed that grew in the deltas of the Nile River in Egypt. The Egyptians made a writing material produced by weaving together strands of the pith of the papyrus plant.

The outer rind is first removed, and the sticky fibrous inner pith is cut lengthwise into thin strips. The strips are soaked in water and then placed side by side on a hard surface with their edges slightly overlapping. Then another layer of strips is laid on top at a right angle. While still moist, the two layers are hammered together, mashing the layers into a single sheet. The sheet is then dried under pressure. After drying, the sheet is polished with a rounded object like a stone, seashell or round hardwood.

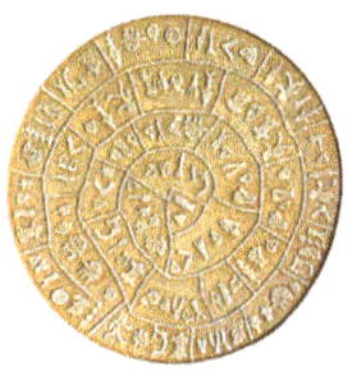

Pre-formed hieroglyphic "seals" were pressed into soft clay tablets. The Phaistos Disc dates from the Minoan Bronze Age, found on the island of Crete. 1600 BC

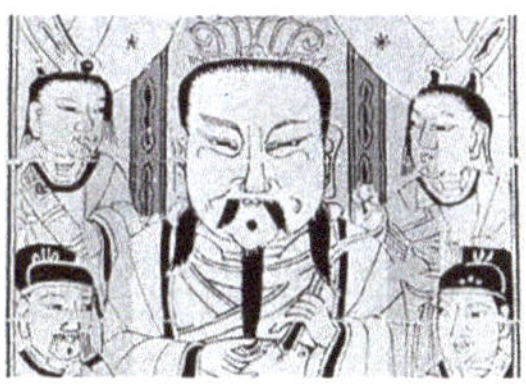

Paper as we know it today, was first made in China in 105 AD, by Ts'ai Lun (Cai Lun).

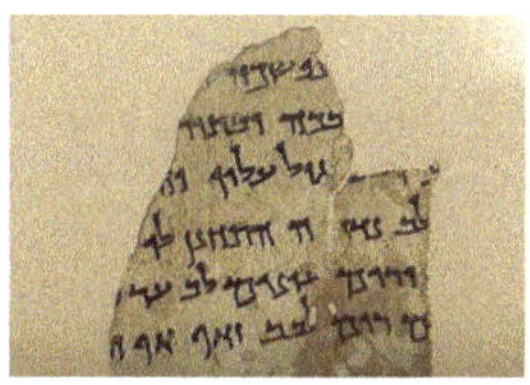

Parchment is made from animal skin, scraped thin, stretched and dried to be an early form of writing material. This image is of a fragment of the Dead Seas scroll.

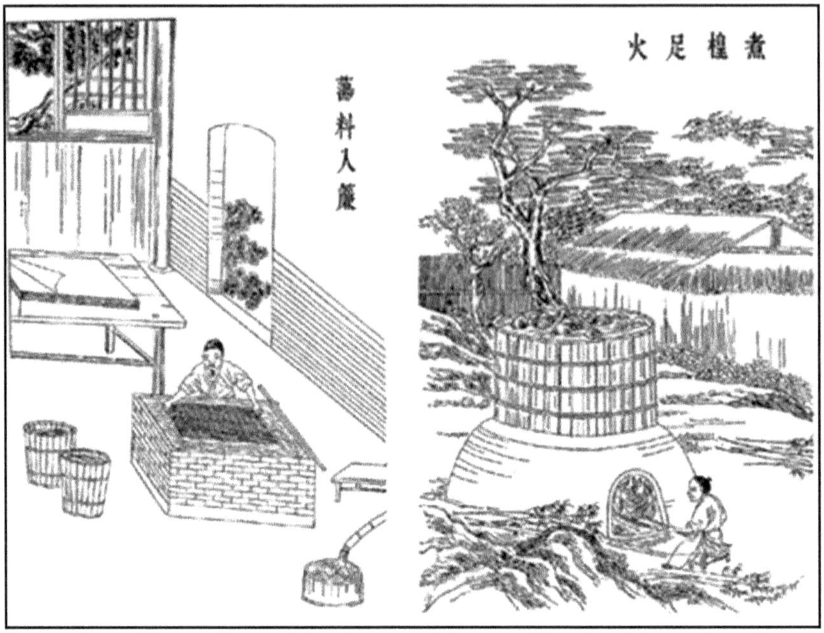

The illustration on the left shows a worker dipping a screen into water with pulp in which a portion is lifted out and dried. At right, the pulp, made from various materials, is "cooked" before it is used to form paper.

Parchment

Parchment was another substrate used by early cultures for writing. Parchment is a thin material made from calfskin, sheepskin, or goatskin. Its most common use is as the pages of a book, codex, or manuscript. It is distinct from leather in that parchment is not tanned, but rather stretched, scraped, and dried under tension, creating a stiff white, yellowish or translucent animal skin. The finer qualities of parchment are called vellum.

Paper

Paper and the way it is made was invented by Ts'ai Lun, a member of the court of the Han Dynasty in China. He used bark of trees, remnants of hemp, rags of cloth, and fishing nets to make paper. The materials were beaten into a pulp and mixed with water. It was then spread on a woven screen that allowed the water to drain and the "pulp" to dry and become paper. Up until this time in Asia, writings and inscriptions were generally made on tablets of bamboo or on pieces of silk called "chih" which is an early Chinese word for paper. The word is composed of the logograms for silk or fabric.

Relief Printing?

Probably the earliest form of "printing" was relief printing in which the image is above the non-image area. An example of this comes from a clay disc called the Phaistos Disc found on the isle of Crete in the Mediterranean. The disc dates from the middle to late Minoan Bronze Age. The Minoan culture flourished from approximately 2700 to1450 BC. It has pre-formed hieroglyphic "seals" probably made from pottery stamps that were pressed into soft clay.

Woodblock

A more commonly recognized form of relief printing, **woodblock printing**, eventually came into being as a method of printing on cloth. The earliest surviving examples from China date to before 220 AD, and from Egypt to the 4th century. Later, in Europe during the 1400s, woodblock printing was also used to print playing cards. In Japan, between the 17th and the 20th centuries, woodblock printing produced a genre of Art known as Ukiyo-e— "pictures of the floating world."

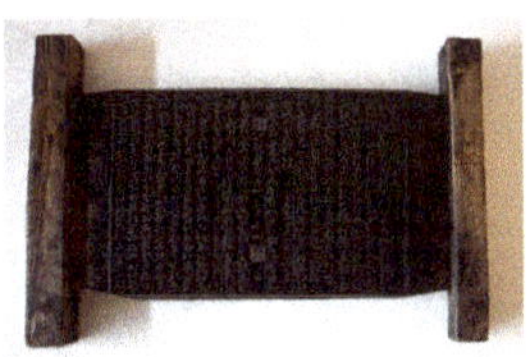

A form of "relief" printing, the non-image area is carved away from the image area. This raised image is inked and used to print from, first on textiles, then later paper.

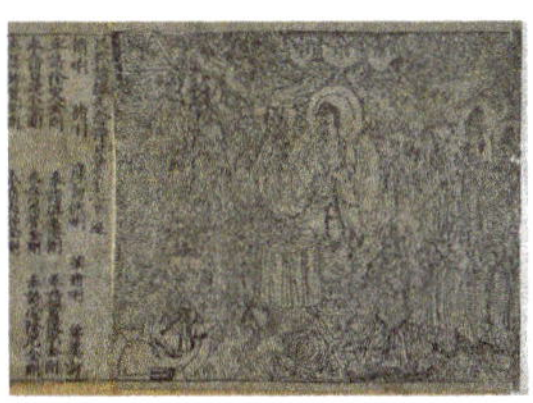

The Diamond Sutra is one of the most important texts in the Buddhist faith, and is the oldest surviving dated printed book in the world. 868 AD

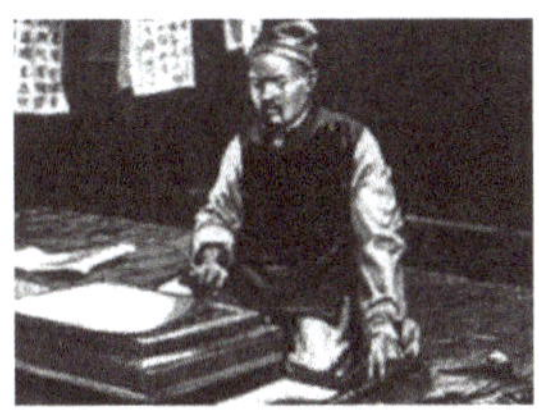

The screen printing method was developed in China in 960 AD. The method has been used since then not only to produce products like posters and flags, but as an Art medium.

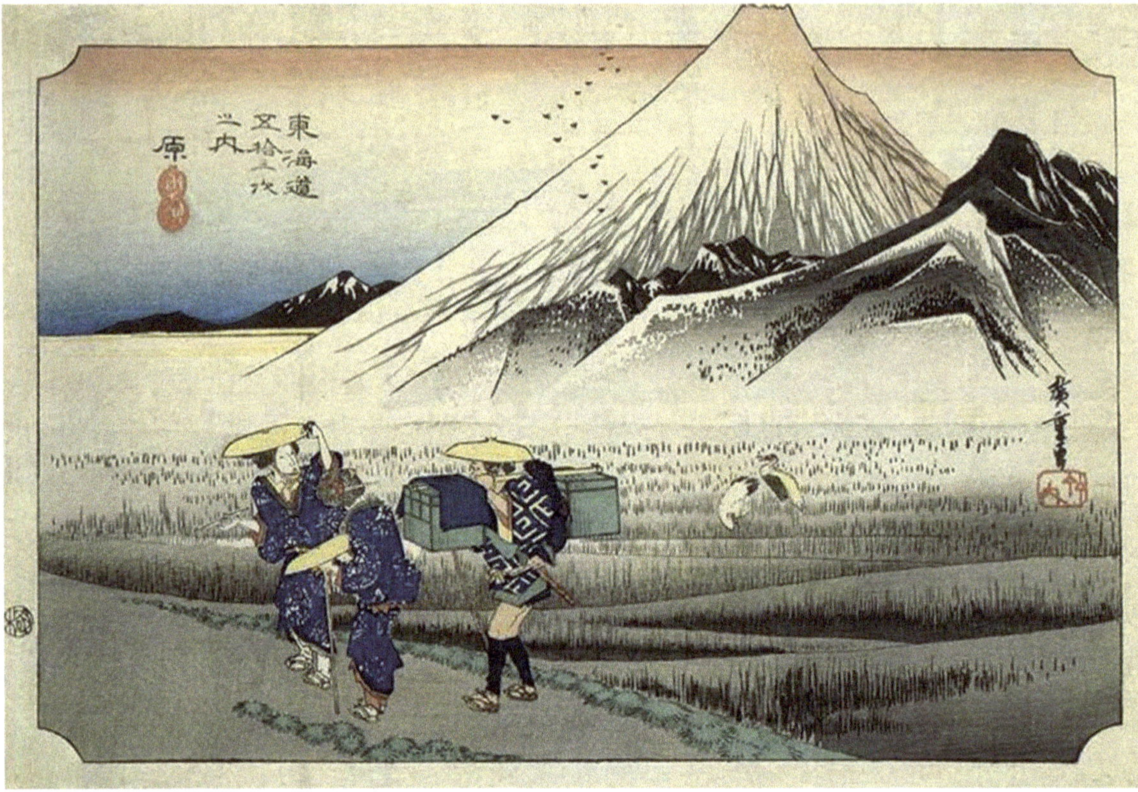

Hara on the Tokaido, ukiyo-e print by Hiroshige. (1797-1858)

Printed Book

In 868 AD, the world's earliest complete survival of a dated book was printed. The Diamond Sutra, was hidden for centuries in a sealed up cave in northwest China before its discovery.

Sutra, literally means a rope or thread that holds things together, and more metaphorically refers to a line, rule, or formula. The book deals with the nature of perception, and describes the religious teaching or sermon, and is most often used to define the teachings of the Buddha.

Seven strips of yellow-stained paper were printed from carved wooden blocks and pasted together to form a scroll that is over 16 feet long. Though written in Chinese, the text is one of the most important sacred works of the Buddhist faith. The word "sutra" is from Sanskrit, the ancient and sacred language of India.

Screen Printing

The **screen printing** method has its origins in stenciling about 960 AD during the Shang dynasty in China. It was a process where stencils were commonly used on cotton and silk for clothing and decorative purposes. However, the silk screening process we know and used today is generally credited to English and American artists in the early-1900s. Samuel Simon of Manchester, England is said to have taken out the first patents related to the modern process of screen printing in 1907. Using sheets of silk and cotton stretched over wooden frames, Simon and William Morris placed single-colored, hand-painted stencils on top of the material to create a design. In 1914, John Pilsworth of the United States took out a patent for multi-colored screen printing.

Commercial screen printing became very popular around the time of World War I and was most commonly used for printing flags, advertising banners and even fine Art. It has continued to be popular for Fine Art as well as for printing on various materials such as fabric, which is known as decorating.

A very recognizable example of 1960s Pop Art style Fine Art screen printing. Andy Warhol, Marilyn, screen print in colors on wove paper, 1967.

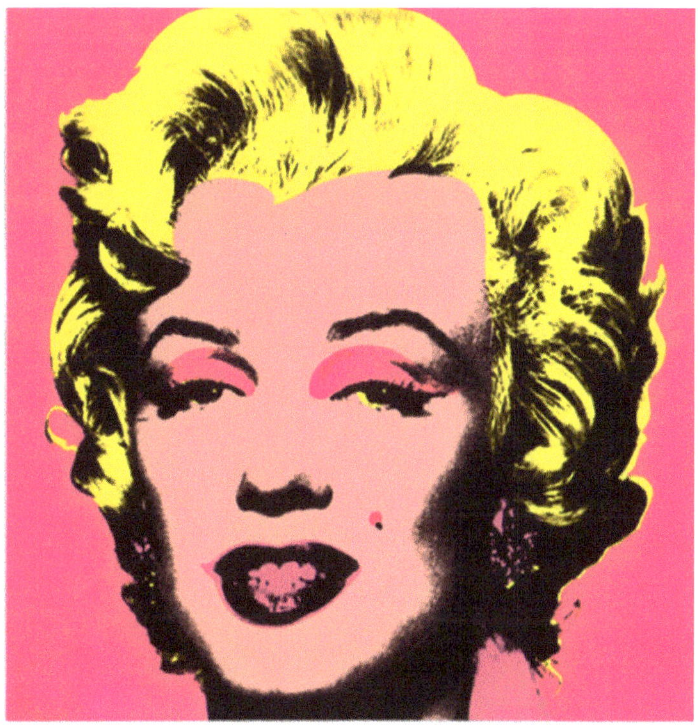

Materials and Methods

Section 2

1000 AD – 1500 AD

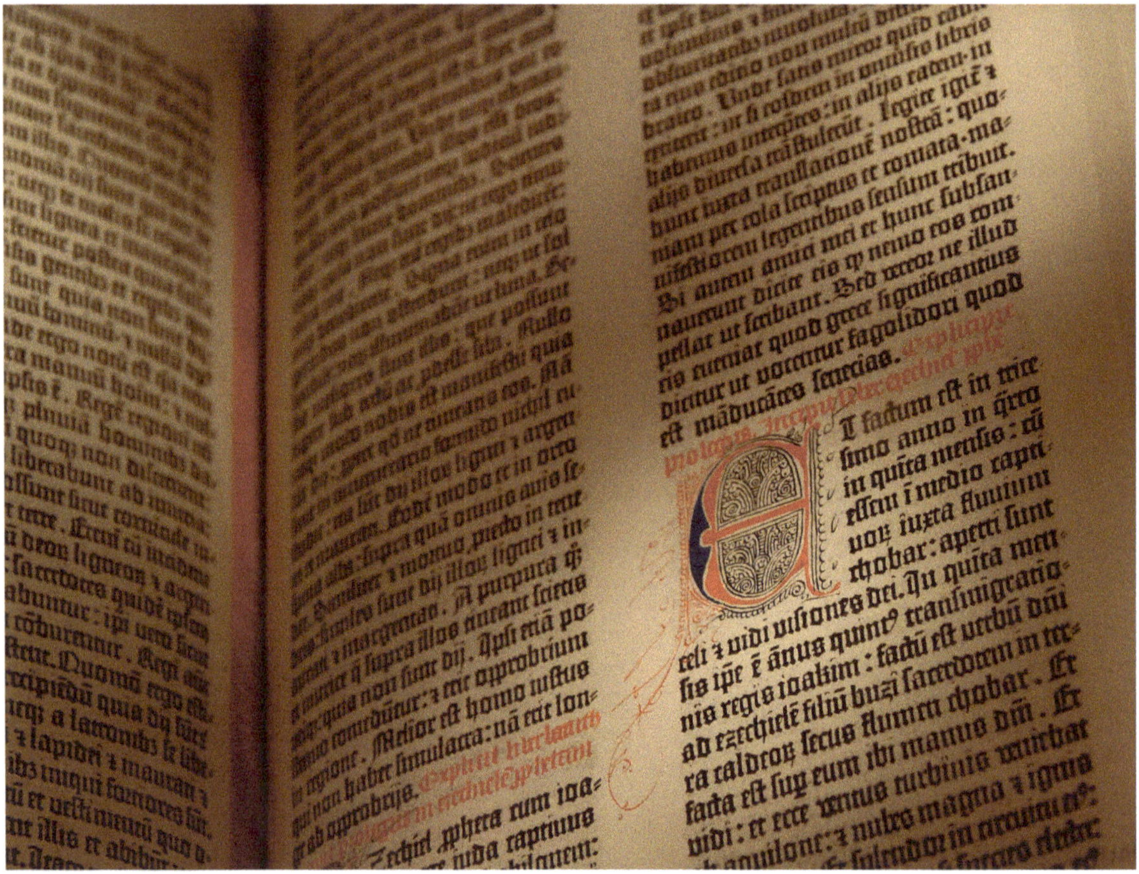

A rare copy of the few remaining Gutenberg Bibles.

Volume paper making of paper by hand, using the method invented in China now with the use of large vats, is documented in both Italy and Germany by 1400. Its use spread rapidly for letters, records, old master prints, and books and manuscript using primarily woodblock printing. The paper making technique "secret" had made its way from Asia to Europe by way of trade routes and the conquest attempts of the Moors from Northern Africa into Western Europe.

Printing from Movable Type

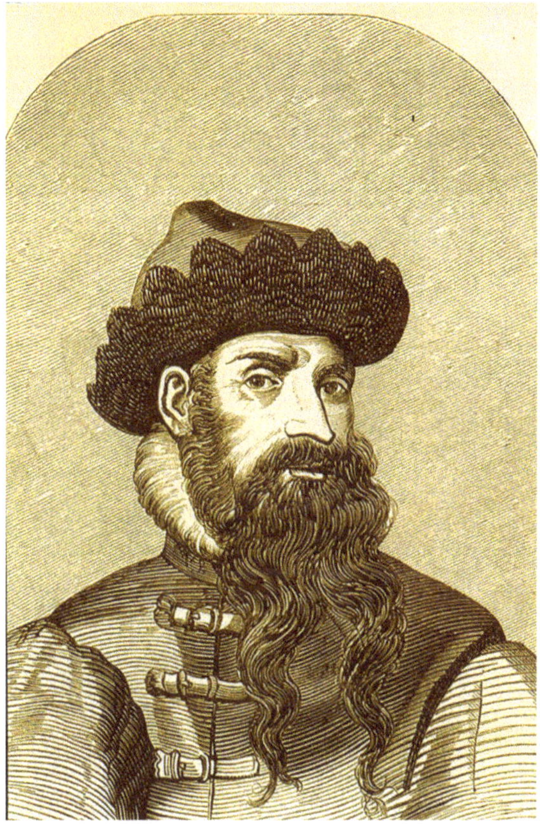

Johannes Gutenberg, named by Time magazine as the "Man of the Last 1000 years, invented printing from individual type characters around 1437.

Johannes Gutenberg, born in Mainz, Germany, was a goldsmith and printer, who is credited with inventing movable type printing in Europe, circa 1437. His major work, the Gutenberg Bible, also known as the 42-line bible, has been acclaimed for its high aesthetic and technical quality.

Before Gutenberg, every book produced in Europe had to be copied by hand. The Chinese had been mass producing books since the ninth century using woodblock printing. But now it was possible to speed up the process without sacrificing quality. We know for certain about this first printed Bible from a letter of March 12, 1455. On that day Enea Silvio Piccolomini, later Pope Pius II, reported that, ". . . in Frankfurt, the year before, a marvelous man had been promoting the Bible. Piccolomini had seen parts of it and it had such neat lettering that one could read it without glasses." Every copy had been sold. — *British Library*

Among Gutenberg's specific contributions were the design of metal movable type, the invention of a process for making type in quantity, the use of an oil-based ink, and the creation of a printing press similar to the screw olive and wine presses of the period. It is then the combination of these inventions into a practical system of printing that is so important.

Gutenberg's method for making type is traditionally considered to have included a metal type alloy and a hand mold for casting type. The use of movable type was a marked improvement on the handwritten manuscript, which was the existing method of book production in Europe, and even woodblock printing. It revolutionized European book-making which was very time consuming. Gutenberg's printing technology spread rapidly throughout Europe and is considered a key factor in the European Renaissance.

Things were not as good for Gutenberg as one might expect. Among other things, he had a financial dispute with Johann Fust, his partner or financier, on their joint work on the Bible. After Gutenberg's court case with Johann Fust, it seems that he got into serious financial difficulty. In 1458 he defaulted on debts incurred in Strasbourg in 1442, of which he had previously paid off regularly.

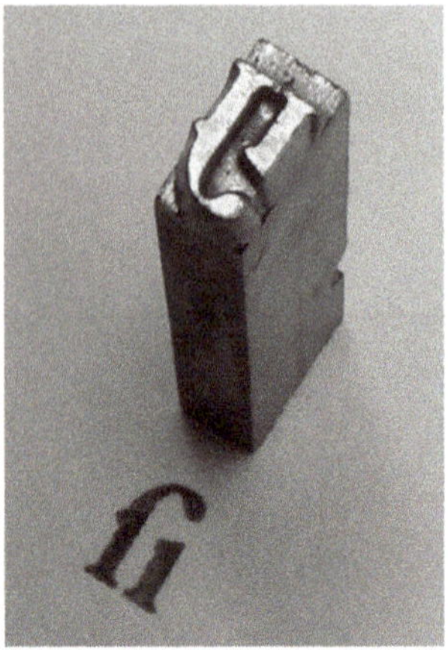

Ligature of F and I characters 12 point Garamond relief type.

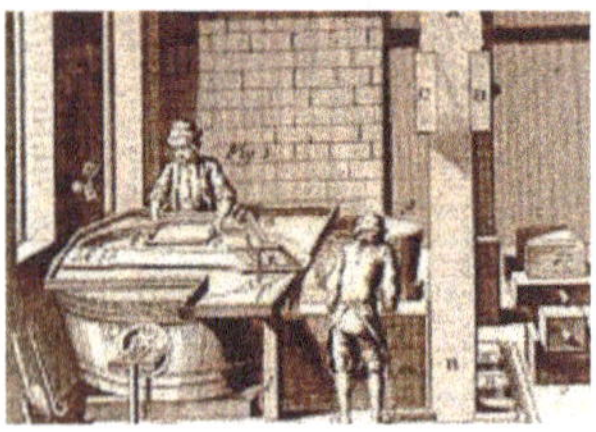

Vat used for paper making in Europe 1200 AD.

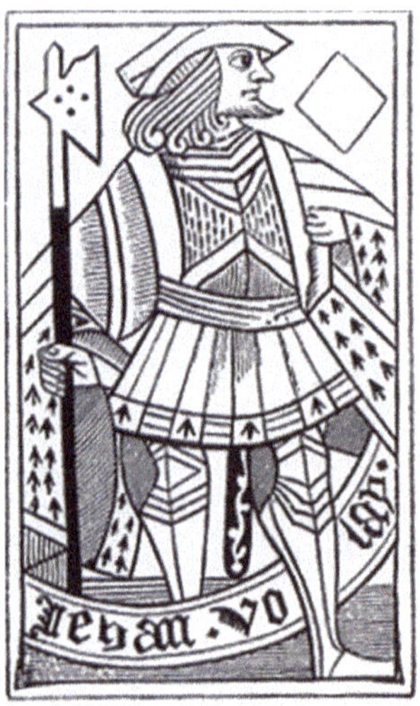

An early product of woodblock printing in Europe were playing cards, circa 1400's.

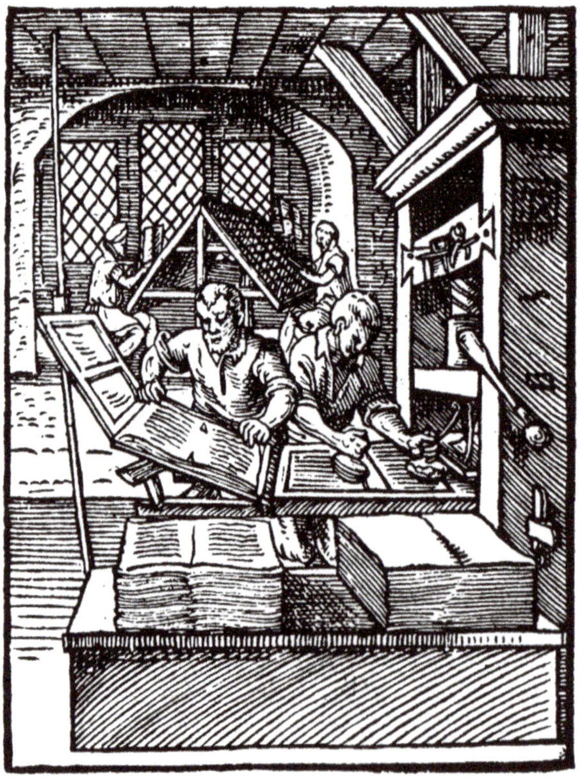

Printing from movable type using a printing press with a design inspired by wine and olive presses.

Into Mass Production

Section 3

1500 AD – 1800 AD

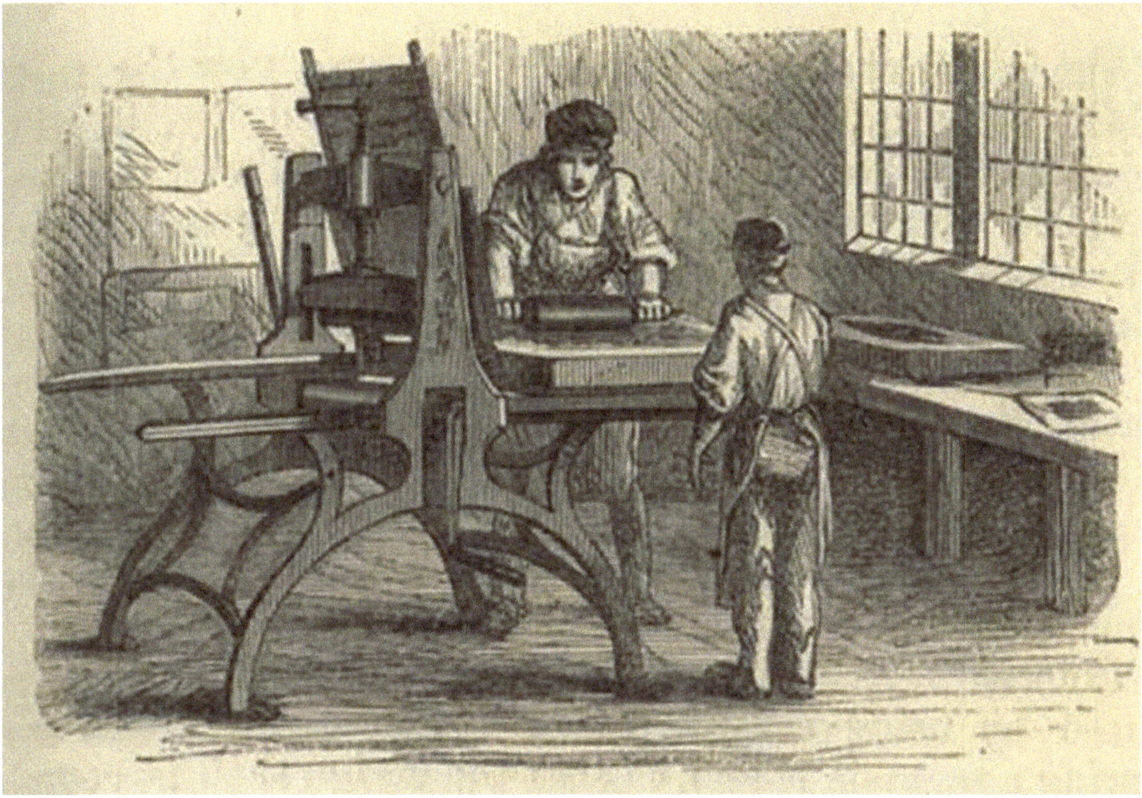

Different than writing ink, a varnish-like ink made of soot, turpentine, and walnut oil was created specifically for the printing press. Once the task of a printer to make their own printing ink, the demand for more printing ushered in a need to produce quantities of ink as printing grew.

Printing Ink

This ink production, the quantity production of paper, and Gutenberg's printing method all coming into existence at about the same time set the table for the rapid expansion of printing.

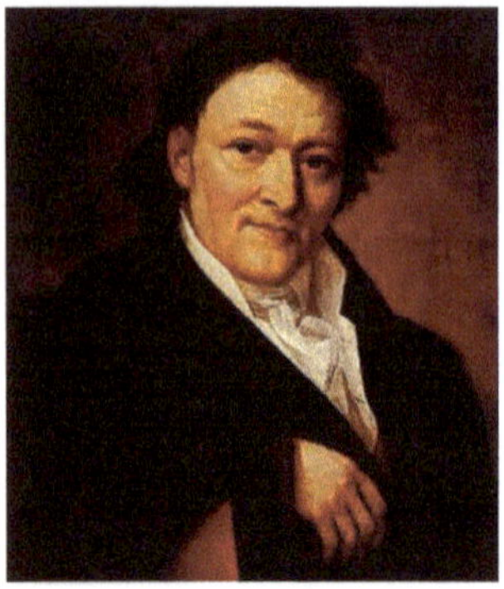

Alois Senefelder
Senefleder was an actor and playwright, that developed the lithographic method of printing in 1796. He was decorated by King Maximilian Joseph of Bavaria and a statue of him stands in the town of Solnhofen, where lithographic stone is still quarried.

Lithography

Printing remained pretty much the same until a new method was developed, "Lithography." It didn't supplant relief printing (printing from a raised surface like Gutenberg's movable type) but rather offered a different means for printing that provided a different "look" to the printed piece, and more options.

Alois Senefelder was an Austrian actor and playwright who invented the printing technique of lithography in 1796. This was an outcome of problems he had with his play Mathilde von Altenstein, which caused him to fall into debt, and unable to afford to publish a new play he had written. To print this play, Senefelder experimented with a novel etching technique using a greasy acid resistant ink as a resist on a smooth fine-grained stone of limestone. He then discovered that this could be extended to allow printing from the flat surface of the stone which an image was created on it by drawing on it with a grease pencil. With water applied to the surface of the stone, (repealed by the oily image, but was attracted to ink), ink was applied by use of a roller. Placed in a press that applied pressure, the ink transferred to paper printing the image.

Lithography would expand in use. In the 19th century, color lithography created a communication revolution and brought art, literature, and music to the masses. The process had a dramatic impact on consumer culture, too, as colorful and appealing product labels began to influence advertising, branding, and customer choices. Everything from cigar boxes to children's games suddenly exploded with color.

Modern lithography method we know today, is the most used method of printing today, overtaking relief printing in popularity in the mid-1950s.

Paper Making

The mass production of paper would begin with the invention of a continuous paper-making machine for making rolls of paper, by Nicholas Louis Robert in 1798. The machine used an oval vat that contained paper pulp was then deposited onto a moving wire screen, much like a conveyor belt, producing paper not in sheets but continuously. The brothers Henry and Sealy Fourdrinier, stationers of London who financed the project, have their name associated with the process, the Fourdrinier process.

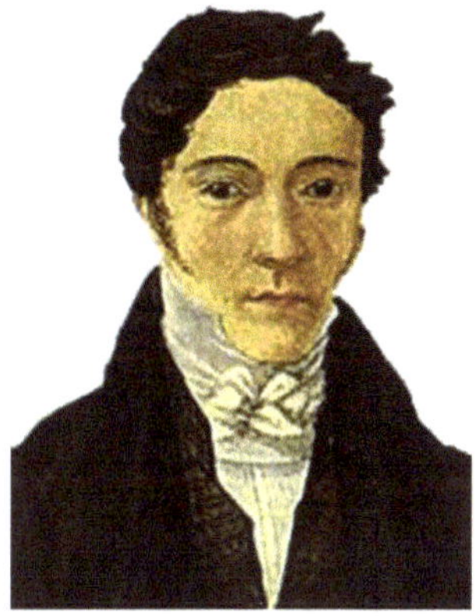

Nicholas Louis Robert
In 1801, Robert and his brother-in-law John Gamble patented the machine in England. They divided the patent rights with their financial backers, Henry and Sealy Fourdrinier. By 1807, with further improvements, it was put on the market.

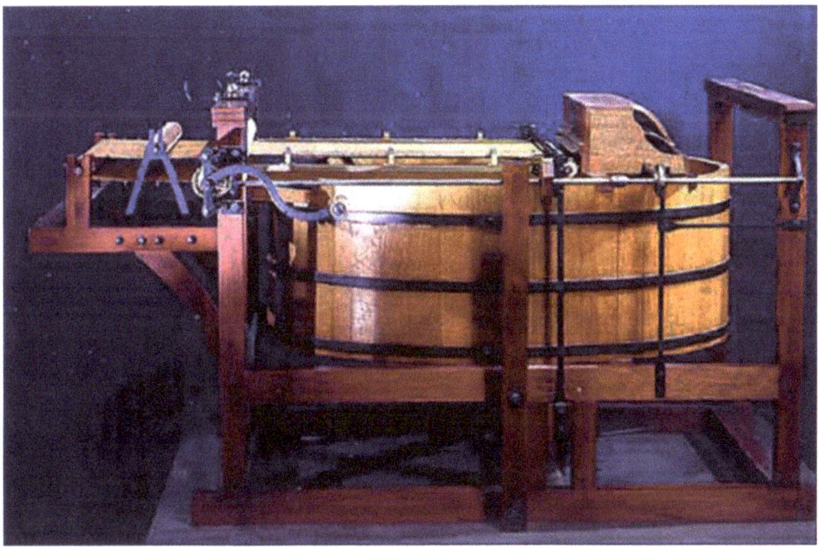

Paper making machine created by Nicholas Louis Robert. The oval vat contained the wet pulp that was transfered on the moving wire screen.

Industrialized Printing

Section 4

1800 AD – 1900 AD

French artist and chemist Louis Daguerre developed one of the first methods of **photography** in 1802. Daguerre first exposed silver-coated copper plates to iodine, obtaining silver iodide. Then he exposed them to light for several minutes. The plate then was coated with mercury vapor and heated to 75° Celsius, to amalgamate the mercury with the silver, followed by fixing the image in salt water. Though the method produced quality and artistic looking images, other more easily used methods would replace it. He is credited with taking the first photo of a person in 1839.

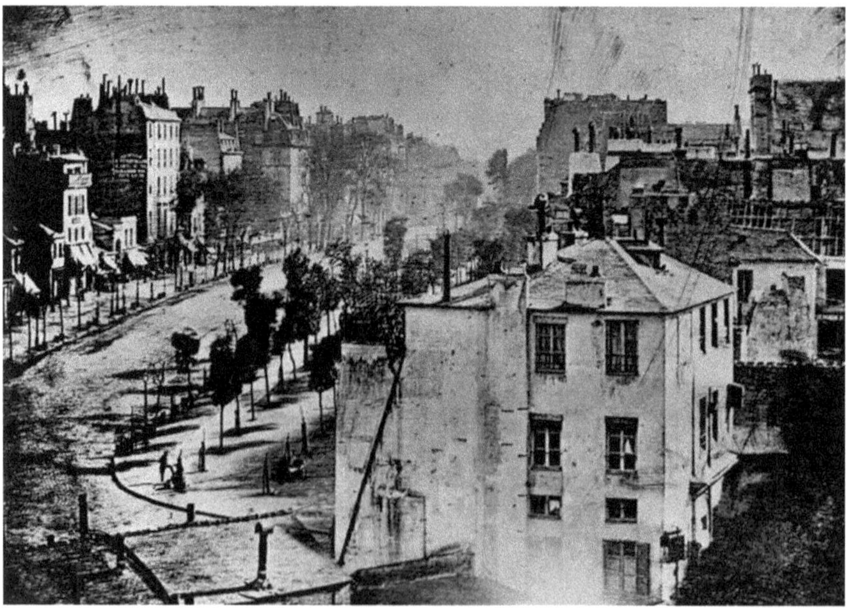

Louis-Jacques-Mandé Daguerre invented the daguerreotype process in France. American photographers quickly capitalized on this new invention, which was capable of capturing a "truthful likeness. Seen in this daguerreotype, is what is considered the first photograph of a person, seen lower left on the corner of the street.

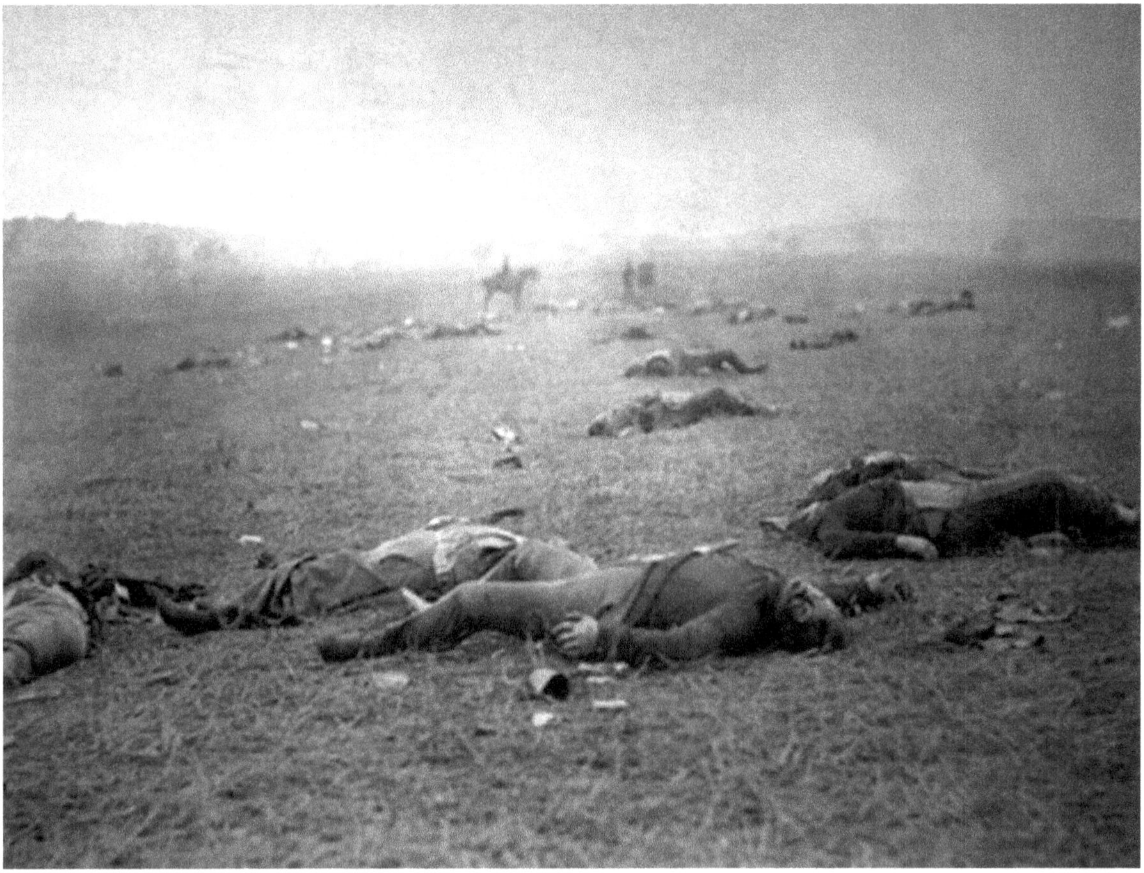

A Harvest of Death is an iconic photo taken by a contemporary photographer of Mathew Brady, Timothy H. O'Sullivan on the battlefield at Gettysburg.

Photography would later have a great affect not only on the graphic arts, but as an Art form, and as a way for us to capture images of our world and the powerful meaning they relate to us. The use of photography during the Civil War is a good example.

Mathew Brady presented an exhibition of photographs from the Civil War Battle of Antietam in his New York gallery entitled, "The Dead of Antietam." Many of the images in this presentation were graphic photographs of corpses (some even posed). This was the first time that anyone had seen the realities of war firsthand (albeit in photographs) as distinct from previous "artists' impressions." The presentation was totally new and shocking to many Americans. After the war, many of the glass plates were used to create greenhouses.

Powered Press

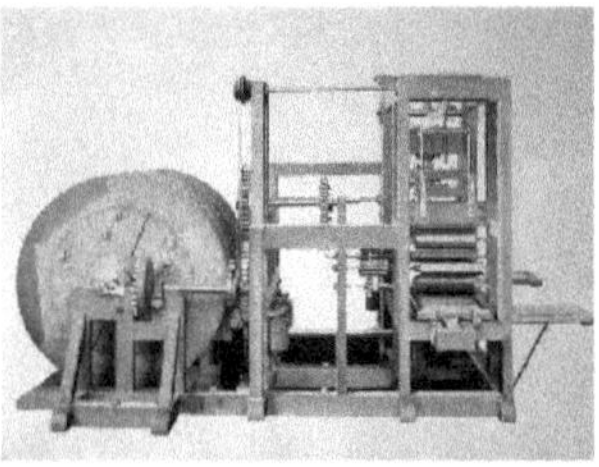

The Friedrich Koenig wooden steam powered press.

With the advent of the Age of Steam, the application of steam power to machines came about. Friedrich Koenig (Koenig means King) built a steam powered wood press which increased the production of printing in contrast to what could be produced using the standard method of printing developed by Gutenberg which by this time had been in use for 400 years.

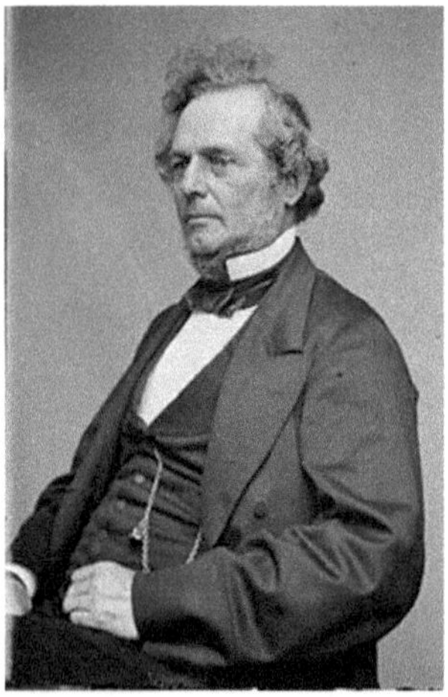

Richard Hoe, developer of a steam powered web press.

Soon to follow in 1843 was the invention of a web press. These presses use a continuous roll of paper and are what most people would associate with a newspaper press. Obviously this increased speed and productiveness for newspapers allowed for greater distribution and influence of the "press." Richard Hoe, an English-born American mechanic, who with his brothers-in-law, Peter and Matthew Smith designed and created the press using steam, which lead to the establishment in New York City of a manufactory of printing presses. Its not uncommon today to find a Hoe press in a newspaper pressroom.

Gravure

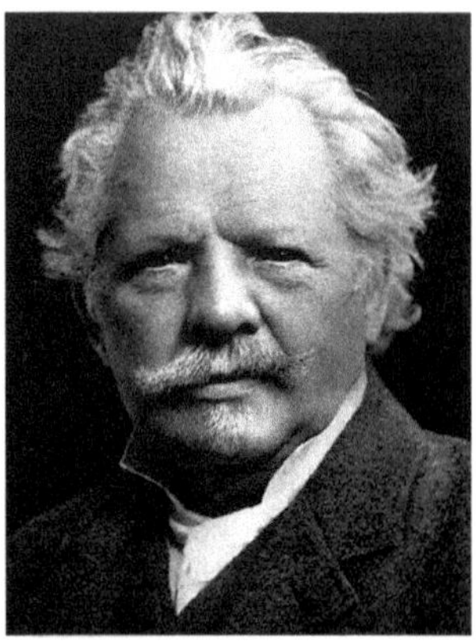

Karl Klietsch, inventor of gravure printing.

Karl Klietsch, was a Czech painter, photographer, caricaturist, and illustrator in Brno, Budapest, and Vienna, and is known as the inventor of **Gravure**, sometimes called, **Photogravure**. He worked many years trying to improve technology of picture reproduction and arrived at this method of printing which uses a series of dots etched into a metal cylinder for the image to be printed. It is in use today for high volume and high quality color printing.

Typesetter

Typesetting was a laborious process assembling individual characters into words, lines, and paragraphs— Gutenberg's invention. A mechanized method was needed to meet the potential that more capable presses and improved paper making had to offer. Ottmar Mergenthaler, a German, created a typesetting machine in 1896 that utilized a keyboard, and matrixes that where filled with molten lead to produce individual lines of type. Prior to Mergenthaler's invention of the linotype, no newspaper in the world had more than eight pages. The machine became the standard of the graphics industry. A competitor to the linotype was the Lanston Monotype of Tolbert Lanston. Even Mark Twain got into the act. After many years and most of his fortune he gained from his books, an inferior impractical machine, the Paige Typesetting Machine failed to gain acceptance.

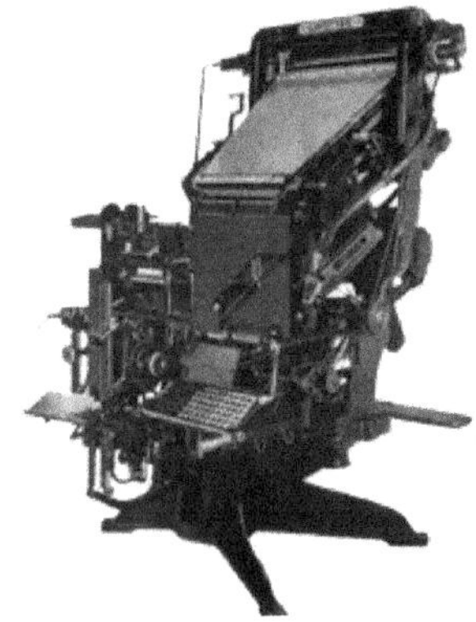

Ottmar Mergenthaler, a German, invented the Linotype typesetting machine in 1884. He got the idea for the brass matrices that would serve as molds for the letters from wooden molds used to make "Springerle," or German Christmas cookies.

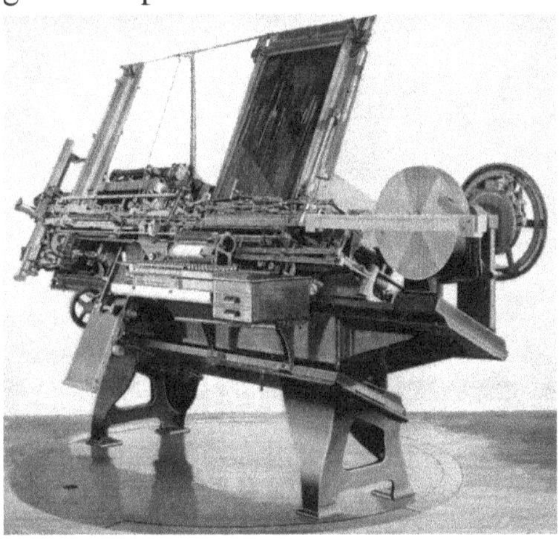

The Paige Typesetting Machine.

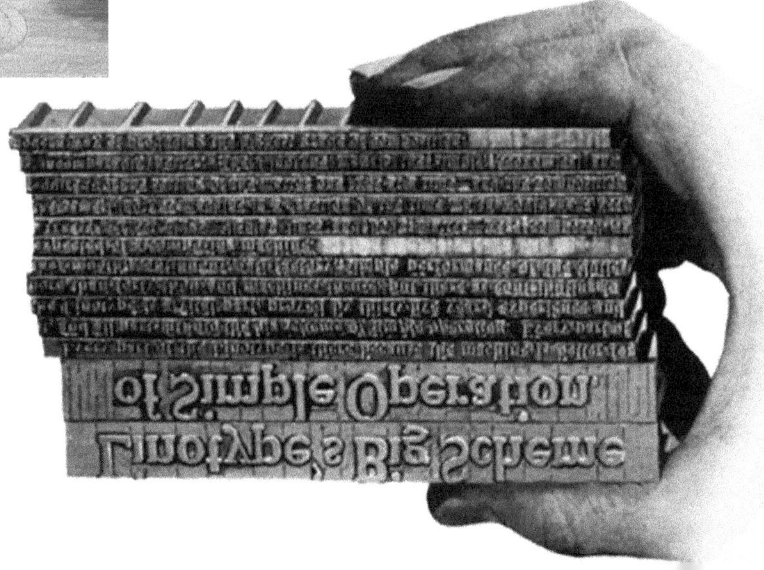

Linotype typesetting. Lines of cast type, called slugs, made from using melted lead.

Mass Communication

Section 5

1900 AD – Present

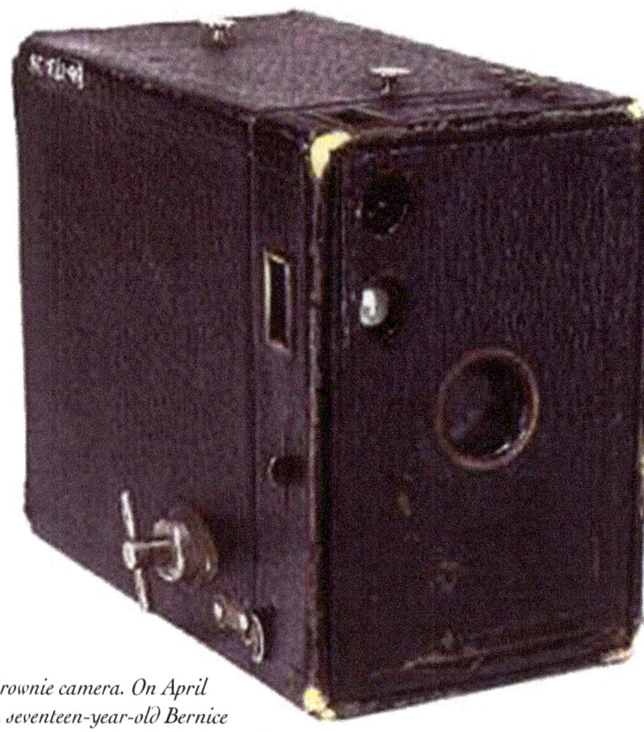

Kodak Brownie camera. On April 15, 1912, seventeen-year-old Bernice Palmer, a passenger aboard the Carpathia, used this camera to document the ship's rescue of survivors of the Titanic.

The first true personal camera was made by Kodak, the company founded by George Eastman. It cost $1 and impacted social interaction much in the same way that the smart phone has our society today. Eastman was first a film manufacturer, but he could see what bringing photography to the masses, especially marketing to young people, via cheap but durable cameras would mean for future film sales and processing. A camera in every home meant a lot of film to be sold and processed.

Offset Printing

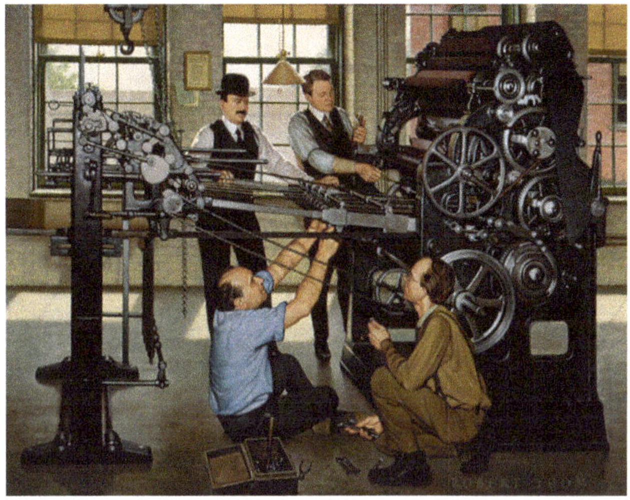

Ira Rubel with his press in a painting by Robert Thom. — Rochester Institute of Technology, library Cary Collection.

Offset Printing was discovered by Ira Rubel in 1906 when running a lithographic press, a printing problem caused the image to be printed on the impression cylinder and then on the back of the next sheet. It was noticed that image was better than that which was being printed. This accident lead to the development of the process of offset printing which when incorporated into the mechanics of a lithographic press provides the quality printing of presses that are in common use today.

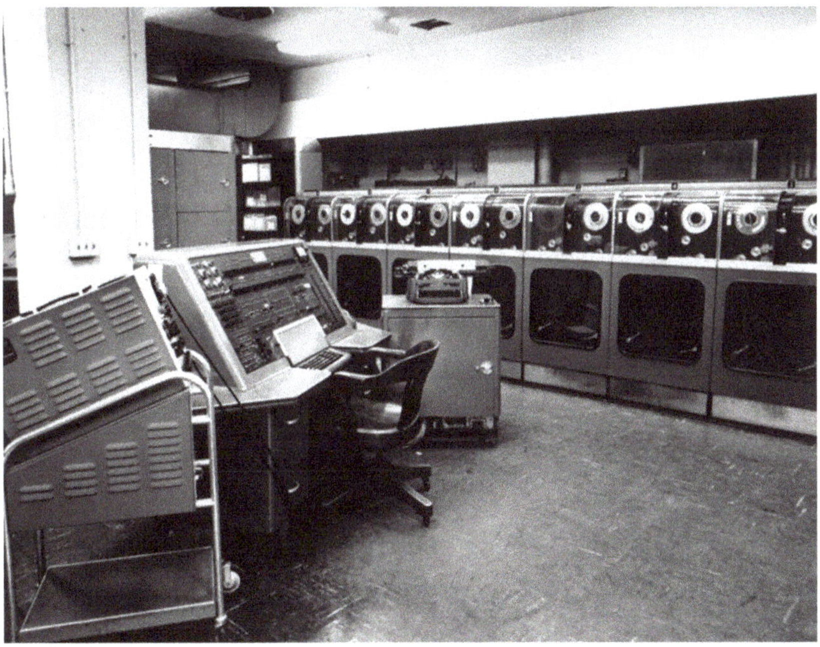

UNIVAC (Universal Automatic Computer).

Computers

One of the first electronic computers made was the UNIVAC (Universal Automatic Computer). The machine was 25 feet by 50 feet in length, contained 5,600 tubes, 18,000 crystal diodes, and 300 relays. It utilized serial circuitry, 2.25 MHz bit rate, and had an internal storage capacity 1,000 words or 12,000 characters. It utilized a Mercury delay line, magnetic tape, and typewriter output. In 1952, the UNIVAC I successfully predicted the outcome of the 1952 presidential election, during a televised news broadcast. The term "bug" in a computer comes from the fact that bugs, real bugs would get caught between contacts of the electromagnetic replays and cause problems.

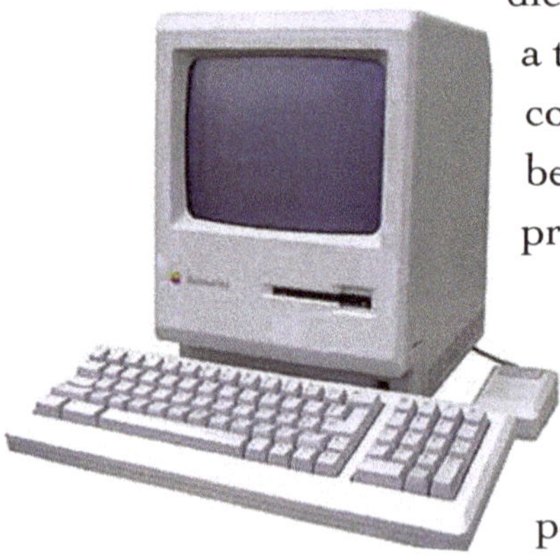

The Mac went on sale in 1984 for $2,495 (adjusting for inflation would make the price almost $5,000), two days after the famous ad aired. It came bundled with two programs designed to show off its graphical interface, MacWrite and MacPaint.

Personal Computer and Desktop Publishing

Desktop publishing would revolutionize the graphics industry in the mid-1980s in which the invention of the personal computer and graphics software provided the ability for the non-professional now to create designs and layouts using a computer.

Professionals also grasped this new technology and transformed the industry from mainly a hands-on skilled craft with extended production times to a modernized technical field requiring artistic and computer skills with on-demand production expectations. One of those technologies was the Macintosh computer. The brand developed by Apple Computer, which

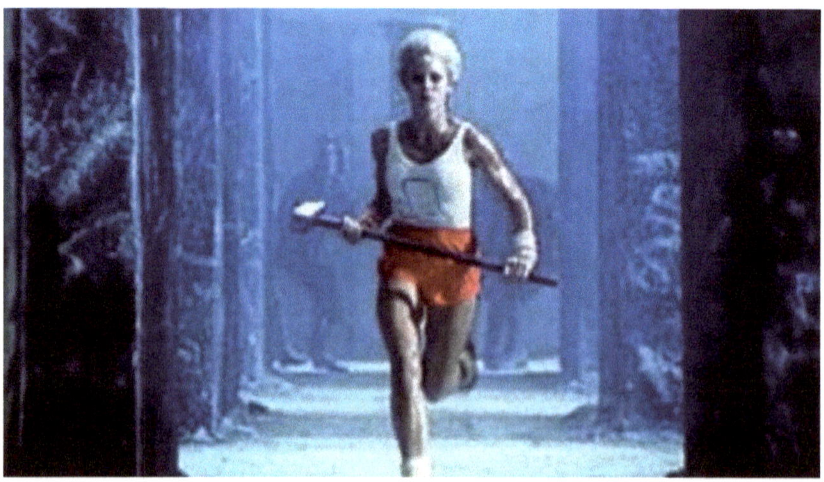

was started by Steve Jobs and Steve Wozniak, was introduced in January 24, 1984 in a famous TV commercial during the Superbowl.

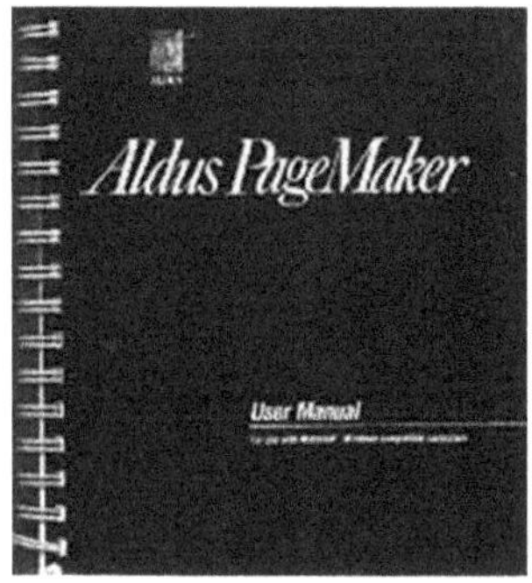

PageMaker was introduced in 1985 by the Aldus Corporation.

The other pieces to the desktop publishing explosion were the software programs Aldus PageMaker, and Adobe Photoshop. Acquired by Adobe in 1994 and since replaced by InDesign the software program PageMaker allowed for the creation of layouts, in particular for publications. This started what would be known as desktop publishing.

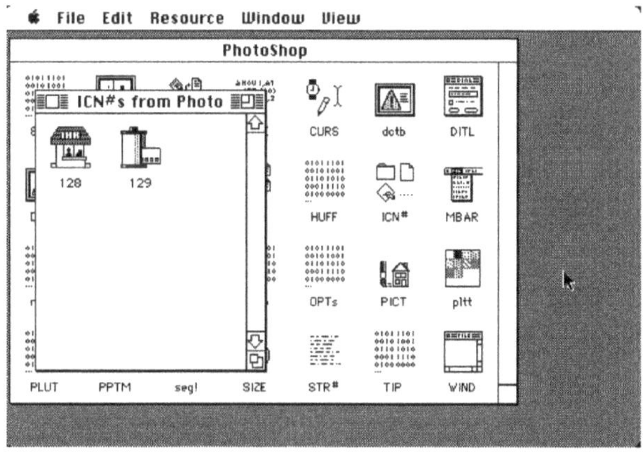

Note the icons for the Photoshop app (which looks like an old drive up film drop off) and a Photoshop file (roll of film).

In 1987, Thomas Knoll, then a PhD student at the University of Michigan, began writing a program on his Macintosh Plus to display grayscale images on a monochrome display. This program, called *Display*, caught the attention of his brother John Knoll, an Industrial Light & Magic employee, who recommended Thomas turn it into a full-fledged image editing program. Thomas took a six month break from his studies in 1988 to collaborate with his brother on the program, which had been renamed ImagePro. Later that year, Thomas renamed his program Photoshop and worked out a short-term deal with scanner manufacturer Barneyscan to distribute copies.

World Wide Web

One of the biggest influences on Graphic Communications and perhaps even human communications itself has been the advent of the Internet and later the World Wide Web. It has transformed the way we interact, share information, do business, and socialize. For the graphic arts, which historically has been a professional realm craft, its impact has been dramatic, both opening opportunities in graphic arts occupational fields,

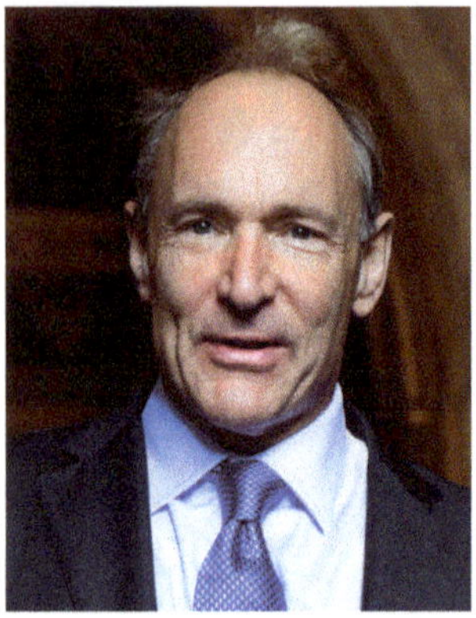

Tim Berners-Lee, was knighted in 2004 by Queen Elizabeth II for his pioneering work.

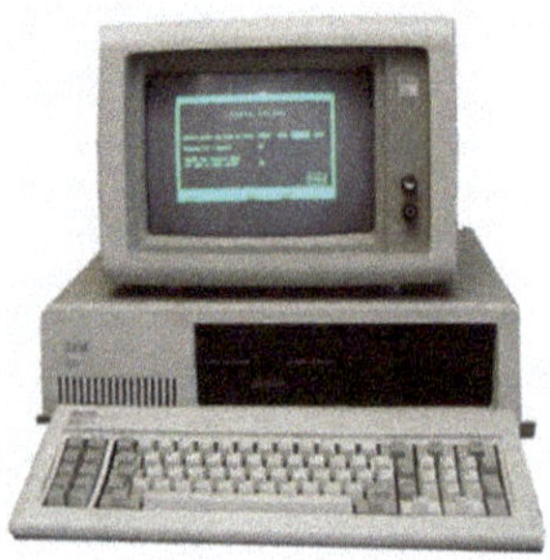

The personal computer PC, early 1980s, before the development of WYSIWYG or "what you see is what you get," graphical user interface.

January 1983, the ARPANET standardizes on the TCP/IP protocols adopted by the Department of Defense (DOD). The Defense Communications Agency decides to split the network into a public 'ARPANET' and a classified 'MILNET,' with only 45 hosts remaining on the ARPANET. Can you spot the aeronautics company Rockwell and the school UC Berkeley?

but also altering or even eliminating traditional methods and processes of graphic communications production.

With foundations in the Internet, which had its early beginnings in the 1950s with Arpanet, the World Wide Web, which is a part of the Internet, came into being with the advent of **Hypertext Mark up Language**, a programming language that graphically describes text and images when viewed in a web browser. This was developed by Tim Berners-Lee, a researcher for CERN— European Organization for Nuclear Research (in French).

The World Wide Web Consortium (W3C) is the main international standards organization for the World Wide Web (W3). It is a consortium where member organizations maintain full-time staff for the purpose of working together in the development of standards for the W3.

The Internet and the Web seem to have no limit. At the start of 2021 there are 4.66 billion users with more joining each day. We are now seeing further use of the Internet by non-humans, the Internet of Things. One can only imagine the communication possibilities.

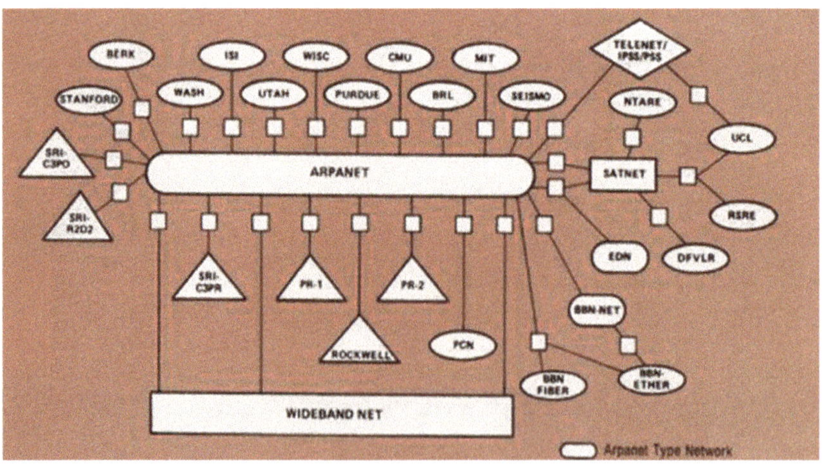

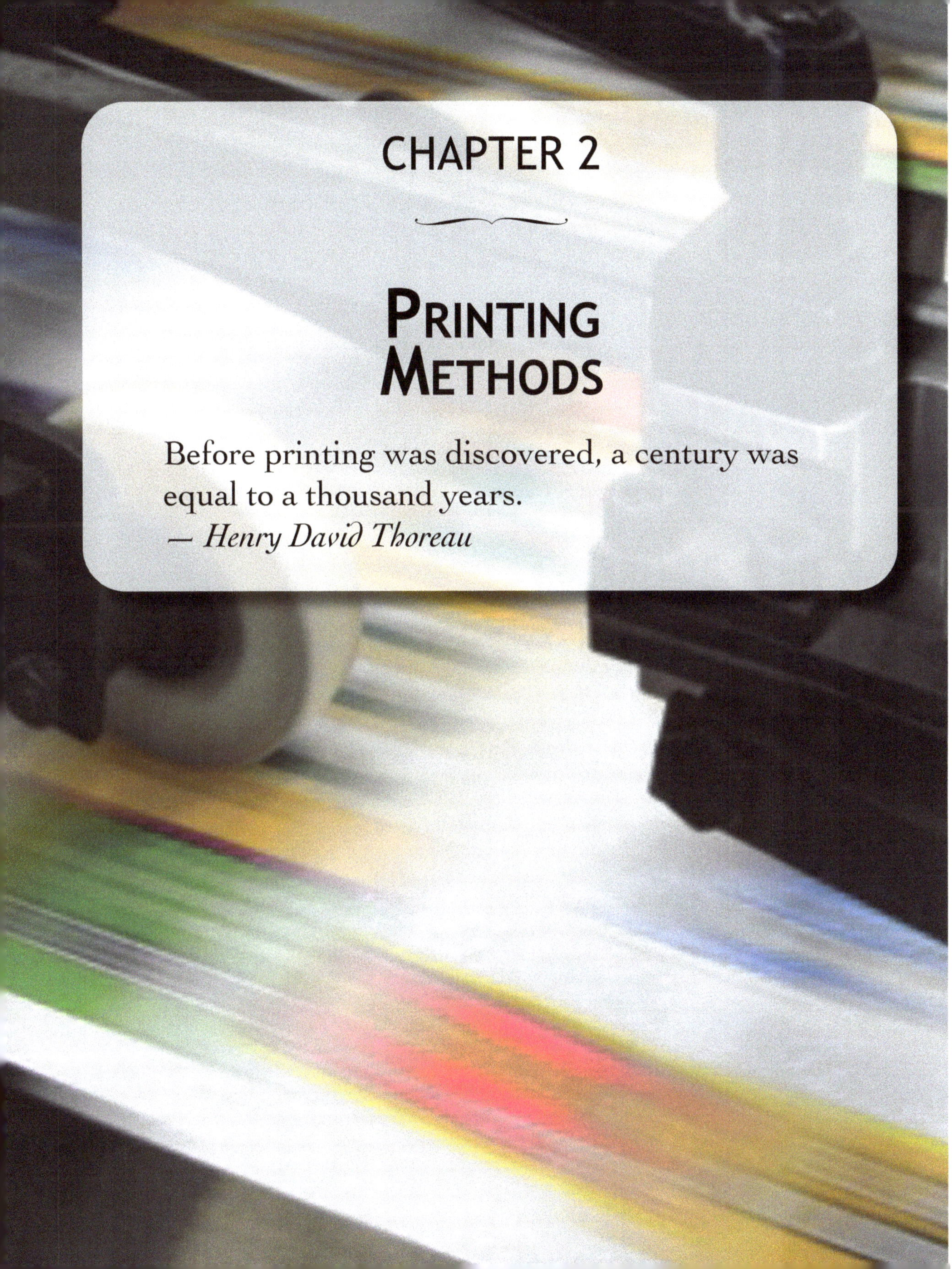

CHAPTER 2

Printing Methods

Before printing was discovered, a century was equal to a thousand years.
— *Henry David Thoreau*

There are five major printing methods: relief, lithography, intaglio, screen, and pressureless. Each has advantages and disadvantages as well as the kinds of products produced by them. Often a combination of these methods are used to produce a product. These methods are defined by the image carrier. That is, the mechanism that contains the image and also the non image.

MOST COMMONLY USED METHODS OF PRINTING			
METHOD	COMMON USES	IDENTIFYING	DESCRIPTION
RELIEF Letterpress Flexography	Commercial printing and imprinting. Specialty printing including embossing, die-cutting, scoring, perforation, foil stamping, and sequential numbering	Raised image on backside. "Ring of ink." Specialty printing techniques.	Printing from a raised or relief inked surface.
LITHOGRAPHY Offset Offset Lithography	Publications, commercial printing including business cards, letterheads, envelops, brochures, flyers, posters, and carbonless forms.	Much use of graphics, photographic images, and color. Sharp clear images. Wide use.	Printing from a flat surface in which the image has been created photographically (or digitally) and reproduction based upon the theory that water and oil do not mix.
INTAGLIO Engraving Etching Gravure	High volume and quality color printing. Money, stamps, fine art, and catalogs.	Raised inked image. All images are made up of dots including type for Gravure.	Printing from a recessed or sunken image area.
SCREEN Silk Screen Screen Printing	Fabric (T-shirts, etc.), posters, fine art, billboards, 3D packaging and various substrates (plastic, wood, metal).	Think layer of ink. Opaque ink most often. Odd shapes, sizes, textures, and materials used as substrate.	Printing by forcing ink through an open image area supported by a screen.
PRESSURELESS Inkjet Other	Package numbering and IDs. Database variable printing.	Much improved image. Small dots identifiable viewed through magnifying glass.	Non-contact printing of droplets or areas of ink or dye, controlled by a computer.

What the Ancients Invented

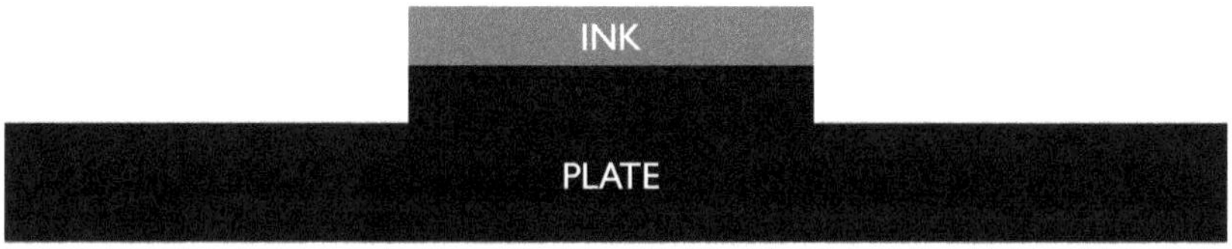

Note how the inked area (image) sets above the non-image area.

Relief

One of, if not the oldest form of printing, **Relief printing** uses an image that is raised above a non image area. In other words, printing from a raised or relief inked surface. We saw in Chapter 1- Section 1, that an early example of what could be considered relief printing was done as far back as 1800-1600 BC, when symbols where reproduced by pressing pre-formed hieroglyphic "seals" into soft clay on the Minoan Phaistos Disc found on the island of Crete.

A more recognizable form of relief printing is **woodblock** printing. It was developed in China and used to print both fabrics, and then later on paper for books soon after paper as we know it was invented.

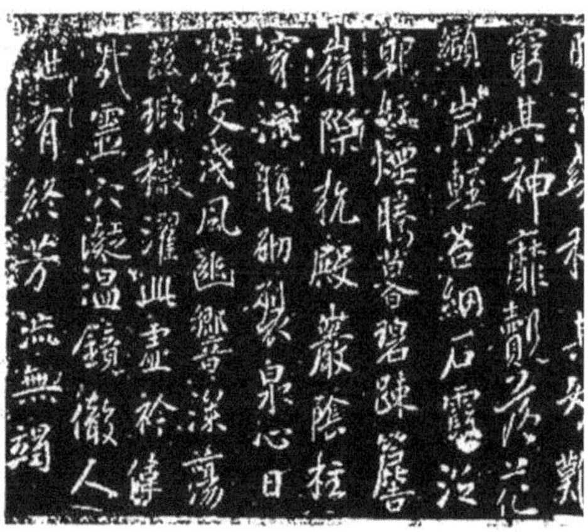

The most extensive of several large projects to preserve authoritative texts was the carving of the Buddhist canon on 7,137 stone tablets or steles -- over 4 million characters -- in an undertaking that continued from 605 to 1096. — http://www.chinaculture.org/

The origin of woodblock printing is linked to the creation of cutting or shaping stamps and seals of stone used to inscribe records. The Chinese found a method of making multiple copies by using paper and ink to create rubbings

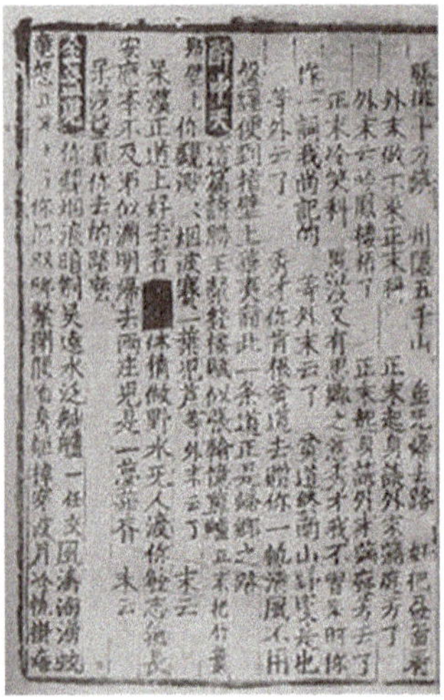

Wood block printing such as this printed fabric from the Chinese Yuan Dynasty (1271-1368).

(also known as inked squeezes) in effect "print" the inscription, making precise copies that could be carried away and distributed in considerable numbers.

These stone rubbings led to the development of more controlled media, that of wood blocks. China is documented as having a completed book created with woodblock prints such as the Diamond Sutra. Japan also had prints dating in the 770's which were printed in an edition of one million, but the plate composition is unknown.

In Europe woodblock printmaking came much later. Printing on fabric with wooden stencils was common for centuries, but woodblock printing on paper began with paper production, somewhere around 1390.

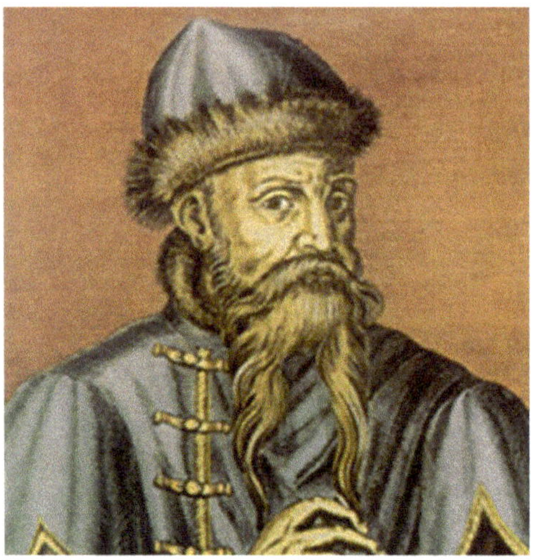

Inventor of printing by use of movable type, Johann Gutenberg contemporaries were artists Sandro Botticelli and Jan van Eyck, as well as King Henry V, and Joan of Arc.

Early European prints were single sheets, used mostly for religious images. They were hand printed and often hand colored, usually using stencils so that the painting would remain clearly visible. These prints started with carved lines, and it wasn't until 1400 that cutting wide areas emerged. — *http://www.arttalk.com/*

The next step in the development of relief printing was Johann Gutenberg's invention of printing from movable type (lead type) and refinement of a printing press. There are some who claim that he was not the first to invent this process but rather a Dutchman named Laurens Janszoon Coster, an official of the Great Church of Haarlem was printing this way as early as 1430, some ten years or so before Gutenberg. Regardless, of who the inventor was, it had a profound impact on the people and culture of Europe catapulting it out of the Dark Ages.

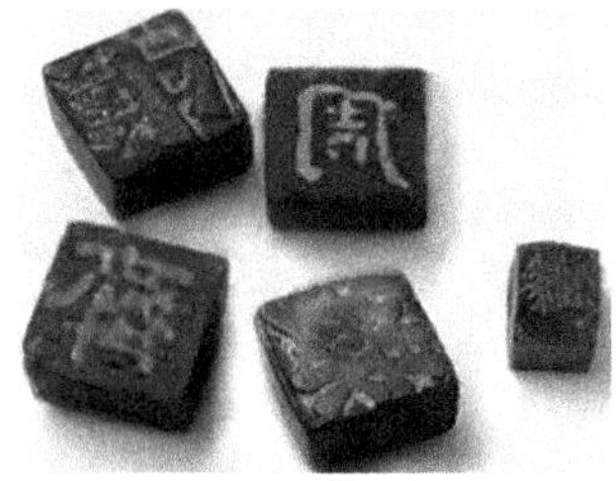

During the Ch'ing-li period (1041-1048) an alchemist named Pi Sheng appears to have conceived of movable type. Each piece of movable type had on it one Chinese character which was carved in relief on a small block of an amalgam of clay and glue. The portion that formed the character was as thin as the edge of a small coin. After the block had been hardened by fire, the type became durable. — http://www.computersmiths.com/chinese-invention/movtype.htm

Of course this method was not new except in Europe. The Chinese had been using individual movable type made of other materials such as wood and ceramics for several hundred years.

Relief printing, commonly known as **Letterpress**, would become the primary method of printing for the next 500 years. It would become more mechanized and with the advent of the industrial revolution, increase in production, speed, and quality. The Linotype machine, which cast lines of type called "slugs," would enhance its ability. The type and other relief elements are locked into a chase (a metal frame) which is placed into a press to be inked and printed from.

Since the mid-part of last century the popularity and use of relief printing has been relegated to specialty printing and finishing methods. The increased development of **Lithography** with its flexibility, use of color and images, as well as cost of set-up proved an advantage over relief printing which was very profitable when primarily columns of type were printed, like in a newspaper.

Relief printing today is mostly used for specialty printing and finishing techniques such as numbering, die-cutting, scoring, foil stamping, and imprinting. Another form of relief printing is **Flexography.** It has a very important role in printing packaging, in particular on materials such as used for bread wrappers that is flexible. It uses a "flexible" nylon/plastic cylinder with a raised image to print.

To Print a Play

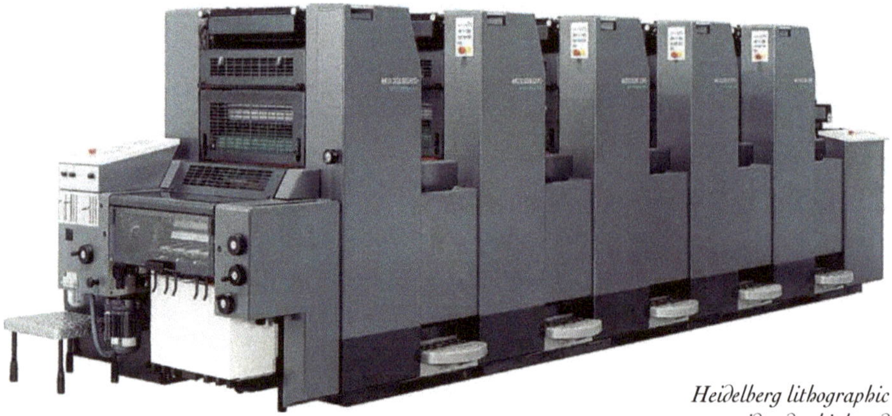

Heidelberg lithographic press, considered a high-end printing press.

Lithography

This method is the most popular method of printing today because of its ability to print a wide variety of products, flexibility, and relative low cost. Lithography means "stone writing." (Greek for stone, *litho*, and *graphein* to write or draw, graph).

Lithography was invented around 1796 in Germany by Bavarian playwright, Alois Senefelder, who accidentally discovered that he could duplicate his scripts by writing them with a greasy crayon on slabs of limestone and then printing them. As described in Chapter 1 - Section 3, the discovery was a solution to a problem he had trying to print and publish a new play. He used a technique of drawing with grease pencil or other tool, on a smooth fine-grained block of limestone. The stone was coated with a thin layer of water. Ink on a roller was ran across the stone. The ink was repelled by the water but

adhered to oily image. Paper was then placed on the stone and put into a press where pressure was applied that transferred the image to the paper.

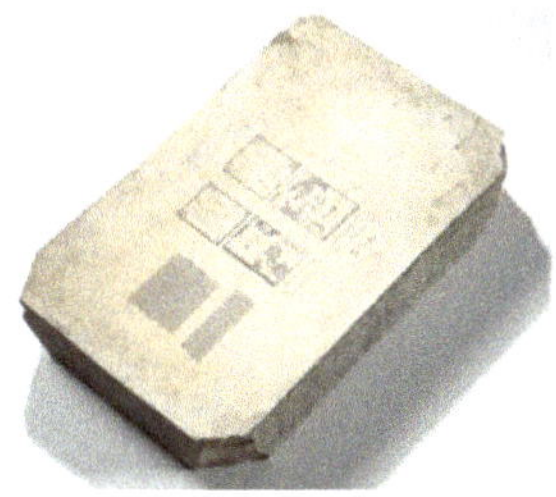

Initial Lithography printing was done from a limestone block that had the surface smoothed. A grease pencil or other tool was used to create an image (in reverse).

Rather than use blocks of limestone, today's modern lithographic presses use metal plates, typically of aluminum with a photographic emulsion. The exposed and processed plates are used to print a wide variety of printing including publications, commercial printing including business cards, letterheads, envelops, brochures, flyers, posters, and forms.

Offset Lithography

Modern lithographic presses also have an additional process that makes them so efficient and able to produce high quality images. It is called **Offset Lithography**. A lithographic press contains three cylinders. One holds the metal plate (plate cylinder) that has water and ink applied to it by a series of rollers. The next cylinder has a rubber blanket (blanket cylinder)

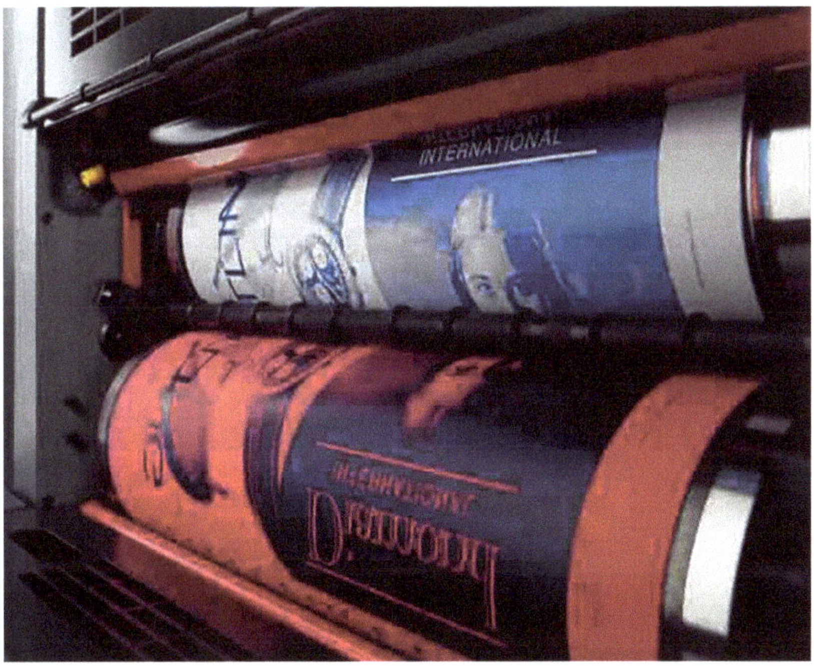

Two of the three cylinders on an offset-lithographic press, the plate cylinder with plate and the blanket (red) cylinder. The impression cylinder is below the blanket cylinder.
— http://www.creativeedgechicago.com/

clamped to it. The image is transferred from the plate to the blanket and then to the paper as it passes through. A third cylinder (impression cylinder) acts as a back for the paper. The process of "off-setting" the image produces a better quality image than if it were printed directly from the plate. The offset process was independently discovered in 1906 by Ira Rubel and A.F. Harris when a sheet of paper miss-fed during printing.

Lithography, with the process of **offset**, is the most popular method of printing today because of its ability to print a wide variety of products with flexibility, speed, and relative low cost.

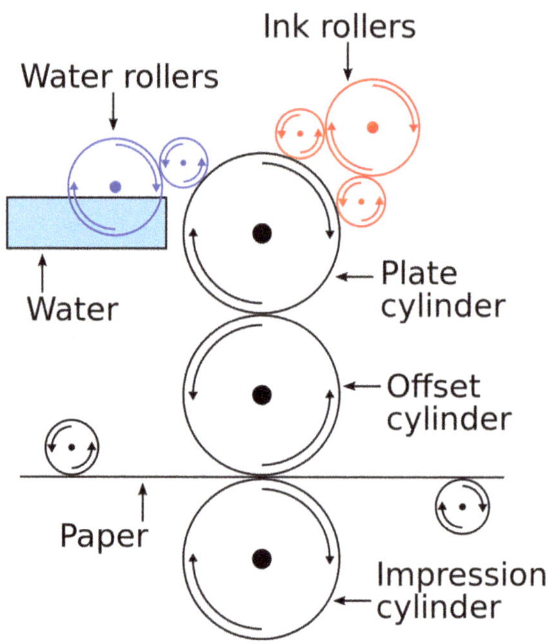

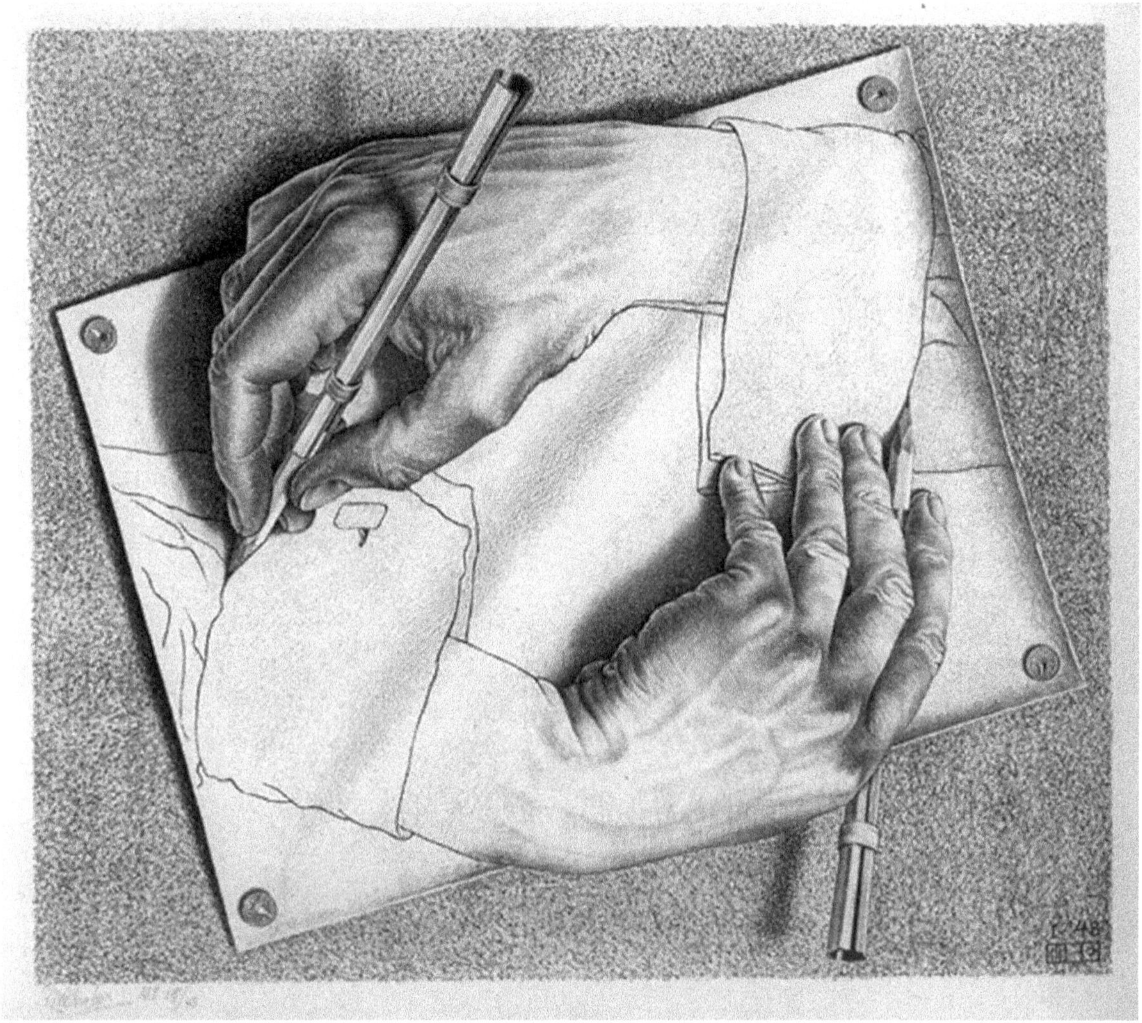

A well recognized print by M.C. Escher, Drawing Hands, 1948, lithograph, 11 1/8 x 13 1/8 inches. — http://www.bocamuseum.org/

A Method to Make Currency

Intaglio

Intaglio is, from *intagliare* to engrave, or cut in Italian, derived from Medieval Latin *intaliare*, and Late Latin *taliare* to cut. Intaglio is also a form of creating designs on gemstones, glass, ceramics, stone, or similar material in which the design is sunken beneath the surface. It is the most ancient form of gem **engraving**—the earliest known Babylonian cylinder seals date from circa 4000 BC. Created for a practical use as a form of signature or administrative tool, but often were worn much like a necklace to keep them close at hand.

Similar to this process of gem cutting, one can see the natural progression and development of intaglio printmaking which

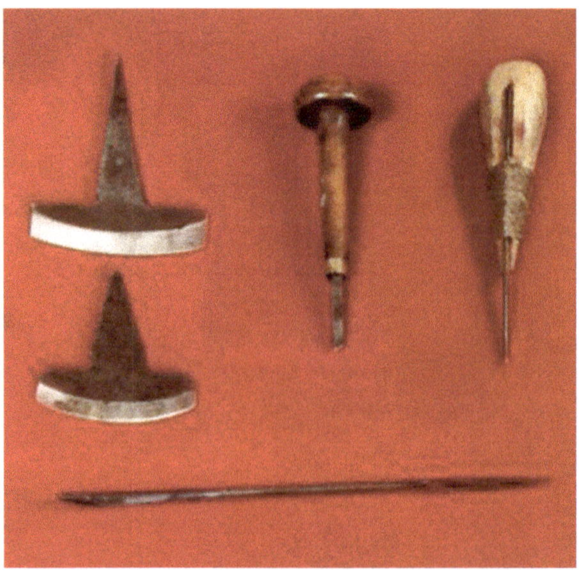

Burins. These tools were used to carve into metal plates for engraving. Similar tools are used today to create master plates to print U.S. currency.

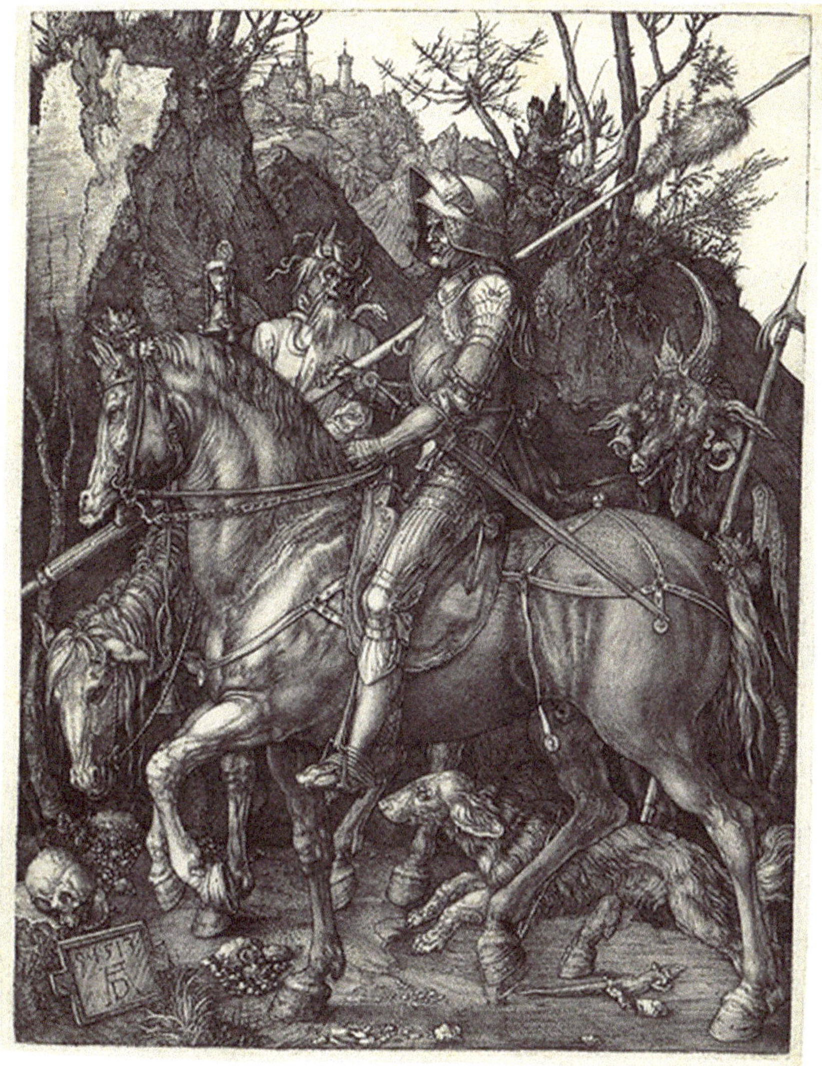

Fine Art print, Knight, Death, and the Devil, 1513–14 Albrecht Dürer (German, 1471–1528). —http://www.metmuseum.org/

coincides with the beginning of paper production in Europe in the late 1300s and the work of goldsmiths and armourers. Cutting and engraving metal using a burin, was common for a long time as well as inking these engraved depressions for decoration. From recording designs by rubbing engraved motifs with or without inking onto paper it was only a short step to using this technique as a way of artistic reproduction.

Engraving

The first copper engravings were done probably around 1430. In engraving, fine lines are cut into a brass or copper plate with burins or graver made from steel. Engraving is when a metal plate literally has an image carved into it by use of these hand tools. Intaglio developed some decades after woodblock printing, resulting from the fact that it was more complicated than woodblock printing. Engraving would become embraced

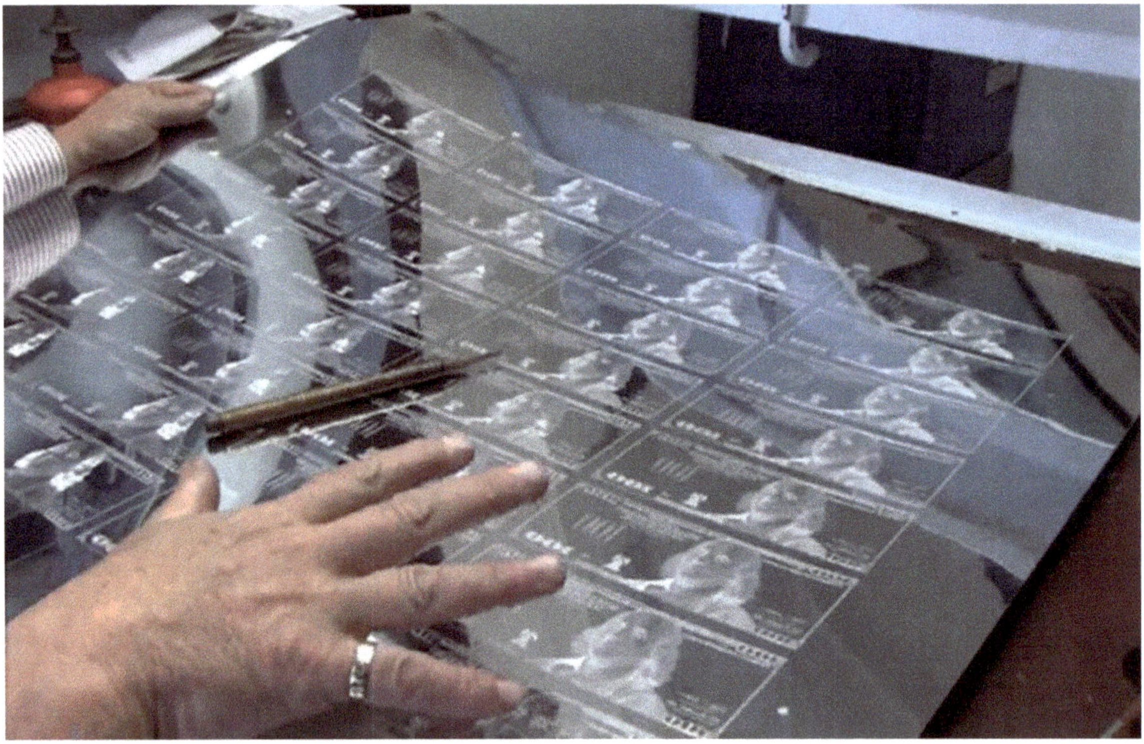

A worker inspects an engraving plate at the U.S. Bureau of Engraving and Printing. The plate is made from individual plastic molds made from the master die that are assembled into one plate containing 32 exact duplicates of the master die. — http://www.moneyfactory.gov/

by artists. The period 1470-1530 is considered the Golden Age of engraving and includes such artists as Albrecht Dürer, Martin Schongauer and Lucas von Leiden.

Engraving obviously has great commercial printing use. A good example is United States Bureau of Engraving and Printing that prints U.S. currency. Master engravers skillfully create master plates that are utilized in a process where the presses print 32 bills on a sheet of specially produced paper before being cut to size. Two other printing methods are also used to produced the finished money— relief and lithography. There are two other forms of Intaglio that would develop later: **Etching**, and **Gravure**. For all of these, ink is applied to the surface of the plate where it also fills the sunken areas (image). Ink is removed from the plate (non-image) leaving only the ink below the surface. Put into a press, pressure is applied whereby the paper is somewhat forced into the sunken area absorbing the ink.

Etching

A second form of intaglio, Etching is mainly used to create fine art. An acid resist, such as wax is applied to a metal plate, usually zinc, copper, or steel. The artist then scratches off the ground with a pointed etching needle where he or she wants a line to appear in the finished piece, thus exposing the bare metal. Rosin is sometimes used as a resist to provide a texture to an area. The prepared plate is put into a tray of acid, which eats into the metal and thus creating an image. Like the other Intaglio methods, ink is applied to the plate including the "etched" areas. The surface is cleaned of ink leaving the remaining ink in the sunken areas. Etching has been an Art media for hundreds of years, starting with Daniel Hopfer, who is believed to have been the first to apply the technique to printmaking.

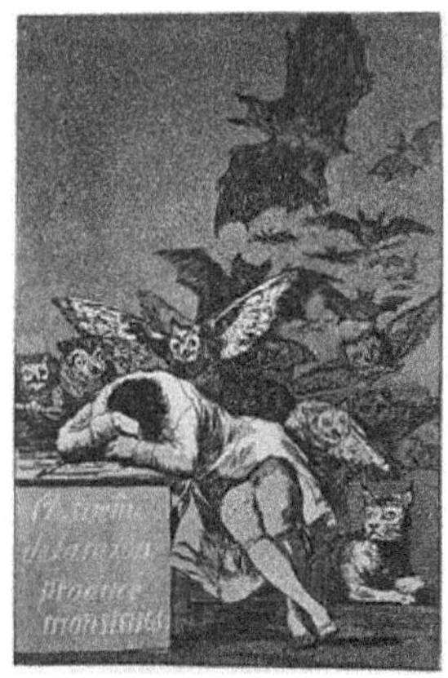

Fine Art etching, "The sleep of Reason Produces Monsters," 1797, an etching by famous Spanish artist Francisco Goya.

Gravure

Gravure, sometimes called rotogravure, is an intaglio printing method used to print high volume, high quality printing, often in color. Common products are magazine, catalogs, and newspaper inserts that may be a million copies or more. The image to be printed is half-toned, in other words the images, graphics, and text are converted into a series of dots which are etched into a polished cylinder on a gravure press. The same size dots have varying depth which allows for more or less ink and therefore lighter or darker color.

The method was invented in 1878 by Czech painter, photographer, and illustrator Karl Klietsch (sometimes referred to as Karl Klic). While living in Vienna, he patented an improved method for applying an aquatint grain to break up the image and allow for deeper etched shadows. In addition, Klietsch invented a technique of transferring the image from a negative, to a copper plate by way of gelatin-coated carbon pigment paper. The results were superior and the Talbot-Klíc Dust-Grain gravure was born. By the late 1880s, Klietsch's gravure process was often used to illustrate high-quality books with photographs—a process technically and artistically far superior to previous methods.

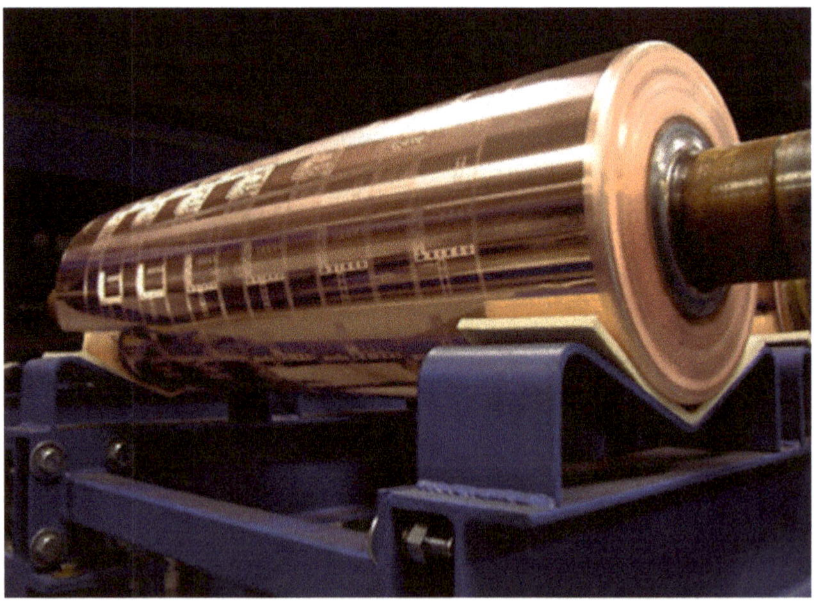

A copper rotogravure cylinder prepared with images, ready to be put on the press. When printing is done, ink is applied to the cylinder with the excess surface ink being removed by a device called a doctor blade.

More Than Just a T-Shirt

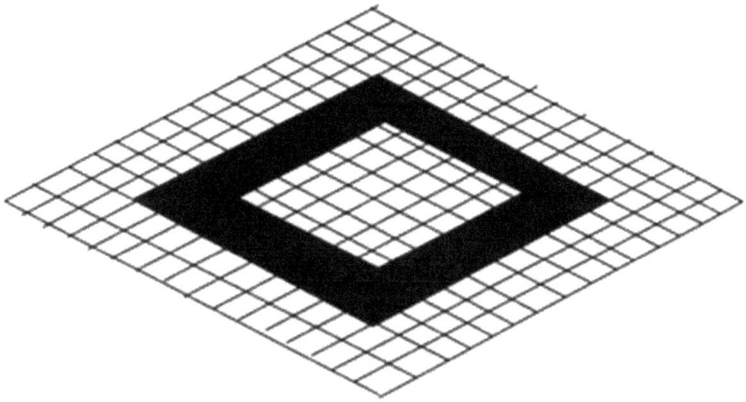

In this illustration, the open area inside, is the image that is created by the stencil (black shape). The remainder of the screen on the outside would be covered by paper or tape before printing to prevent the ink from going through.

Screen

Screen Printing, Silk Screen, or Stencil is printing by forcing ink through an open image area supported by a screen. The mesh is typically a synthetic "cloth" commonly used today, with fairly large opening between treads. It is stretched tight and secured to a frame. Wire mesh is used for long runs whereby silk is rarely used anymore. A stencil, as simple as a piece of paper with a hole cut in it is placed on the bottom of the screen. Photographically made and hand cut stencils are more commonly used. A squeegee is drawn across the top of the screen forcing the ink, which most often is an opaque ink, through the mesh where it is not blocked by the stencil onto what is being printed. This is great method for printing on products of odd shapes, sizes, textures, and materials. Typical products and materials include fabric (T-shirts, etc.), posters, fine art, billboards, 3D packaging and on various substrates (plastic, wood, metal).

Screen printing is a form of stenciling that first appeared in China during the Sung Dynasty (960–1279 AD). The crude method was adopted and refined by Japan and other Asian countries but would not be introduced to Europe until the late 1700's. It still would take quite a bit of time before being widely accepted. In 1907 an English man by the name of Samuel Simon officially patented the screen-printing technique. Originally Simon's method was used to print high quality custom wall paper or to print on silk or linen material, primarily for the wealthy.

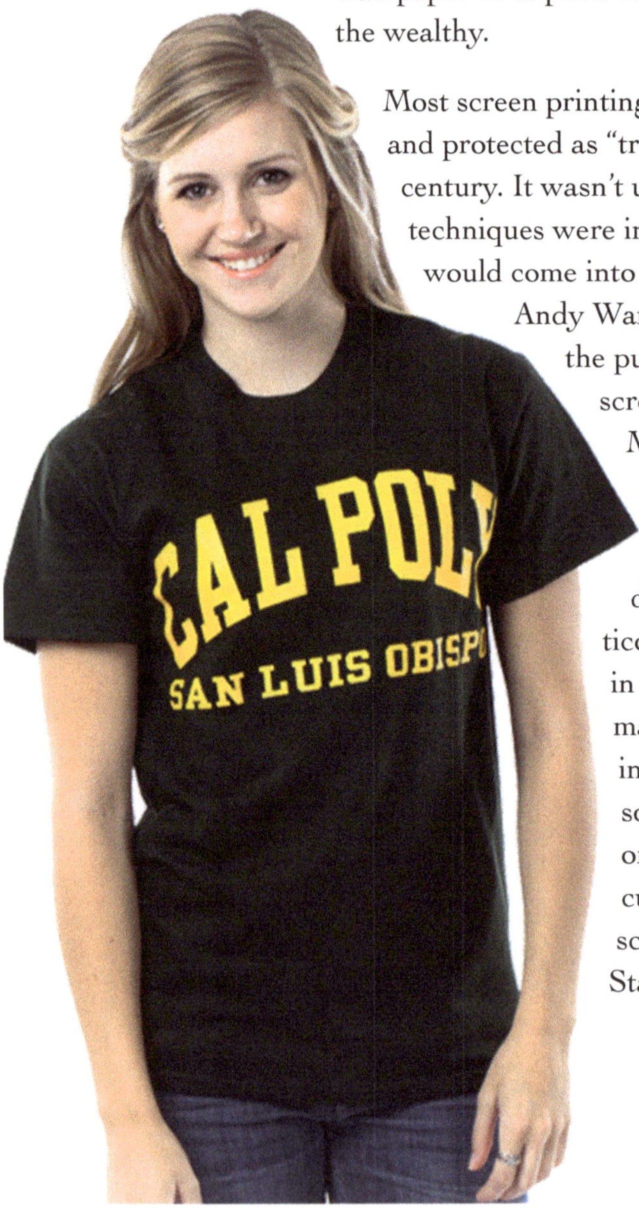

Most screen printing techniques were kept confidential and protected as "trade secrets" for much of the twentieth century. It wasn't until the early 1960's that new stencil techniques were incorporated and the printing method would come into the mainstream. We can now credit Andy Warhol for bringing screen printing into the public eye with his famously gaudy screen printed depiction of Marilyn Monroe shown in *Chapter 1 - Section 1.*

An American entrepreneur, artist and inventor Michael Vasilantone, developed and patented a rotary multicolor garment screen printing machine in 1960. The original rotary machine was manufactured to print logos and team information on bowling garments but soon directed to the new fad of printing on t-shirts. Screen printing on garments currently accounts for over half of the screen printing activity in the United States. — *http://www.edcmktg.com/*

Is That all There is?

Pressureless

Though these two **pressureless** methods don't have the glamour and tradition that the main four printing methods described in earlier sections of this chapter do, they certainly have a role and importance in reproducing printed documents.

Electrostatic

Electrostatic"printing" has been around since 1938 when Chester Carlson received a patent for his electrophotography

Xerox Machine circa 1960 . David Owen, author of "Copies in Xerox Machine circa 1960 Seconds: Chester Carlson and the Birth of the Xerox Machine," said, "It was a product no one knew they needed until they had it."

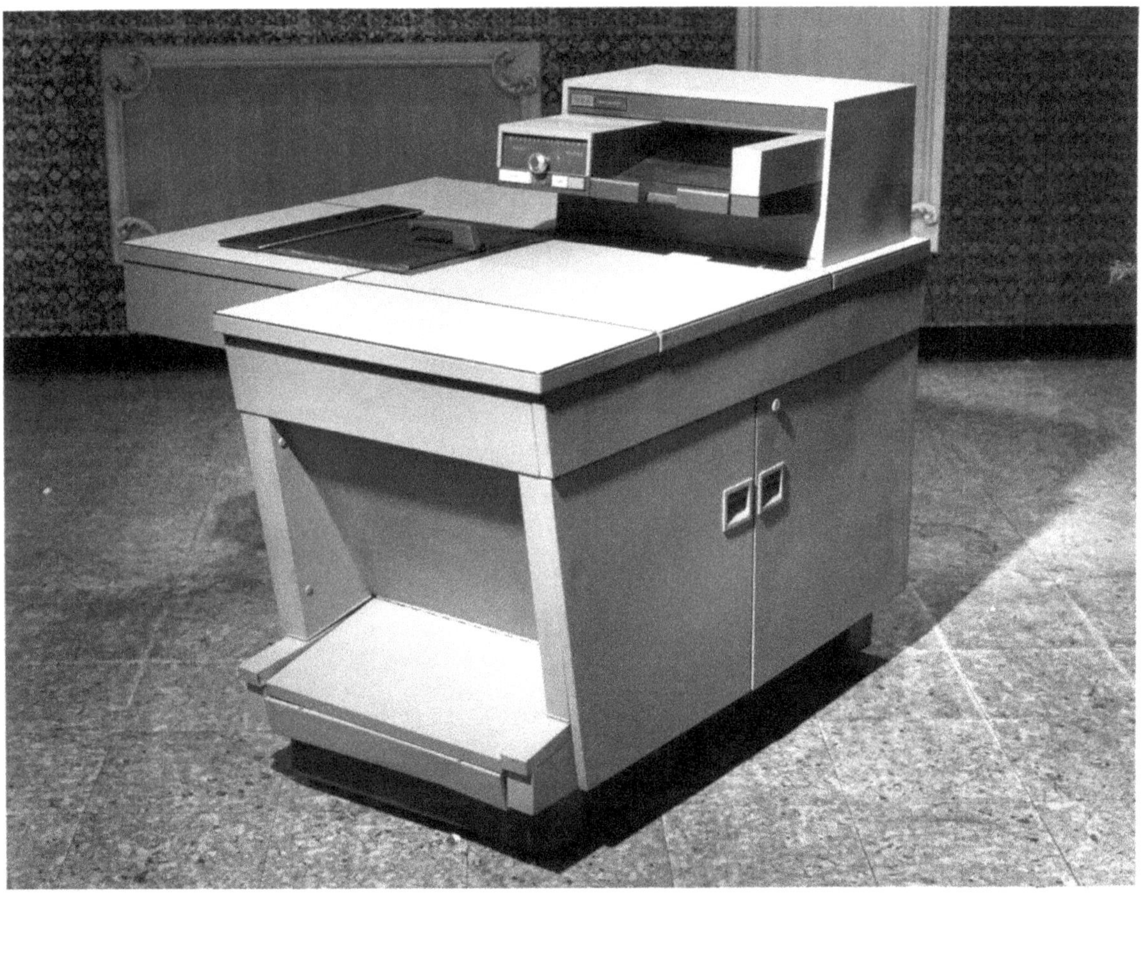

invention which was later named xerography, from the Greek words *xeros* "dry" and *graphia* "writing." The company, Xerox was founded in 1906 in Rochester as The Haloid Photographic Company, which originally manufactured photographic paper and equipment.

Joseph C. Wilson, credited as the "founder of Xerox," took over Haloid from his father. He saw the promise of Carlson's invention and, in 1946, signed an agreement to develop it as a commercial product. So successful was this electrostatic method that it is commonly referred to today as xeroxing. That wasn't always the case. The earliest models were so unreliable that Xerox's repair crews got emergency calls almost daily.

The basic process works like this. The image to be copied is placed into the electrostatic or xerox machine. When started, a sheet of paper enters the machine and goes through an area known as a corona, that electrically charges the paper. Next a light scans the original image to be copied. The light is reflected and strikes the charged paper uncharging the paper in those areas. The dark areas of the original don't reflect light so no light strikes the charged paper leaving those areas charged. The paper then goes through an area where a metallic toner comes in contact with the paper. The toner is electrostatically attracted to the areas that remain charged and not the uncharged areas. Think image and non-image. Lastly the paper goes through rollers that apply heat and pressure, affixing the toner to the paper providing a resulting copy of the image. Surely you've used a copier that has jammed. Upon pulling out the stuck paper you have noticed that the toner comes off or hasn't adhered to the paper—having not gone through the rollers.

Electrostatic printing is a cheap, fast, and useful method for producing short run "printing." Typically in black, with advancements in technology, quality color printing is often done for both individuals and businesses.

The typical desktop Laser printer uses a similar method to print copies though a laser is used to image a charged drum rather than reflected light.

Inkjet

Inkjet has made leaps and bounds lately. Once the domain primarily of cheap desktop computer printer it is forging new and exciting ground. Current trends in printing see more and more adoption and use of the ink jet printing method given the increased quality of machines and development of inks, in particular, the size of the droplets of ink that are "sprayed" onto paper and other substrates, creating printing of high quality.

At a recent printing show in Chicago, Print/Graph Expo 2013, an inkjet newspaper press was demonstrated for a local newspaper company, the first inkjet newspaper press in the U.S. At the demonstration tabloid additions of a local Polish newspaper, Spanish language soccer newspaper, and an edition of the Wall Street Journal one after another with little set-up time. The press is capable of printing tabloid and broadsheet papers of up to 72 pages. The ability to change from one job to another is demonstrated in this quote from the company president,

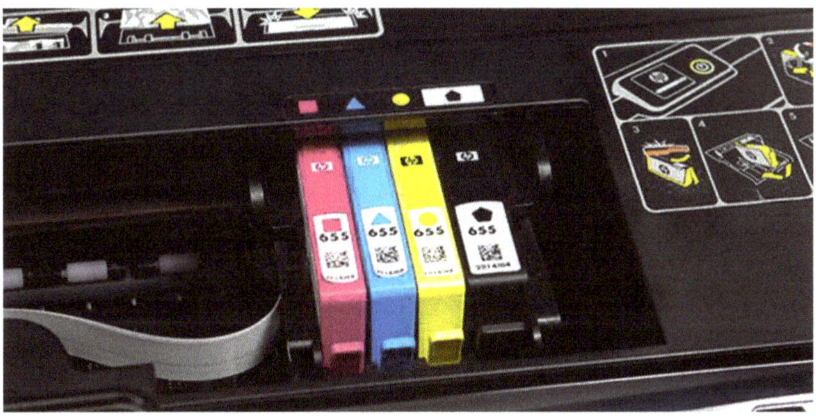

The most expensive part of owning an inkjet printer are the replaceable ink cartridges.

"the accumulated waste for one week of printing was exactly one newspaper copy."

The flexibility of inkjet printing has been known and used for a long time. Packaging and labeling of boxes, coding, individual addressing of mailers are examples of its use. The inkjet print market is currently worth $80.4 billion, and is expected to reach $118.2 billion in 2025 according to latest Smithers' report 'The Future of Inkjet Printing to 2025'. Signage is the largest market sector for inkjet, representing 57% of the value in 2011. But this proportion is steadily falling as the [digital] printing is being selected to print books, transactional and direct mail, packaging and labels, and commercial products, which are all growing strongly. *—https://www.smitherspira.com/market-reports/*

Inkjet is well established in visual communications using wide-format equipment, but the really dynamic sector is in high-speed inkjet, with many print providers moving away from high-volume mono laser printing. Not only high volume but personalized high volume. The Smithers Group, in an article on inkjet printing, provides an example of inkjet is being used in magazine production, whereby, 300,000 copies of the November 2016 edition of Popular Mechanics magazine was sent to US subscribers with a personalized cover. An outsert from HP greeted the subscriber by name and showed a scene specific to their home town. This process of utilizing a database of information to create the individualized printing is known as Variable Data Printing or Variable Data Publishing (VDP). A further description of VDP will be done in Chapter 9 - What's Next.

Certainly, pressureless or inkjet could soon be counted among the top printing methods used. **This book was printed by on-demand printing.**

CHAPTER 3

COLOR

I found I could say things with color and shapes that I couldn't say any other way - things I had no words for.
— Georgia O'Keeffe

Color My World

The role of color in visual communication is complex. It is undoubtedly the most researched, most visually powerful, and since the advent of computers, the most technical of all elements of design. It enhances the viewer's response on a variety of levels; it heightens our perception and intensifies emotional and psychological reaction. It is certain that to become proficient with color, you must spend time studying it and working with it. *—"Exploring the Elements of Design," Evans and Thomas*

Color has historically been very important to humans. An example is the coloring of food to make it more attractive. Coloring food was not an invention of contemporary society. Spices and condiments were probably used as colorants as long as 3,000 years ago. It is likely that colorants taken from naturally occurring minerals, plants and animals were developed along with spices which played such a prominent part in the development of early civilizations. Unfortunately in the 18th and 19th centuries, unscrupulous food manufacturers began to exploit the value of color to sell foods which were of poor quality or spoiled. Pickles often owed their appetizing green color to copper sulfate, a poison which killed unknown number of consumers. The rainbow hues of candy in shops were due to highly toxic salts of copper and lead. Thorn leaves, dried and colored with toxic verdigris (copper oxide), were sold as China tea. Used tea leaves were tinted with black lead and other chemicals, dried and sold as "fresh" tea. Even as late as 1900, a yellow color was sometimes added to milk in London to disguise "watering."

Color is a very important design decision for many diverse manufacturers. Consider the automobile industry. Automakers consider colors for future model years. PPG Industry, a major manufacturer and supplier of paint for the automobile industry, provides forecasts for paint colors. In response to continued demand for color innovation in automotive coatings, PPG introduced 64 exterior shades to manufacturers for consideration in styling 2018-2019 model year vehicles. Titled "AMPLIFY," the collection includes four color-trend story palettes: *Hyper HD* is a colorful and impactful theme that welcomes self-expression, performance and modern technology, *IM Perfect* is a global trend named as a play on words, celebrating the perfection of imperfections and authenticity in individuals living their best lives and focusing on their uniqueness with an emphasis on wellness, *Knight's Watch* is a stronghold theme providing sturdy reassurance for safety and security through traditional colors representing refuge and confidence, and *Lucid Dreams* reflects calmness, sensitivity and privacy, portraying a refuge from technology overload with fluid, graceful design. After more than a decade as the world's favorite car color, silver is falling in popularity to white. PPG Industries, the leading supplier of automotive paints, says 25 percent of the vehicles it supplied paint for the 2013 model year were white, up 3 percent from the prior year. — *http://finance.yahoo.com/.* Certainly the trend has continued since then.

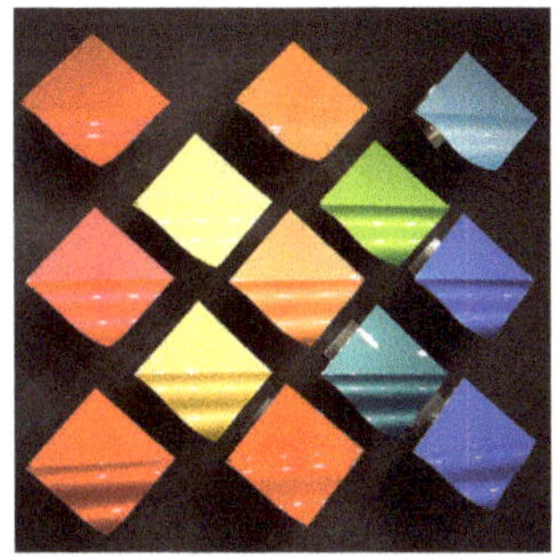

PPG's forecast of automotive paint colors.

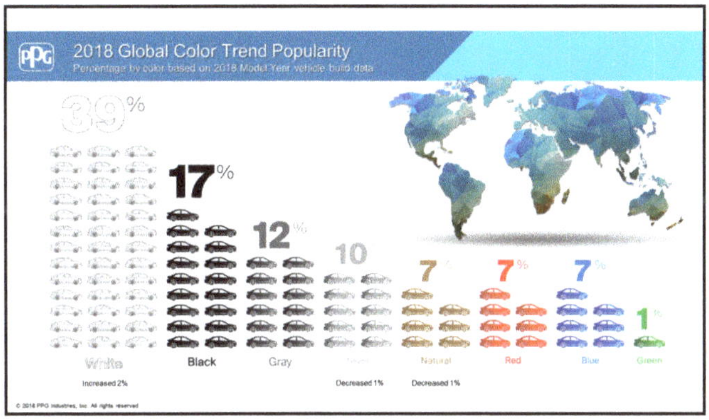

© 2018 PPG Industries

Color forecasting is not relegated to the automobile industry. The Color Marketing Group, since 1962 has been providing advanced color information, interpretation of past color movement, the interplay of design and color or new solutions to current marketing problems for color professionals. The non-profit organization publishes each year a two-year look ahead at color for automotive, communication/information, home furnishing, home utility products, as well as fashion. They also describe the impact color will have on industries including retail, hospitality, health care, and office.

Color most certainly is important in the graphic communications field both for print as well as digital products. Think of the packaging industry with the varied designs needed for the production of packaging. The average American supermarket stocks over 17,000 products, each competing for the consumer's attention and ultimately their dollars. Design specialist are constantly challenged to capture the buyer's eyes by making packages more appealing. Packaging color plays a major role in a products success, considering an approximate 80% failure rate for new products.

jetBlue®

The use of blue not only relates to the name of the airline but evokes the feelings of being trustworthy, dependable, secure, and responsible. Certainly attributes desired of an airlines.

Approximately two-thirds of all purchases made in a supermarket are non-planned. Impulse buying— encouraged by effective packaging which includes the choice of colors. Color is certainly an important part of capturing the consumer's attention. The ubiquitous red and white Campbell soup cans, Seven-Up green, and Hershey brown are attention-getters and easily recognized.
— *http://www.pantone.com/*

Lastly, color is critical to the design of a logo for a company, business, or organization. Research has found that different colors, provoke very different reactions in people. The most prominent brands in the world are defined by their colors. Think of McDonald's golden arches, the name Jet Blue, and UPS' slogan, "What can Brown do for you?" These companies, and many others, strategically use colors in their logo, website, and product to appeal to customers. It's important to think about how you utilize colors and what the colors you choose say about your business.

Color Theory

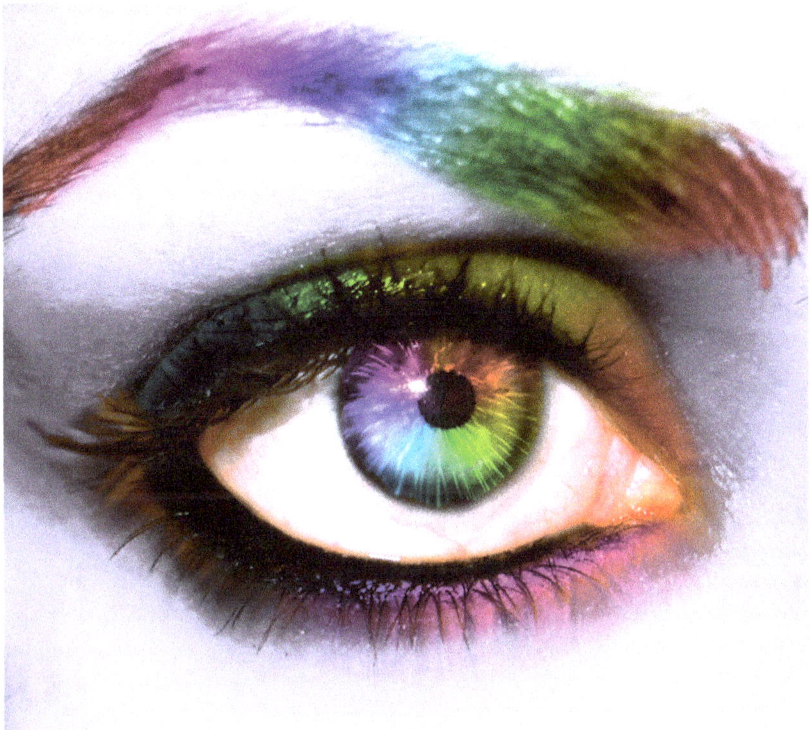

Our eyes provide us with our most important sense that we as humans have, sight. We rely on sight not only for routine activities, but for our very survival. Our eyes are comprised of a number of parts that direct the light to nerves that send that "light" information to the brain for interpreting the color that we "see." It works like a camera. The eye contains an iris that opens and closes to let more or less light in through the pupil depending upon the brightness of the light. A lens focuses the light which strikes the back of the eye or retina which contains nerve endings. There are two types of nerve endings called rods and cones. These nerves are receptive to the wavelengths light in different ways. They serve the task of detecting the intensity and the frequency of the incoming light.

Red plus Green Equals Yellow

There are three kinds of cone cells that roughly correspond to the colors red, green, and blue. When you see a color, each cone sends its own distinct signal to your brain. For example, suppose that yellow light, that is real yellow light, with a yellow frequency, is shining on your eye. You don't have a cone specifically for detecting yellow, but yellow is kind of close to green and also kind of close to red, so both the red and green cones get activated, and each sends a signal to your brain saying so. Of course, there is another way to activate the red cones and the green cones simultaneously: if both red light and green light are present at the same time. The point is, your brain receives the same signal, regardless of whether you see light that has the yellow frequency or light that is a mixture of the green and red frequencies. That's why, for light, red plus green equals yellow. —*excert from the Youtube video "How we see color", by Colm Kelleher*

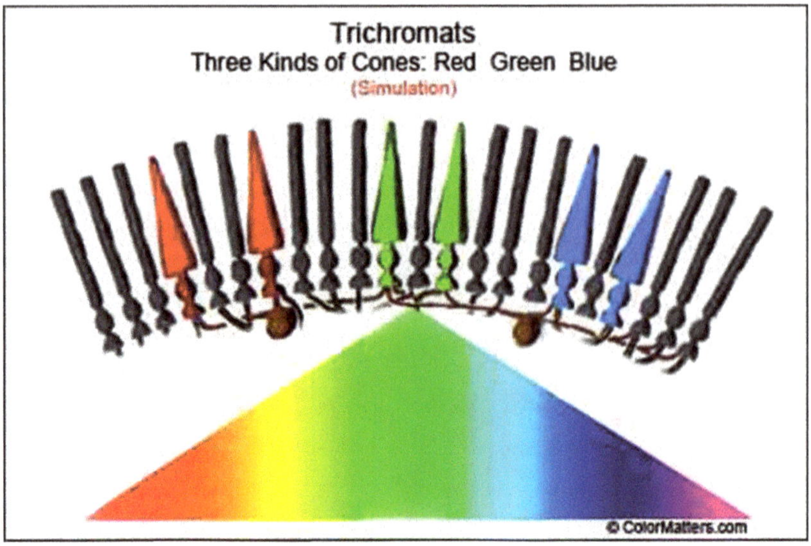

An adult eye is typically equipped with up to 120 million rods that detect the intensity of light and about 6 million cones that detect the frequency of light. These rods and cones send nerve impulses to the brain. The nerve impulses travel through a network of nerve cells. There are as many as one million neural pathways from the rods and cones to the brain. This network of nerve cells is bundled together to form the optic nerve on the very back of the eyeball.

Rods are receptive to lightness and darkness. At night, often we see things simply by movement, that is a change in lightness and darkness of images in their locations. People that have a hard time seeing at night, often called night blindness, have a reduced number of rods.

Cones are receptive to the three primary color components of light—red, green, and blue and transmit the color they "see" to the brain. The information from the cones and rods are passed to the brain via the optic nerve.

Wavelengths are a form of energy that makes up the visible spectrum of color we see. They are part of the electrometric field which produces microwaves, radio waves, infrared radiation, and X-rays. When light strikes an object some of the color wavelengths are reflected to the eye. The spectrum of visible light can be broken into three primary colors: red, green, and blue. When we see white all three color wavelengths are reflected or transmitted. When we see black, no wavelengths are reflected or transmitted.

Varying degrees of the three primary colors provide the vast spectrum of colors with minute variation from one "color" to another. If we use just the three primary color one can see the relationship that they have to one another. Further discussion on this principle will be done when we look at color systems later in this chapter.

Fine artists for millennium have studied color, and more specifically light and how color is dependent upon it.

Claude Monet, the famous French painter who is considered the father of the "Impressionism" style of painting, was one such artist. In the 1890's he began a series of paintings that depicted haystacks over and over again—but the interesting thing was that the paintings were not about the haystacks, but

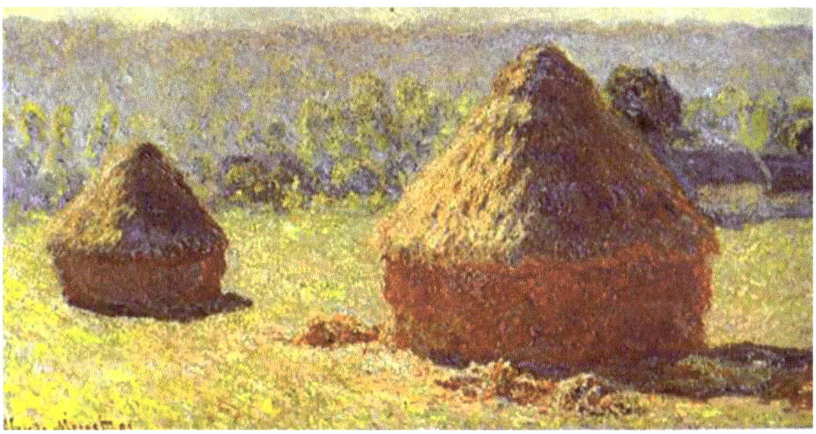

Claude Monet, "Haystack End of Summer Morning, 1891, Oil on canvas. A series of paintings that are a study of how light affects color.

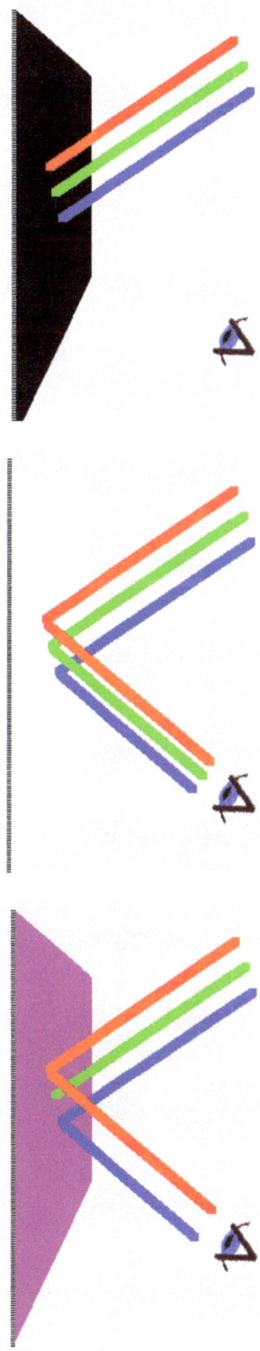

Combination of two primary color provide a third color.

rather an investigation of how the light during different times of the day, or different seasons of the year, changed the way the haystacks looked. It's the artist's eye that critically judges light and color and is able to represent its differences in works of art.

Color differentiation is not only important to the artist, it is important to the graphic artist that creates design and to the those that reproduce print and digital media. Studies have shown (Cal Poly, San Luis Obispo, Graphic Communication department, Brian Lawler), that visual artist tend to have a better ability to differentiate color than the average person. A common test for this is the Farnsworth-Munsell test.

Another more common test that tests our ability to see color based upon color theory, is a color blindness test. Unfortunately, some people lack the ability to see color as most do. There are many different types and degrees of color blindness - more correctly called color vision deficiencies. These people have a deficiency or lessen sensitivity to wavelengths of light by one or more of their "cones."

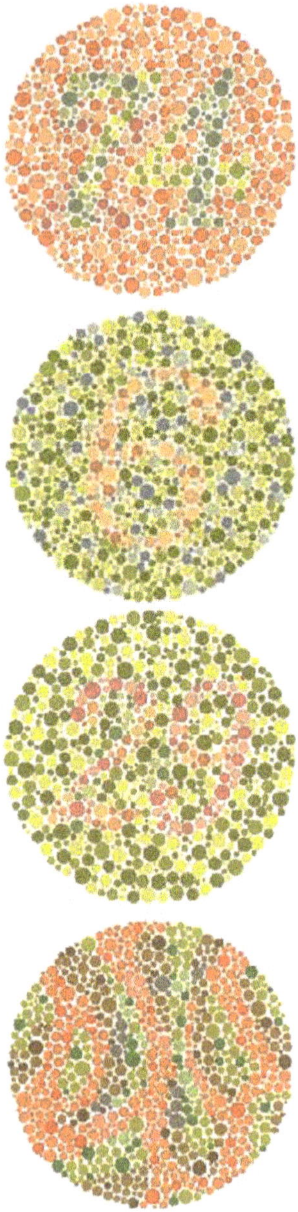

Ishihara Color Blindness Test—Can you see the numbers? How about the bottom one? If you can't, that's a good thing, if you do, then please see an optometrist.

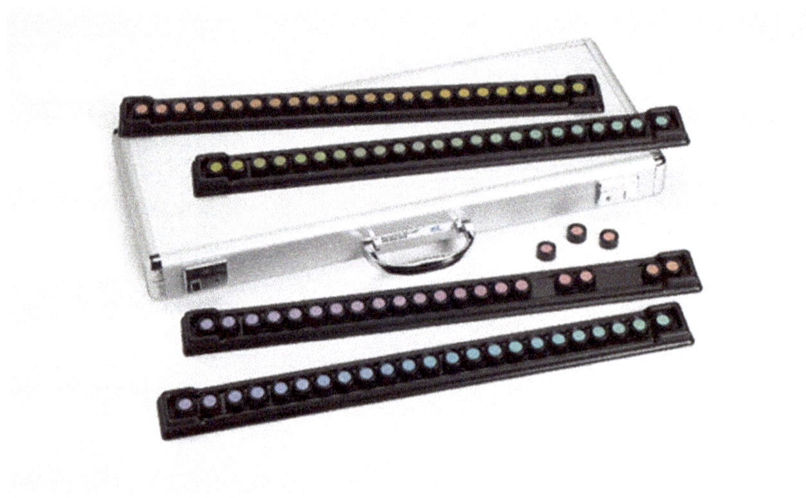

The Farnsworth-Munsell 100 hue test is a color vision test that tests hue discrimination, in which the color chips are arranged in order of one end color to another by the person being tested.

Color Psychology

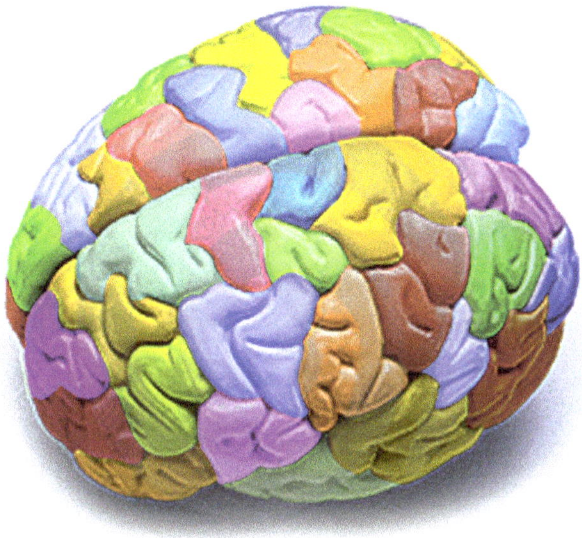

Color evokes understanding and emotion based upon learned, cultural, and human perceptions. The meaning of a color therefore varies depending on many factors.

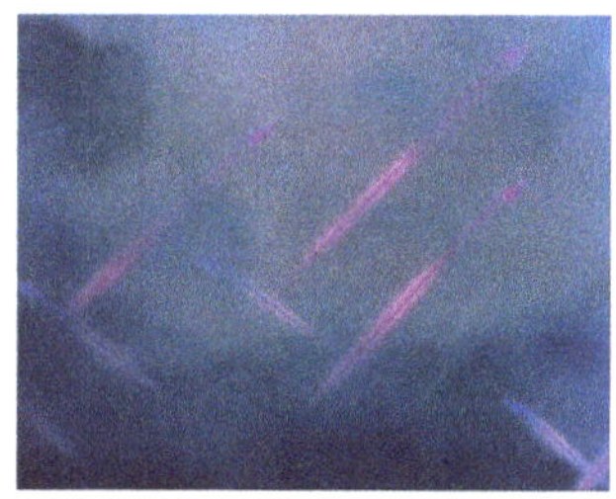

Disney's Fantasia — Visual interruption of music in color for the music Toccata and Fugue.

Psychology plays an essential role in deciphering the meaning of color in visual communication. Color psychology involves the affective nature of color— how color makes a person feel. This is a powerful dimension of color in all of the visual arts. Color psychology encompasses symbolic and cultural associations that also affect how individuals feel about certain colors. Color has even been associated with the sound of music. Think about the classic movie *Fantasia*.

Color is more emotional and subjective than intellectual and objective. Consider this, the color wheel was developed more from views of human perception and psychological response to color than to any scientific theory. *Experts from — "Exploring the Elements of Design," Evans and Thomas.*

People are affected and influenced by color in many obvious and not-so-obvious ways. We use color to describe feelings: "I'm in a blue mood," "She's green with envy," and "He's got me seeing red." It's used to identify everything from military organizations (navy blue), to business (IBM, "big Blue"), to life stages (baby blue). Beyond words and images, color communicates instantly and powerfully. "A world without color would be a world without emotion," Richard Palatini, instructor at Kean University, New Jersey states this and lists the following four points about color.

The "life" of color

People develop feelings about color that change and evolve as they reach different life stages and they also relate to color in different ways during each stage. Adolescents are drawn to colors that are more outrageous, intense, and used in unusual ways. The same red that children are drawn to, is the same color adults perceive as dangerous.

Wide World of Color

Culturally, often people have different associations with color. As example, the color white is associated with mourning by the Chinese, yet in America, white is the color of wedding gowns. Considering our mobile global society, people will bring their color "baggage" with them when interacting cross-culturally like in business or travel. In these situations, people need to assimilate into their new societal environment by emulating the new colors they find.

Color with Feeling

For a graphic designer, marketing executive, advertiser, or one trying to communicate visually, what is the emotional response one wants to elicit from an audience? Excitement, serenity, power? Greens, lavenders, and blues can communicate peacefulness and serenity. Dense purples, deep reds, and intense pinks are sensually provocative.

Crimes of Color

Sometimes breaking the "laws" of color can be the right thing to do. In creating a distinct identity, being different might be better than using the right symbolic color. Think of these car rental businesses which have created their own distinct yet appropriate color personality: Hertz (yellow), Avis (red), and National (green).

Sight is a precious gift. In of itself, sight is an incomplete dynamic. The other half of sight involves perception— how we understand and filter what has been sensed visually, so that we can identify and understand what we're seeing. (see Chapter 6, Coming Up with a Design). Often too, color may suggest sensations. Warm— red, oranges, and yellow stimulate appetites. Many musicians such as Strauss, Mozart, and Liszt sometimes ascribed to color to explain or plot their compositions. Our brains utilize a number of things to make sense of the world and what we see including size, shape, figure/ground, form, texture, patterns, and color. From birth onward, perception is intricately tied to learned information. While color is closely connected to how we recognize and understand reality, it is but one piece of a very complex process.

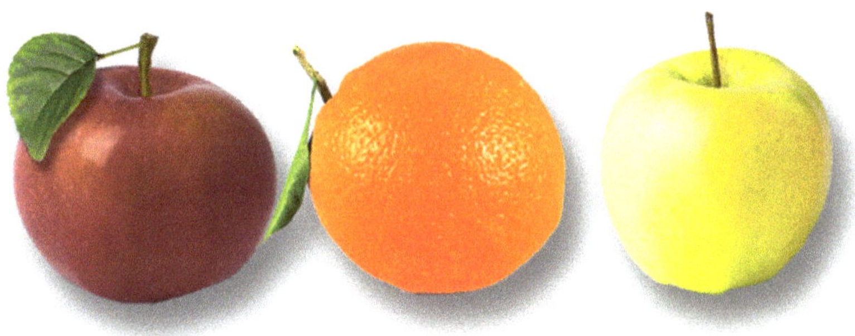

Color has psychological implications that are both innate and learned. Scientists have proven that we all have inherent, unlearned psychological reactions to color stimuli. — *Experts from "Graphic Communications Today," Ryan and Conover*

Mauve
Bold, Stylish, Worldly, Impressive, Somber

Magenta
Romantic, Enchanting, Sensitive, Optimistic

Crimson
Powerful, Aggressive, Dynamic, Dramatic

Scarlet
Bright, Believable, Vivid, Positive, Effective

Poster Red
Popular, Dangerous, Exciting, Loud

Coral
Wild, Fiery, Passionate, Glorious, Explosive

Orange
Tangy, Tempting, Lively, Zesty, Tart

Amber
Mellow, Abundant, Fertile, Prosperous, Contented

Gold
Joyful, Sunny, Rich, Lavish, Uncertain

Yellow
Exciting, Inspiring, Sour, Anxious, Sharp

Lime
Young, Fresh, Naive, Sharp, Lively, Clean

Here are some examples of color and associated color psychology associated with each color as described by Jean Bourges in his book, "Color Bytes: Blending the Art and Science of Color".

Leaf Green
Natural, Dependable, Safe, Secure, Healthy

Sea Green
Mature, Strong, Urbane, Moving, Restless

Emerald
Brilliant, Beautiful, Expensive, Wise, Eternal

Teal
Primitive, Intuitive, Ancient, Aesthetic, Sharp

Cyan
Sharp, Clean, Cold, Hard, Analytical, Intelligent

Sky Blue
True, Honest, Good, Calm, Clean, Peaceful

Ultramarine
Fabulous, Compassionate, Stately, Moving, Soulful

Violet
Moody, Serious, Thoughtful, Quiet, Reflective

Purple
Grand, Regal, Leader, Superior, Majestic

Color Description

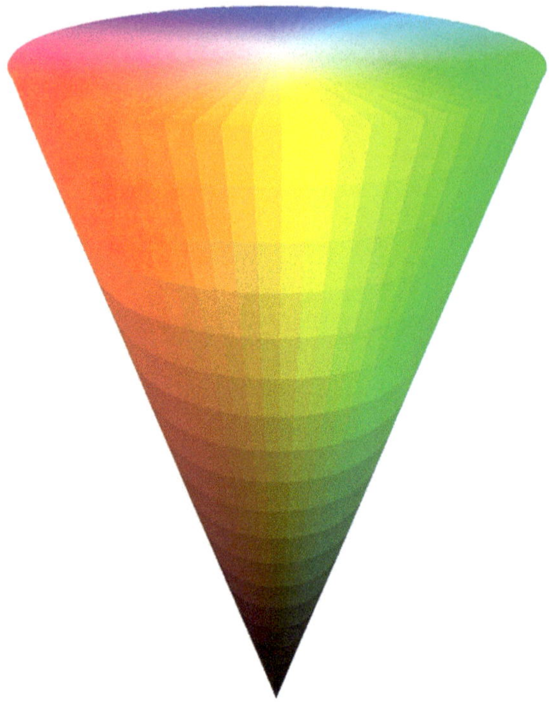

You learned in *Color Theory*, that color is a small portion of the electro magnetic spectrum, and that our eyes have nerve endings, called rods and cones, that are receptive to the wavelengths of light and transfer that information to our brain where it is interpreted as colors. In this section we'll look at the three components that make up color, models in which color is described, harmonious color combinations, and what a color gamut is.

Color has three components: **hue, saturation,** and **value**. The term hue is derived from the ancient Gothic word *hiwi,* which means "to show." It is the color such as red, blue, or purple. Saturation is how intense the hue is, and value (Photoshop refers to this as brightness) is the lightness or darkness of the hue. The relationship of these three components can easily be seen by looking at the color picker in Adobe Photoshop. The

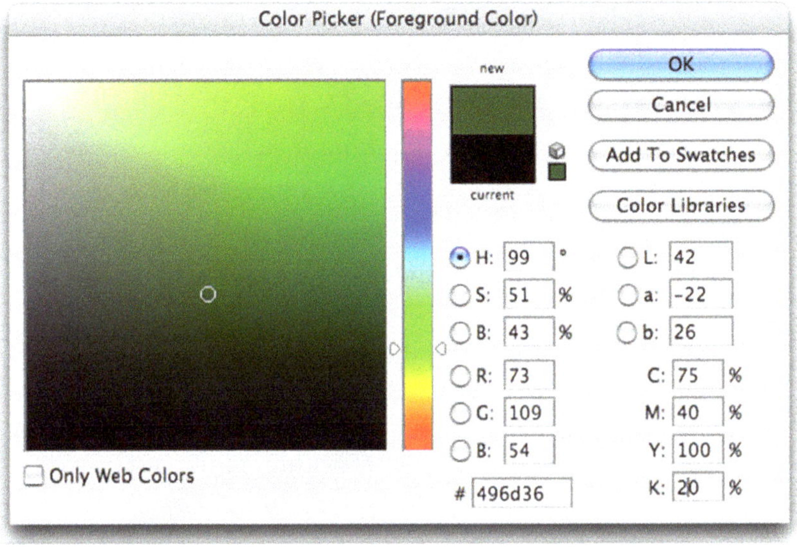

The color picker can be used in Adobe software to specify color. In this example the color picker indicates specifications of five color modes for the particular green selected.

rainbow stripe is the hue, left to right in the color block is the saturation, top to bottom is the value or brightness. Specifications are indicated for five color modes, some used for print media (CMYK) and some for digital media (RGB and HEX). The other two modes are more specific to the description of the color.

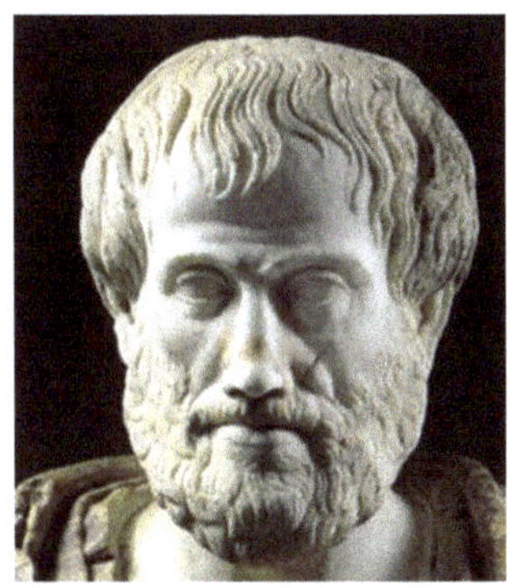

Aristotle (384–322 B.C.E.) is among the greatest philosophers of all time. He considered color as if "color is in body, and therefore in an individual body (for if it were not in any individual, it would not be in body at all)."

Color as important as it is to humankind, has been described historically in scientific, cultural, and philosophical terms. Early interest and investigation into what color is may start with an interpretation of Pythagoras's teachings, which maintained that the root of all harmony was to be found in the positions of the planets between the earth and sphere of fixed stars; the linear arrangement of colors according to Aristotle, who was probably the first to investigate color mixtures; and finally a personal interpretation of Plato's color-system taken from his Timaios, according to which the eye does not receive light, but rather transmits a ray of vision towards an object. Well, not really the way color is understood and described today nor as Sir Isaac Newton discovered.

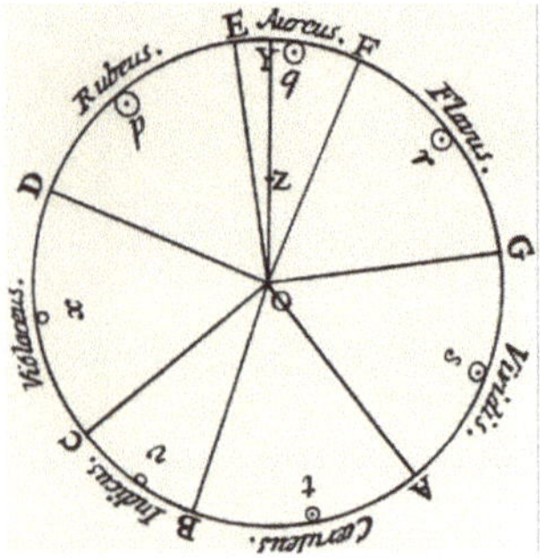

Newton's famous circular arrangement of spectral colors appeared in 1704 in his central work, Opticks.

After Newton had used a prism to separate daylight and count seven individual colors, it appeared to him that, when considering color-hue, this was a closed system. By taking the violet end of the spectrum and linking it to the red start-point, he thus created a convincing circle of colors. With Newton's circular shape, the transition between the one- and two-dimensional color-system is complete. It is helpful to realize that although this step was made by a physicist, it actually has little to do with physics; it is our brain that, out of the straight line of physics, makes the circle first drawn by Newton.

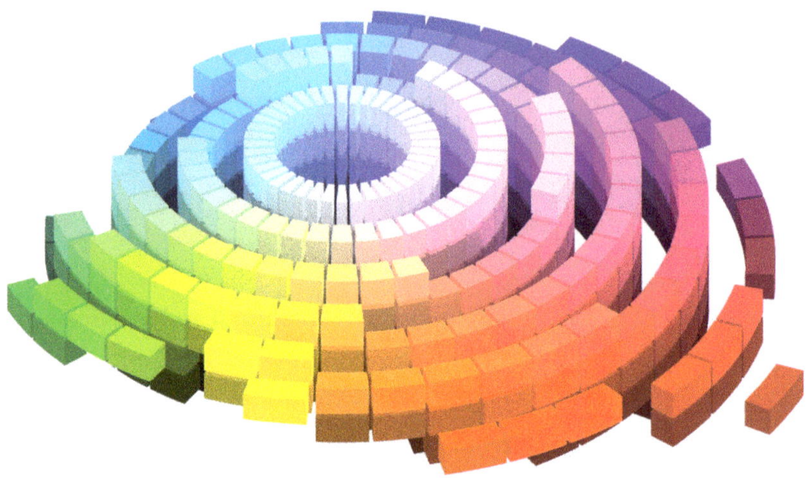

A modern graphic depiction of the Munsell Color System, which describes color three- dimensionally.

One of the most widespread—and nowadays most utilized—color-systems, the **Munsell Color System**, was developed by the American painter Charles Munsell between 1905 and 1916. Remember the Farnsworth-Munsell Color Discrimination Test described earlier in this chapter? The Munsell Color System is based on a unique color-solid arrangement which more accurately demonstrates hue, value and intensity of color. In this system, a color's hue is given a number/letter destination which locates it on the Munsell Color Wheel. Value is designated by a number from 1 -11 corresponding to a scale from black to white. Saturation, also called chroma, is designated by a number from 1 - 15 (the higher the number the greater the hue's intensity). This System is often used by paint, ink, colored paper, and other manufacturers because its alpha-numerical system of notation allows for accurate description of a color's hue, value and intensity (saturation) between various remote parties.

Prior to this, others had developed their theories on color discounting the Newton theory resulting in different systems of color such as the Schopenhauer/Goethe Weighted Color System. Johann Goethe, the German poet and dramatist devised a color system of six equal parts (our common primaries and secondaries). Arthur Schopenhauer, the German philosopher, much to Goethe's dismay, modified Goethe's system by changing the equal distribution of the hues around the color wheel in favor of a distribution of unequal amounts. In Schopenhauer's version the hues were given weights based on their lightness or darkness; that is, their perceived weight. Each complementary pair shares 1/3 of the color wheel, just as in the Prang and original Goethe systems. But in Schopenhauer's modification the complementary pairs are assigned different proportions of their third based on this weighting. Yellow occupies 1/4 and violet 3/4 of their respective third. Orange is assigned 1/3 and blue 2/3 of their third of the color wheel, and red and green each are assigned 1/2 of their portion. The hues, in their order on the color wheel, are yellow, orange, red, violet, blue and green and each are assigned a numerical value or 3, 4, 6, 9, 8,and 6 respectively.

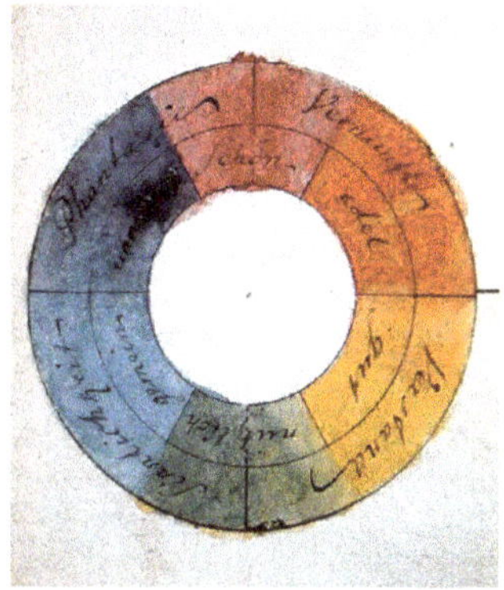

Goethe Color Wheel.

It was Goethe who first understood that color is more than just a physical problem at a time when, artists and scientists were cut from the same cloth.

"When the eye sees a color it is immediately excited and it is its nature, spontaneously and of necessity, at once to produce another, which with the original color, comprehends the whole chromatic scale." — *Goethe, Theory of Colours*

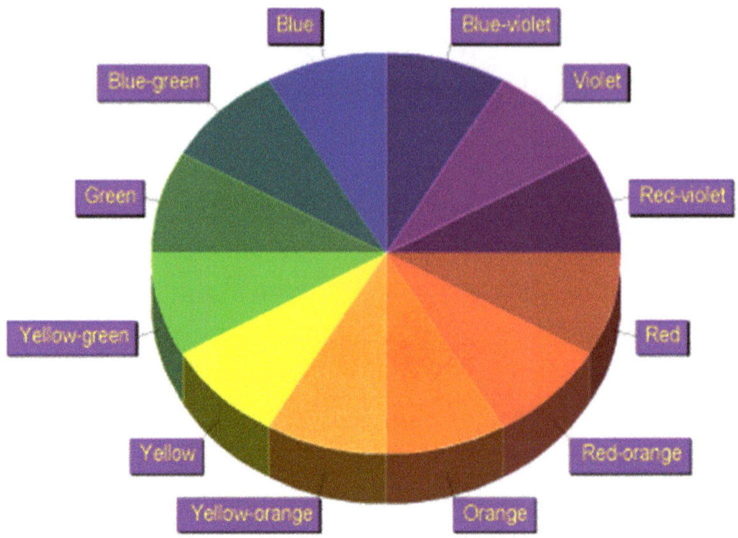

Traditional color wheel that we remember from our early years of school.

The various color description systems that have been described in this section are reflected in a traditional color wheel familiar to most of us which includes 12 hues in the spectrum. In this system the three main hues are blue, yellow, and red. These are known as **Primary Colors**. They are colors that cannot be combined from mixing any colors together within the color wheel. **Secondary Colors** are created by combining two of the primary colors. These colors are green, violet, and orange. The remaining hues, Yellow-green, blue-green, blue-violet, red-violet, red-orange, and yellow orange are **Tertiary Colors**. They are made by combining a primary and a secondary hue. The color name has the primary color name listed first. One could also combine two secondary colors to create a tertiary color. That color would not be included among the 12 hues of the traditional color wheel.

Combination of colors on the color wheel, either traditional or digital, can also be described and used in other ways to create palettes of colors.

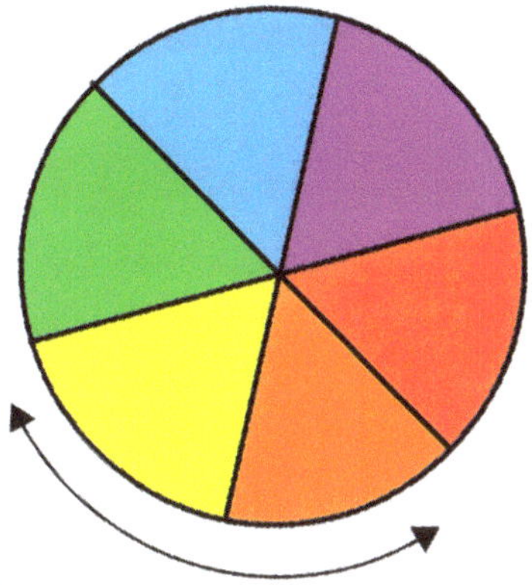

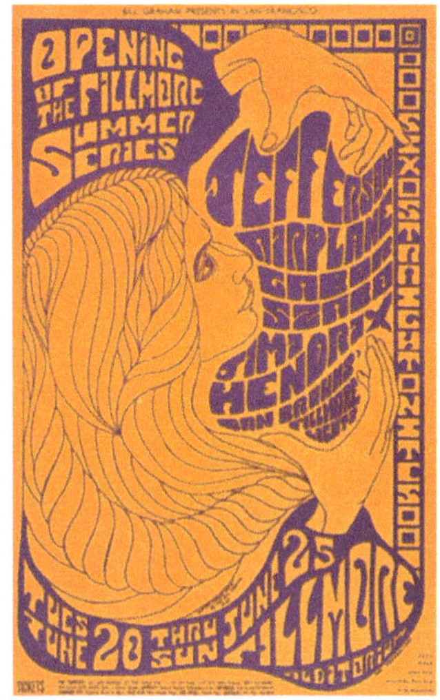

Analogous Colors

Analogous Colors are composed of colors next to each other on the color wheel. These colors share an undertone of the same color, creating a harmonious combination.

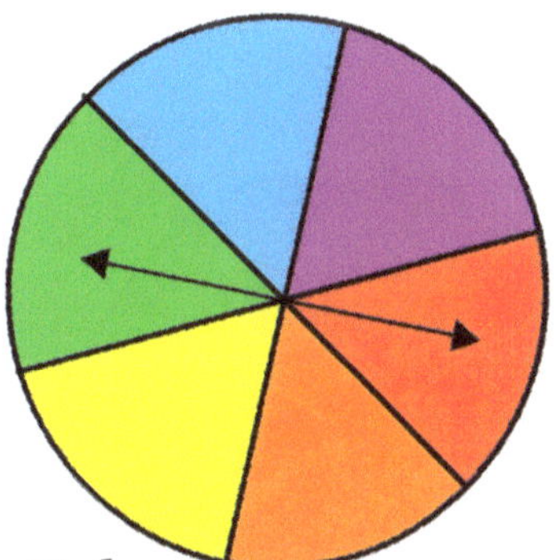

Complimentary Colors

Another often used combination is colors are **Complimentary Colors**. These are colors that are opposite on the color wheel. This "difference" provides excitement in their use. This drama is due to their contrasting warm and cool hues. Red and green, yellow and violet, and orange and blue are examples of primary complimentary colors. A very effective use of these color combinations can be found in the psychedelic posters of the 60s. These contrasting colors provide a vibrant almost visually vibrating design. Another example of their use are in team colors such as the contrasting orange and blue of the NFL Chicago Bears.

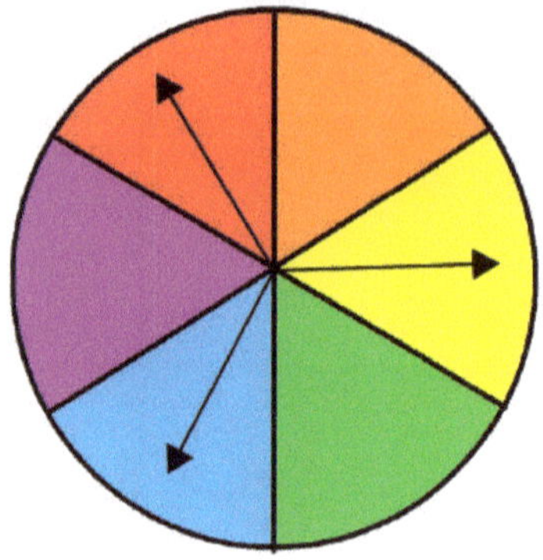

Triads

As the name implies, this harmony in **triad colors**, uses a combination of three colors, each of which is at the point of a visualized equilateral triangle placed on the wheel. As the triangle is turned to any position on the wheel, it points will designate the three colors that are compatible. Primary and secondary colors are triads.

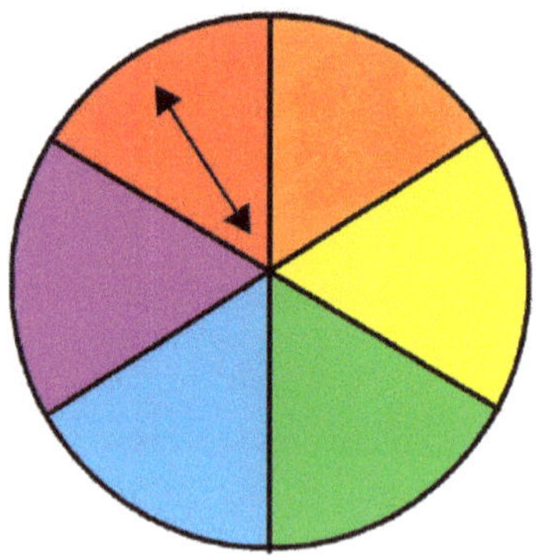

Monochromatic Colors

Lastly, **Monochromatic Colors** provide harmony in the simplest way to obtain color unity and unity in design. It is constructed from different values of the same color. Remember, value is one of the three components that make up color. It is the lightness or darkness of a color.

Digital Color

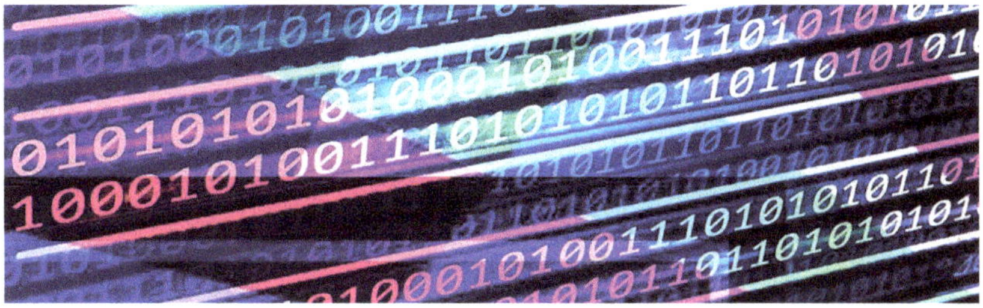

With the invention of the computer and its use in the mid-80s to create graphics and layouts, color became described and produced using digital information. Computers use a binary system for coding and processing of information. The system is quite simple in what we often think of as a complex electronic device, the computer. In essence the system is based on electrical current either on or off though the various components and in the manner in which the processed information is described. It is expressed using zeros and ones. Each is referred to as a bit of information. Eight **bits** of information is called a **byte**. Typically images are displayed and reproduced digitally using this eight-bit method known as bit-depth.

Given the combination of zeros and ones in the system, there are 256 possibilities. That means a pixel (a contraction of picture element) is turned on with varying degrees of intensity. They can have 256 levels of intensity from all "off," 00000000, which would be no light, to all "on," 11111111, which would be the brightest light the pixel can display.

Mimicking the red, green, and blue rod nerve ending receptors in our eyes, color is displayed on computer and television monitors using these colors. Since each of these color pixels can have 256 levels of intensity, their combination of all three provides 16 million color possibilities. Quite a few, but consider this, Adobe Photoshop can also describe color using 16 and 32-bit depth color modes!

On web pages, color is described using hexadecimal colors. This is a system of red, green, and blue values like that are described using alphanumeric pairs of 0-9 and A-F for each color such as: #ff0099 which is a rose color. The first pair, ff, is

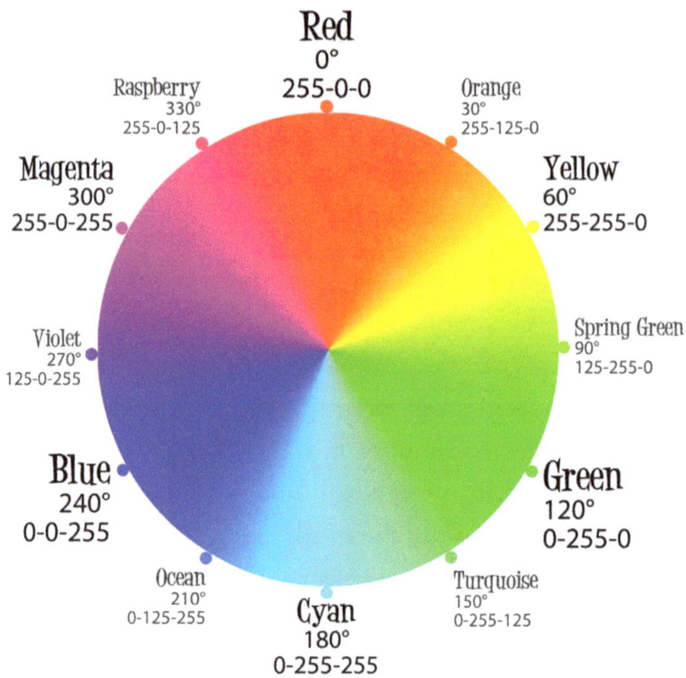

for red, 00 for green, and 99 for blue. More recently, R,G,B,a is being used. The "a" refers to the alpha or transparency level. The color wheel for digital color differs from the traditional "artist" color wheel described previously. Considering that the primary colors are red, green, and blue and not red, yellow, and blue, there is a difference also in secondary, complimentary, and triads that more accurately define digital color. Notice in the illustration the relationship between complementary colors red and cyan, blue and yellow, and green and magenta. This will help to explain the process color or subtractive color system used in full color printing that is explained in the following section.

Color Systems

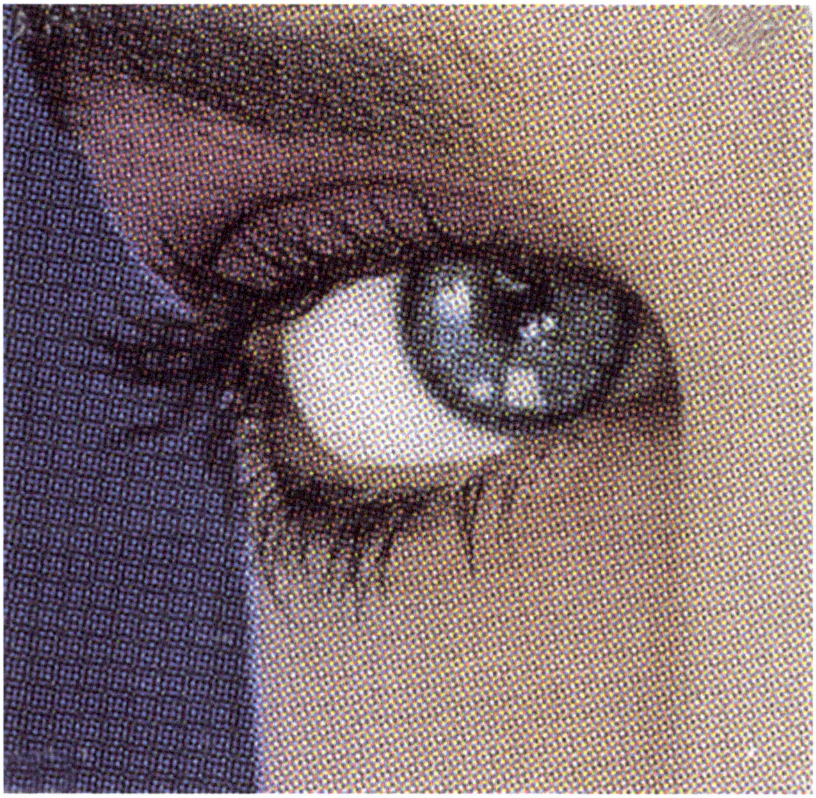

In the printing industry, there are two ways in which color ink is printed, process color, sometimes called four-color, and spot color.

Process Color (subtractive)

Process color uses four colors of ink— cyan, magenta, yellow, and black, commonly referred to as CMYK. Yes black. In the terms of printing, black is a color. To print a spectrum of colors using just four colors, combinations of the colors composed of solids and or tints of a color are used. Typically printing inks used to print process color are transparent so printing a solid or 100% yellow on top of or underneath a 50%

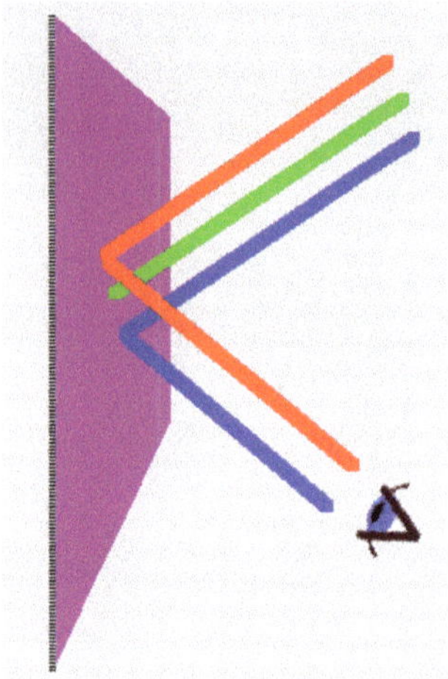

Use of a green filter to separate out red and blue providing the magenta printer.

magenta would give us orange as an example. To print photographic images, a color original image is "separated" into the four colors by creating four separate **halftones** (see Halftones sidebar below). Color filters are used to separate out each of the colors. Blue provides yellow, green provides magenta, and red provides cyan. The process in essence subtracts out two colors. As example the green filter "subtracts" red and blue which when combined together provide magenta. This process of color separation is known a Subtractive Color. But wait! There are four colors. What about black? All three color

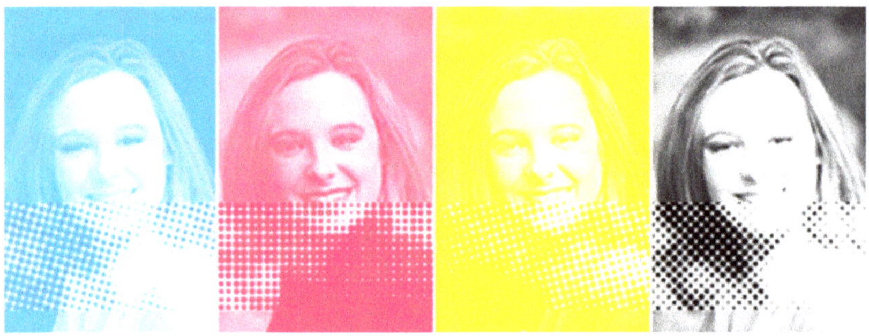

Halftone Process

Halftones are made by exposing the image in a large camera known as a process camera with a halftone screen covering the film, and then developing the film (old school). The screen has soft-edged dots so the brighter the area on the original the larger the dot created, darker areas produce smaller dots. These varying size dots provide the tonal range replicating the original. Initially this is a negative so when the printing plate is exposed and processed the large dots become small one (remember brighter area on the original) and small dots become larger. Today most often a computer and/or scanner generate the halftones without a film intermediate— going directly to the imaging and processing of the printing plates.

filters, red, green, and blue are used which subtracts out all the color leaving no color or black. Black provides that sharpness and definition that using only cyan, magenta, and yellow can't.

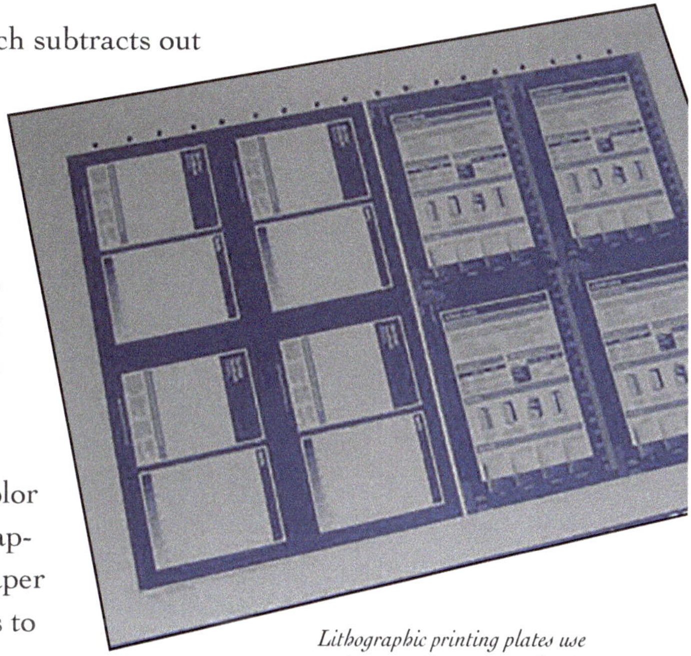

Lithographic printing plates use a photographic emulsion that is imaged to produce image to print. The coating is receptive to the ink. In this example, the blue is only the color of the emulsion, not the color of ink that can be printed from the plate.

Printing is done using a four-color press, in which there are four separate printing units in which each one prints one of the colors. The presses are very expensive so some printing companies only have a single color press. So printing process color requires them to clean up the press and apply different color ink four times. The paper then, is sent through the press four times to print each of the colors.

As you learned in Chapter 2— Lithography, printing plates are made that have the image to be printed. This means making four separate printing plates whether for a single or four-color press.

Spot Color

Rather than using the process or four-color method for printing color, spot color may be used by itself or in combination with process color. In this system, much like mixing house paint, a combination of base color inks are physically mixed. The formula for colors is described using a color system such as the popular Pantone Matching System. Other common systems used include Dainippon Ink and Chemicals, and Toyo. In these systems, color books are used by graphic designers to specify and printers to mix color. In the Pantone system, 14 basic color inks are used such as warm red, Rhodamine Red, yellow, process blue, and black. The color books have colors printed on both coated and uncoated paper. With each color

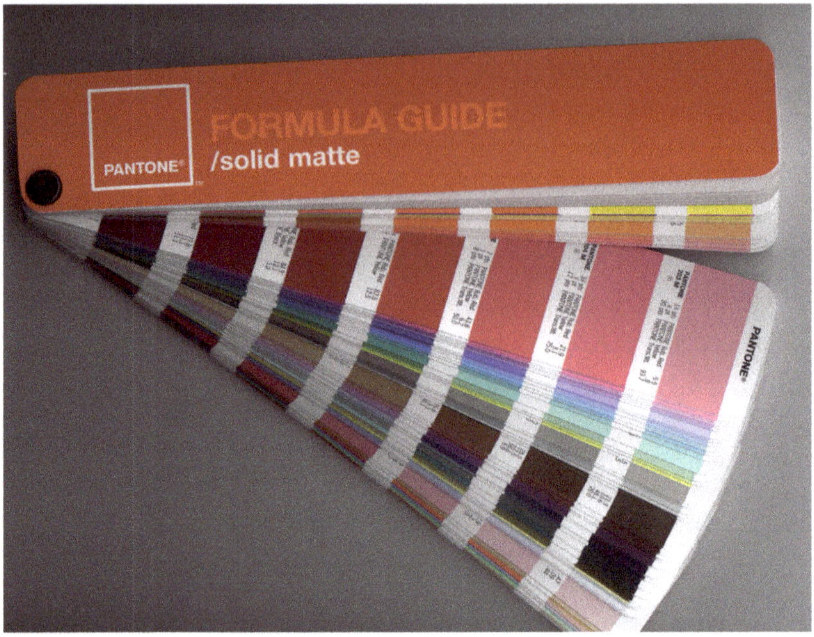

One of many color selection books offered by Pantone®. Some have metalic colors, others are for specific non-printed products such as for the fashion industry.

sample is a formula that indicates how many "parts" of each basic color is used along with a percentage value of those inks.

To indicate the color chosen, a number is used in conjunction with a letter that indicates the color and the finish of the paper it is intended to be printed on. As example, Pantone 300 U, often described as PMS 300 U, specifies a blue color to be printed on uncoated paper.

This manner of describing color allows designers and printers universally to refer to and use the same color without saying, "it's kind of a lemon yellow."

CHAPTER 4

TYPOGRAPHY

"Of all the achievements of the human mind, the birth of the alphabet is the most momentous."
— *Frederic Goudy, Typographer*

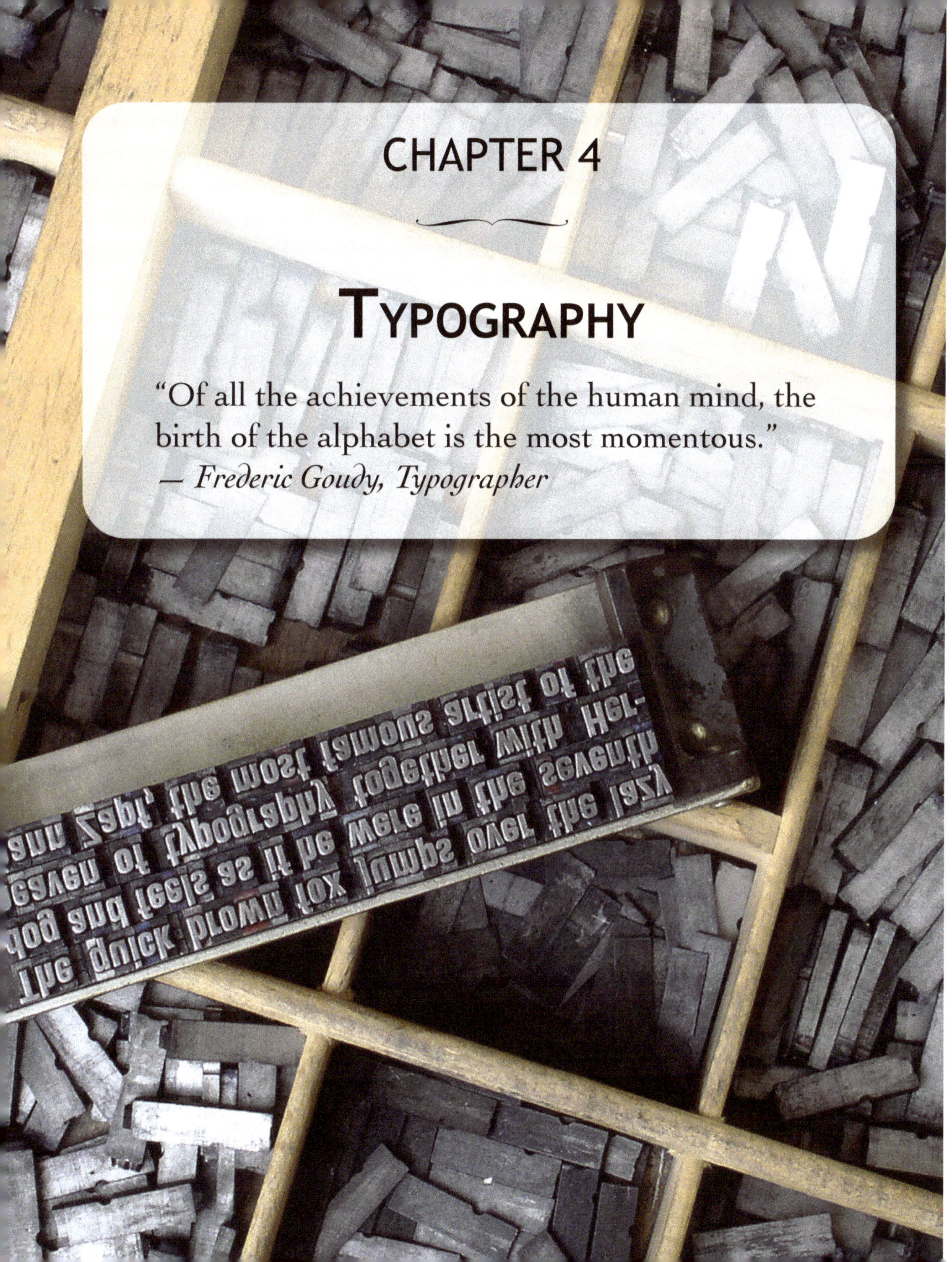

Representational to Symbols to Characters

Early representational images eventually evolved into stylized and simplified images known as symbols. These pictograms (paintings) and petroglyphs (carvings on rocks) would be used to represent things, ideas (also know as ideographs), eventually to represent sounds in a language. An early example of writing using symbols is the well known Egyptian **Hieroglyphics**. Hieroglyphics is Greek for "sacred inscription."

Unfortunately, the meaning of what was written in Hieroglyphics and an understanding of the language itself became lost over time as Egypt's power waned. With the discovery of the pyramids and Sphinx, scientists and Europeans, in general, became fascinated with Egypt and sought to decipher the Hieroglyphics. The Rosetta Stone, an irregularly shaped slab

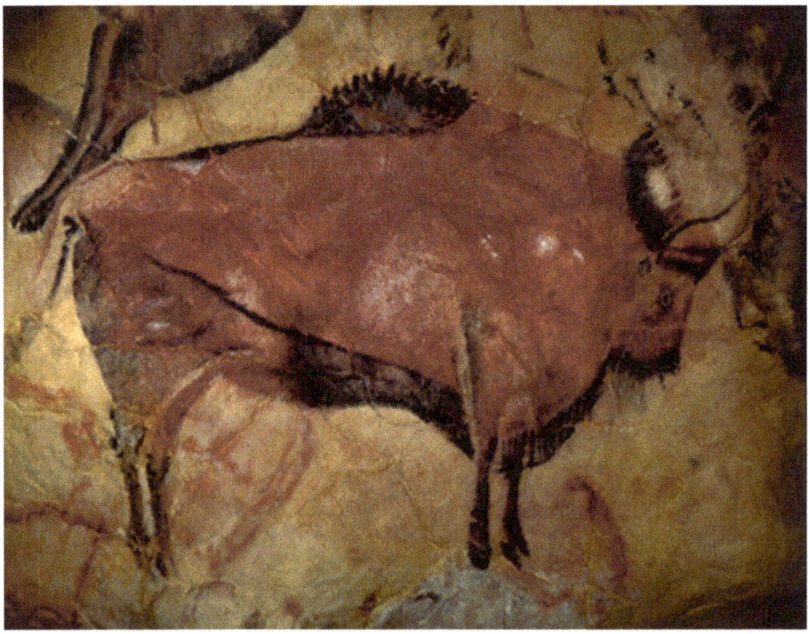

Picture of bison painted on cave wall in a cave near Altamira, Spain — the beginnings of early human visual communication.

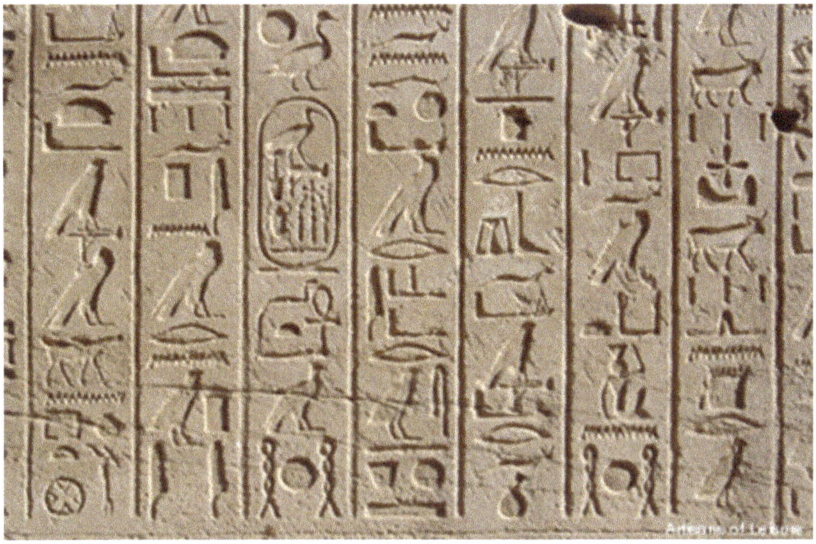

Hieroglyphics and the Rosetta Stone (below) that was the key to deciphering them.

of rock weighing about 1,700 pounds, was discovered by Napoleon's troops when they were preparing to build the foundation for Fort Julian (later known as Fort Rashid) on the West Bank of the Nile near Rosetta, Egypt in 1799.

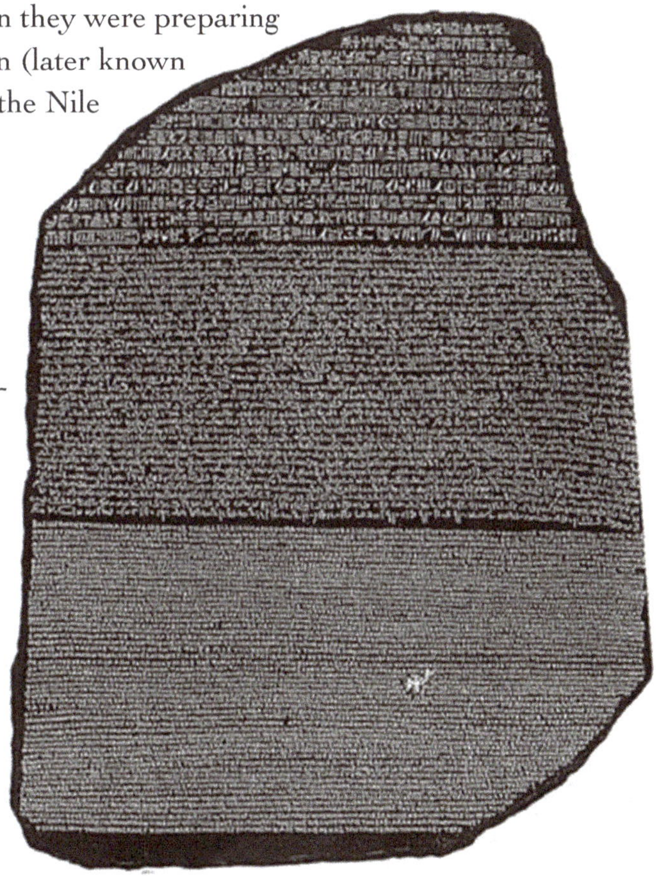

The carved inscriptions on the stone, which dates from Ptolemaic Period, 196 BC, included hieroglyphics – the written language of ancient Egypt (both hieroglyphic, formal and demotic, which was a common or informal form of writing)– and Greek, which was readily understood. The three texts, all stated the same Decree. (Since these three languages were all used at the time, the Decree had to be "published" in all of them.) In 1822, Frenchman Jean-Francois Champollion, using this knowledge was able to unlock the mystery of the hieroglyphics, and ancient Egypt.

Wedge-shaped Cuneiform glyphs pressed into clay.

Cuneiforms

It was the end of the Stone Age, and the beginning of the Bronze Age or the Age of Metallurgy and Writing about 3000 BC! The ancient Sumerians believed in education and record keeping was very important to them and they wanted their sons to learn how to read and write. Their written language began as pictographs, pictures of things that acted as words. Pictographs worked, but they were rather cumbersome so the clever ancient Sumerians started to use wedge-shaped symbols for objects and ideas instead of pictures. The cuneiform script is one of the earliest known forms of written expression. The Cuneiforms were written on clay tablets, on which symbols were drawn with a blunt reed, called a stylus that had a shaped end. The impressions left by the stylus were wedge shaped, thus giving rise to the name cuneiform, "wedge shaped," which comes from the Latin word "*cuneus*."

There is a great deal known about the ancient Sumerian civilization because of the written records they left behind both in stone and clay. The ancient Sumerians kept excellent records and lists of things. They listed their household goods, court activity, and their sales and purchases. They even kept a list of their kings that was updated from time to time, as new kings came to power.

Who's on first, What's on second?

Like the old comedy routine of comedians Abbott and Costello, "Who's on First," it certainly can be confusing as to how type and the written word has developed over the past several thousand years. Lets take a look at some major steps.

Until the discovery of two inscriptions on rocks in Wadi el-Hol, Egypt, in 1999, it was generally held that the beginnings of alphabetic writing could be traced to around 1600 to 1500

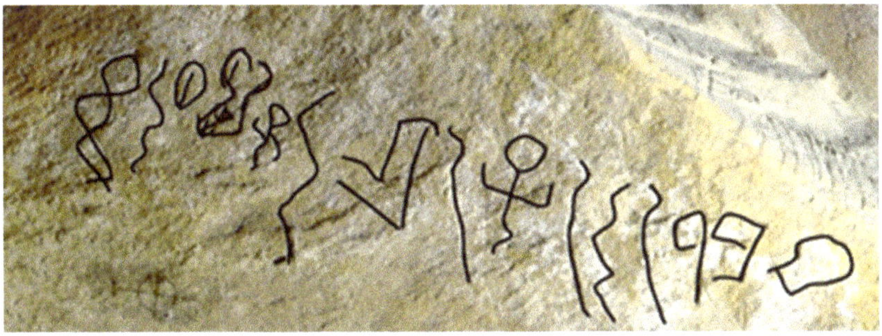

Inscriptions from Wadi el-Hol, Egypt. Graffiti or earliest-known phonetic alphabet discovered in the "Gulch of Terror"?

BC, to the Phoenicians, a people of traders who lived on the coast of today's Lebanon and Israel. However, the 1999 discovery reveals that, rather than the early Semitic alphabet being developed in their homeland of Syria-Palestine, it may have instead been developed by nomadic Semitic-speaking people then living in Egypt. This strengthens the hypothesis that there must have been ties between Egyptian scripts and their influence on those early Semitic or proto-Sinaitic alphabets. If then this is true, it pushes back the origin of the alphabet to between 1900 and 1800 BC.

But the Phoenicians are generally accepted as the creators of the first formal alphabet. The Phoenician alphabet was probably developed to be a quick and easy way for a ship's captain to read notes that a merchant had given him, on his trips along the ports of the Mediterranean and to record sales.

The Phoenicians were traders who created a loose empire of city-states along the coasts of Africa, Spain and Sicily that

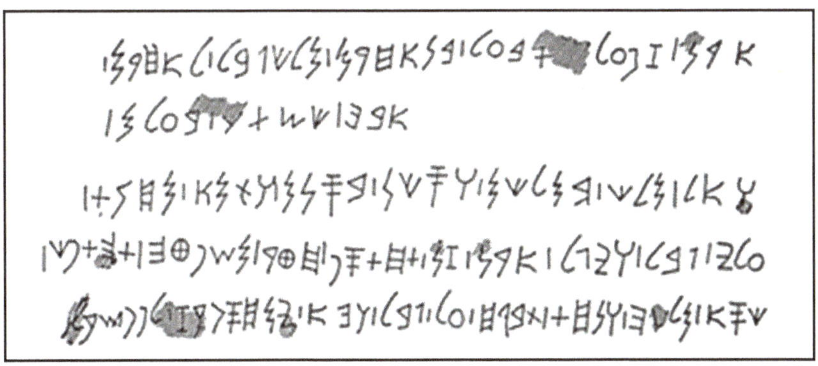

Phoenician inscription, late 11th century BC.

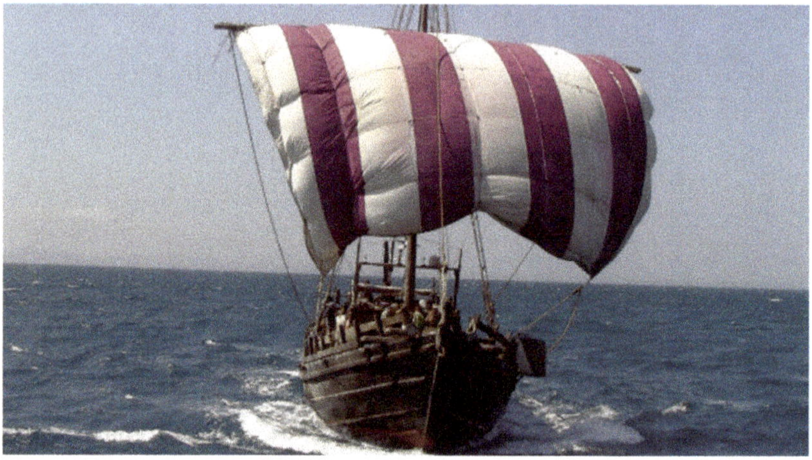

Replica of Phoenician Sailing Vessel— Courtesy of Danille Eubank

they visited. Carthage is probably the best known of these Phoenician colonies. They owed their initial rise to power to a simple snail that can still be found on the coast of Lebanon and that, left rotting in the sun, could be used to make purple dye — thus the Greek-coined Phoenician or purple people, from *"phoiniki,"* meaning purple or crimson. The dye and clothes dyed from it were a prized commodity to be traded. The Phoenician alphabet dates to 1000 BC and is an evolution of characters derived from earlier symbols.

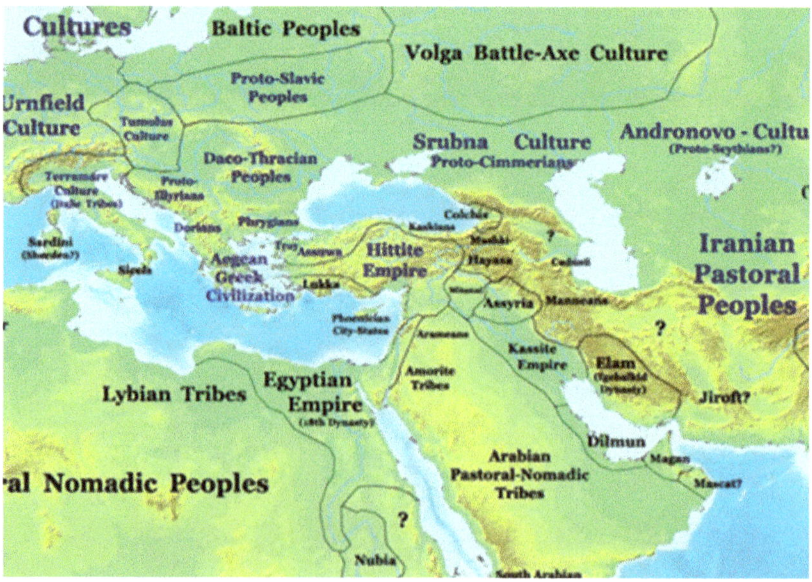

Eastern Europe and the Middle East, 1300 BC.

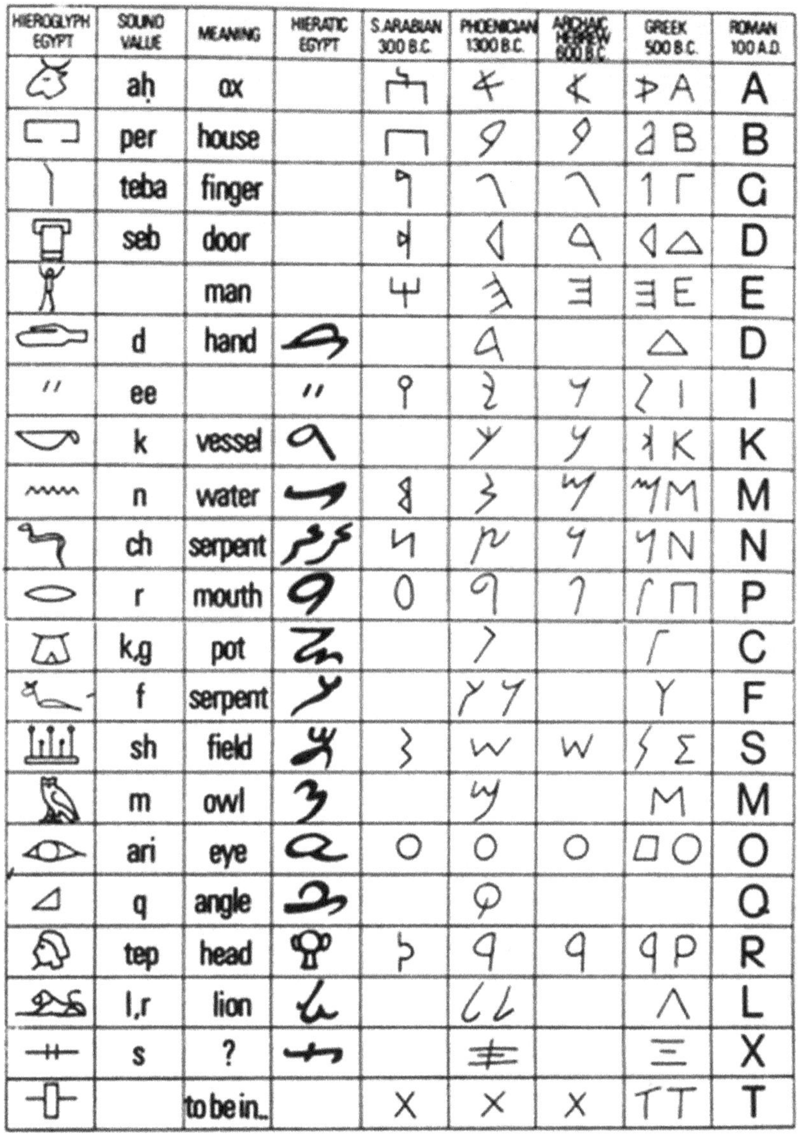

The chart above describe the evolution of the character starting with the symbol writing of hieroglyph to the Roman letter. Note the similarity of the glyphs as they are incorporated by the different cultures.

The chart that follows, shows how type and writing has progressed in its development and added various styles and structures. First is the Phoenician alphabet. Some of the char-

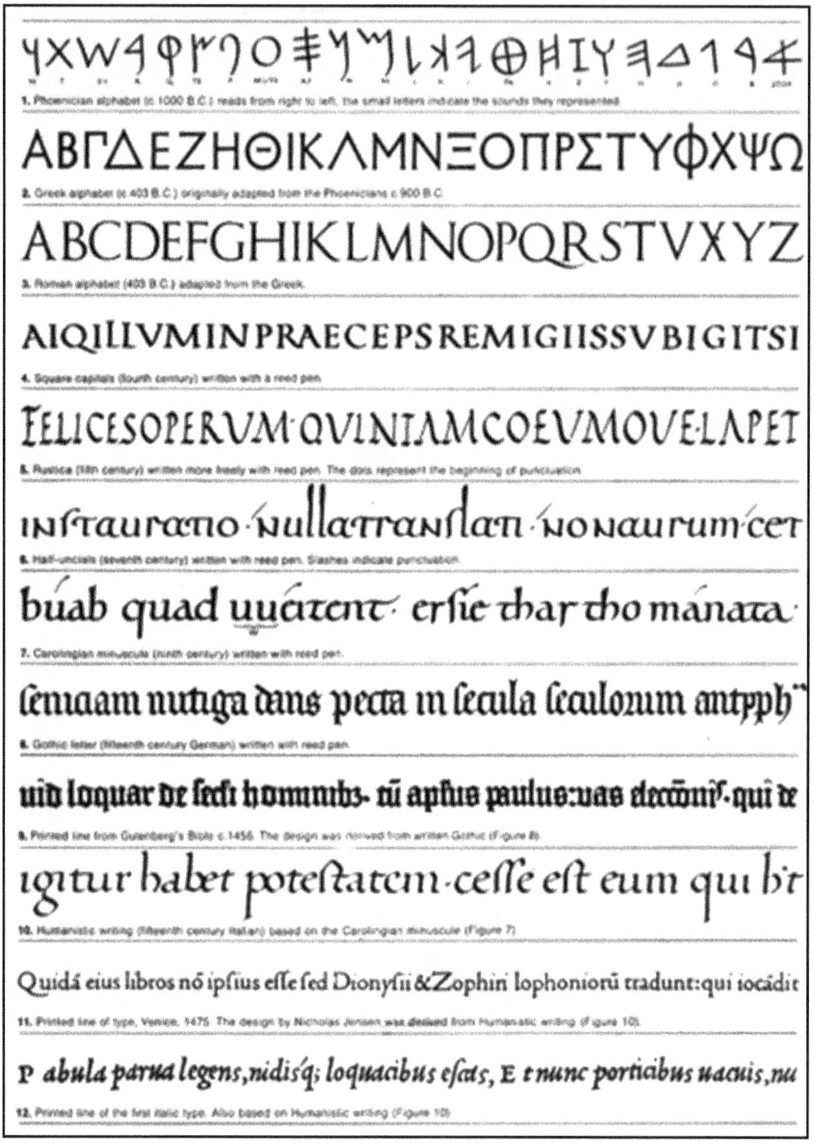

1. Phoenician alphabet (c 1000 B.C.) reads from right to left, the small letters indicate the sounds they represented.
2. Greek alphabet (c 403 B.C.) originally adapted from the Phoenicians c 900 B.C.
3. Roman alphabet (403 B.C.) adapted from the Greek.
4. Square capitals (fourth century) written with a reed pen.
5. Rustica (fifth century) written more freely with reed pen. The dots represent the beginning of punctuation.
6. Half-uncials (seventh century) written with reed pen. Slashes indicate punctuation.
7. Carolingian minuscule (ninth century) written with reed pen.
8. Gothic letter (fifteenth century German) written with reed pen.
9. Printed line from Gutenberg's Bible c.1456. The design was derived from written Gothic (Figure 8).
10. Humanistic writing (fifteenth century Italian) based on the Carolingian minuscule (Figure 7).
11. Printed line of type, Venice, 1475. The design by Nicholas Jenson was derived from Humanistic writing (Figure 10).
12. Printed line of the first italic type. Also based on Humanistic writing (Figure 10).

acters are fairly recognizable in relationship to our present day Western alphabet. Though flipped or rotated characters like the A, D, E, K, and L have similarities. In this illustration are indicated associated sounds. No longer are they symbols that relate to things. Note in this case, the reading is from right to left. Actually, the Phoenician writing as well as other early forms would be read right to left, left to right and so on.

That is, back and forth which is called Boustrophedon (pronounced- *boostrefedon*) - "as an ox turns in plowing."

Next in this chart, one finds the Greek alphabet. "Like a good neighbor" or rather a change in power in the region and their dominance, the Greeks borrowed characters from the Phoenician alphabet, modifying and designing them with Athenian Early Classic style circa 400 BC. These are very recognizable not to mention in use today by fraternities and sororities.

Around the same time the Romans began to develop their own characters based upon the Greek alphabet and eventually developed their own style. The refinement of the style can be seen in Trajan's Column, a Roman triumphal column in Rome, Italy, which commemorates Roman emperor Trajan's victory in the Dacian Wars. At the base of the column, letterforms represent an elegant, and certainly the most celebrated, example of the Roman letter.

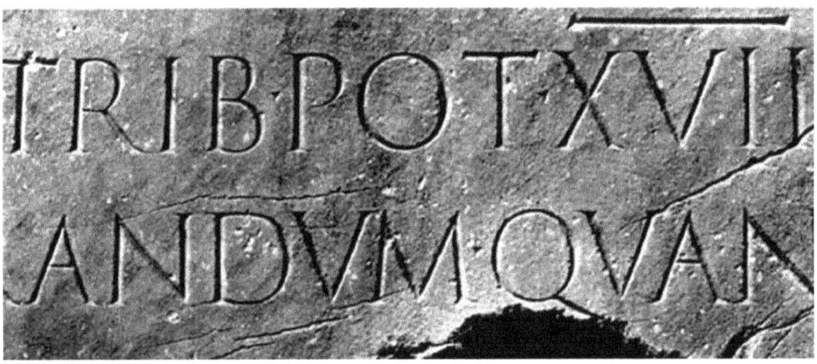

Inscription from Trajan's Column.

Look at the Roman alphabet and what do you notice? Well some letters are missing that are included in our modern day alphabet like the J and W. Notice also that the letters are all capitol letters, and have no space between words. Yes, one had to just know when one word ended and another started.

By the fourth century less stylized and formal writing was being done by the use of a reed pen on parchment (a material made from thinly scarped and dried animal skin). The example in the chart, #4 are **Square Capitols.** This is followed in sample #5 by **Rustica** which includes dots— the first use of punctuation. In sample #6, Half-uncials, from the seventh century, lower-case letterforms have now appeared along with further embellishment of punctuation. The **Carolingian minuscule** from the ninth century, sample #7, shows more definition of words and punctuation.

By the fifteenth century the **Gothic letter**, #8, was in use in northern Europe. This type of lettering was used by the scribes when copying writings such as religious materials. Can you hear the Gregorian chants, envisioning the monks sitting around in a circle doing calligraphy? By the way, Square Capitols, Rustica, Half-uncials, Carolingian minuscule, and the Gothic letter are common forms of calligraphy that have been done by artist for many years.

The invention of printing by movable type by Johann Gutenberg around 1437 ushered in a major increase in the amount of written material that could be reproduced. This dissimulation of information to the masses helped spawn the Renaissance. Since much of the written word at the time was religious material, naturally a book like the Bible would be printed. Gutenberg printed the bible in the 1450s. There are still about 50 copies of the famous Gutenberg bible, also known as the 42-line bible, remaining today.

Gutenberg and the Paragraph?

As a side note to this application of printing the written word, the paragraph was born. Most of what was printed during the mid 1400s was religious material, which was in the Latin language. Since most people couldn't read or speak Latin, during mass the reading of scriptures, like the gospel, would be first read in Latin and then spoken in the native tongue of the parishioners who attended church. To aid in the understanding of the readings, printed religious materials began being printed with space between passages. This was done so that one could write in their language what the priest and interpreted. This separation eventually became the paragraph. And you just thought some third grade teacher came up with the idea of a paragraph?

From the chart we can see further development of type characteristics ending with #12 a printed form of Humanistic writing #10, that is a form of Italic writing.

What a long path type and the written word has come in its development considering how we take it all for granted today.

Font to Foundry to Photoshop

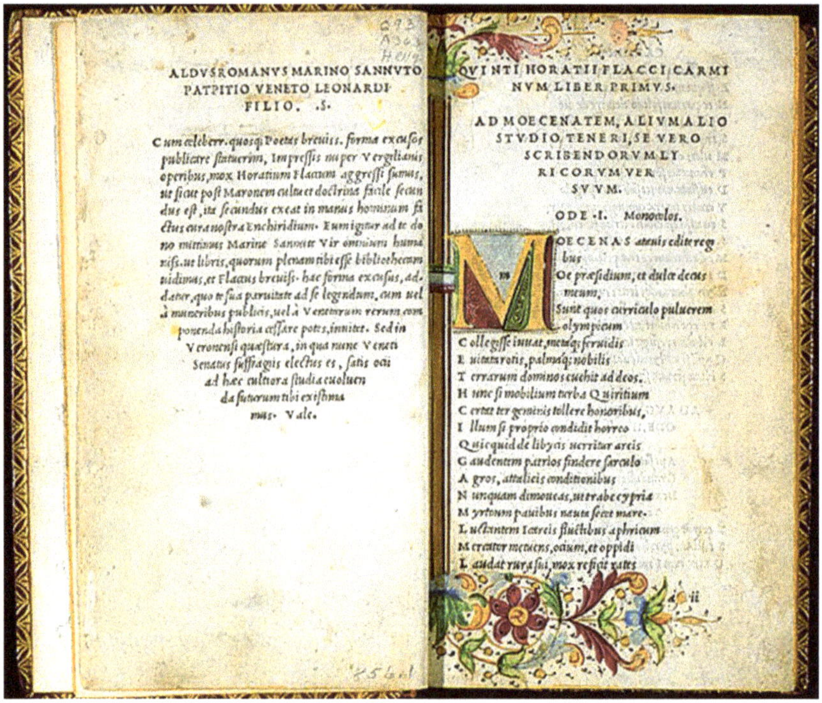

Book of Horace by Aldus Manutius, Venice, 1501.

As innovative as Gutenberg's invention of printing from movable type was and the enormous affect on communication and humankind it had, the process would basically remain the same until the latter part of the 19th century. Early type was cast from molten metal poured into carved molds done by typographers. Gutenberg himself fashioned a font containing over 300 characters, including flourishes and ligatures, to simulate the look of hand lettered Gothic script. He also invented a variable-width mold to cast type from metal and perfected a blend of lead, antimony, and tin that resulted in very durable type.

As printing flourish, printers often were their own typographer making the fonts to print from. Some would go beyond and create new styles. Nicolas Jenson (1420-1480), a printer and publisher, would develop the first standardized typeface for printers– known as Old Style. Later on in this chapter we will look at categories of type, Old Style being one of them.

Others that influenced typography and the development of new forms of type design include Francesco Griffo (credited with developing Italic type) who designed type for Aldus Manutius (1450-1550), a publisher and printer that founded the first successful mass market publishing house. In 1530, Claude Garamond (1490-1567) established the first metal type manufacturing factory and began to produce fonts for printers.

With the invention of the first steam press in 1814 to replace hand-operated presses and in 1868 of the rotary steam press, the need arose for more type to be used to meet the demand of the increased production of printing. As the Industrial Revolution was peeking, entrepreneurs and inventors began working on machines that could set type.

The Linotype was probably the most successful typesetting machine. It was developed in 1884 by a German watchmaker named Ottmar Mergenthaler. Using a keyboard of 90 character keys, the operator set single lines of raised type, called a slug. The machine assembled matrices, which are molds for the letter forms into which molten lead was cast. The process became known as "hot metal" typesetting.

The Linotype would be the workhorse of the printing industry, especially publications like newspapers and magazines

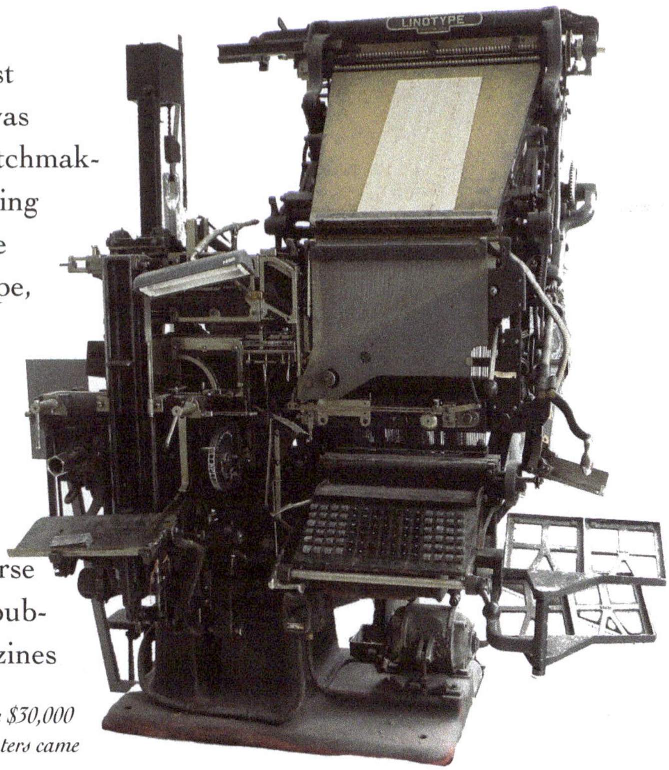

Ottmar Mergenthaler's Linotype machine. At one time $30,000 machines, they would become "boat anchors" as computers came into the industry.

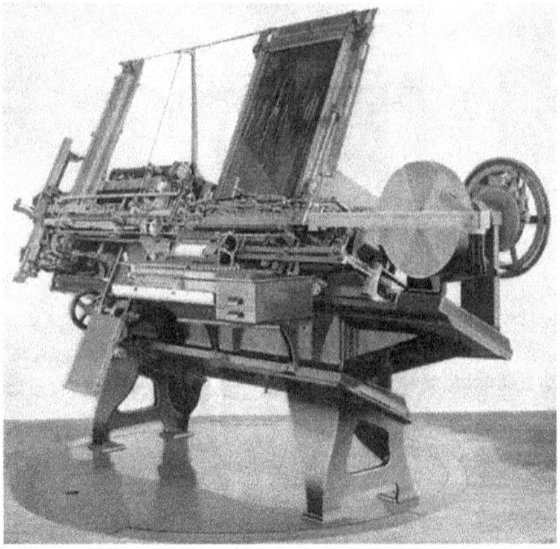

Paige Typesetting Machine, one of several "Rube Goldberg" type contraptions invented to set type.

until the Lithography process of printing would overtake relief printing as the primary method of printing and later phototypsetting equipment in the 1960s.

Competing typesetting machines included the Monotype which set individual characters rather than single lines, which allowed for more control over kerning and was particularly well suited for typesetting books. It consisted of two separate machines. First, a keyboard produced a perforated strip containing all the information needed to compose the text. This strip was then used to pilot a typecasting machine.

In a way, the technologically more "advanced" Monotype was a precursor of computer techniques, in that it "coded" the text before its creation.

Then there is the Paige Typesetter and its unlikely connection to none other than Mark Twain. Yes the famous author.

James Paige finished the development of his typesetting machine by 1887. The costly endeavor was heavily bankrolled by Mark Twain who as the principal investor was putting $3,000 a month towards creating a machine that would be more efficient and less expensive than human compositors. He had invested $50,000 by this time and would eventually buy the rights to it in 1889.

The machine never was a success because it often broke down due to the fact it had 18,000 parts. This and other speculations and investments lead to Twain becoming bankrupt!

The next advancement in typesetting began with the invention of the computer and its adaptation to the process. With its early beginnings in the 1950s, Phototypesetting as it was known, came into more mainstream use in the mid-1960s into the 70s. Using a monitor and a keyboard to input type and code, the machine exposed photographic paper with the use of film strips, disks, or a matrix that contained the font. The paper was developed and used to create layout designs using a "cut and paste" process that would be used in creating layouts for Lithographic printing.

One of those popular typesetting machines made by Compugraphic Corporation, was the Compugraphic EditWriter 7500. It could also be used off-line for text entry and phototypesetting using 8" floppy disks storage.

Of course by the mid-80s the personal computer, and in particular the Macintosh, along with Adobe Photoshop and Aldus PageMaker brought typesetting and layout to new levels of ease and even use by non-professionals.

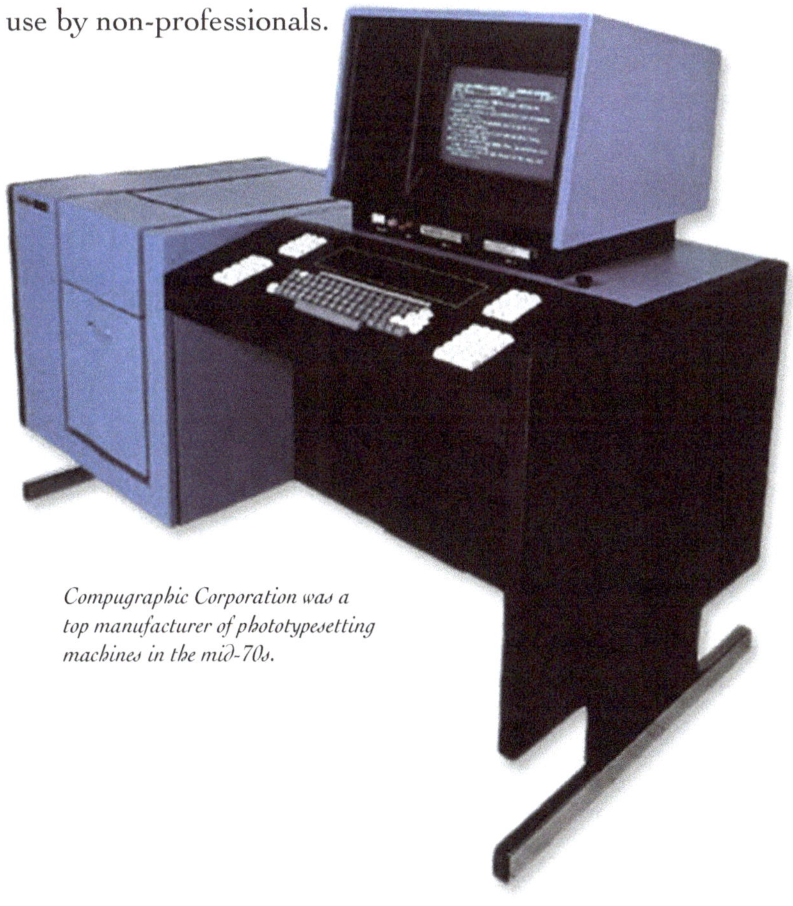

Compugraphic Corporation was a top manufacturer of phototypesetting machines in the mid-70s.

The Importance of Typography

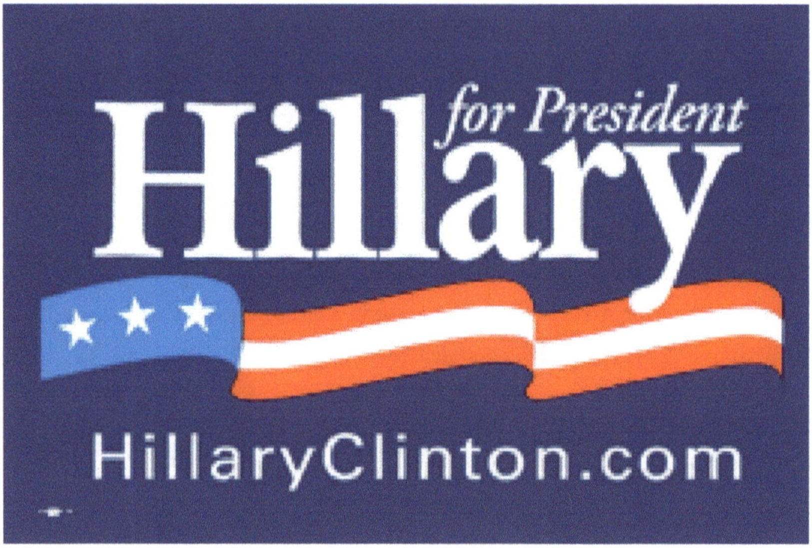

Hillary Clinton 2008 election campaign poster. The serif typeface used is New Baskerville, which is commonly used by book publishers, law firms, and universities. Was this an appropriate choice for her?

Typography is derived from two Greek words, *typos* "form" and *graphei* "to write." In other words giving form to the written word. Good typography adds to the message that is written strengthening clarity, and intrinsic meaning. Typography matters because it helps conserve the most valuable resource you have as a writer—reader attention.

A good example is the choice of type made by designers for political campaigns. So few words to say so much. Think about these choices from past candidates. Sen. John McCain's sans serif Optima is more recent, 1957, than Baskerville which dates to 1757 that was used by Hillary Clinton. Optima has been described as "classic, quirky, elite and just a little bit old-fashioned"— adjectives that certainly fit McCain's cultivated image as a maverick.

Former President Obama used Gotham in his 2008 campaign. The typeface has a vague familiarity to it. It's like the sign atop

CHANGE

WE CAN BELIEVE IN

Gotham, the type of choice for former President Obama's 2008 campaign.

a building that you pass by everyday but never really noticed. John Berry, an author on typography says,"It's funny to see it used in a political campaign because on one hand it's almost too ordinary, yet that's the point, it has that sense of trustworthiness because you've seen it everywhere."

Clearly the main purpose of type is to be read. No matter what the medium used— newspaper, magazine, billboards, Web page, or book, type is used to accomplish these five objectives:

1. Attract and hold the audience.
2. Be easy to read.
3. Prioritize and emphasize important information.
4. Maintain harmony and unity among elements in a design.
5. Create and establish recognition, creating identity and maintaining continuity in the message.

Type, after all, comprises about 80% of most designs so it is not only important as the vehicle for the written word, but an essential part of most visual communication.

With this importance of typography in mind, a designer makes choices based upon the following criteria: Readability or Legibility (how easy the text is to read), Appropriateness (does it have unity with the overall design?), Reproducibility (depending upon the print method or its digital use), and Practicality (is it legally purchased or available).

The Anatomy of Type

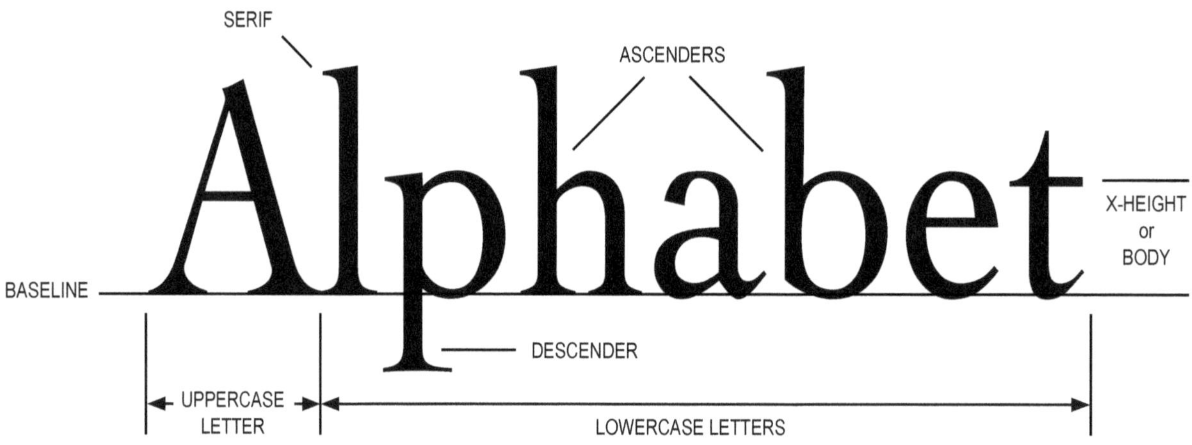

In order to examine and describe the design characteristics of typefaces, one needs to know the various parts that define the letterforms. The variations and subtle differences of these parts of type distinguish typefaces.

Baseline

This is an imaginary line in which the characters lay on. Some characters like the p, a, b, e, and to some extent t, in the example above, actually are a little below the line. This is because the round portion of the letterform presents an optical illusion and would make it look higher up than the other letters.

X-Height or Body

The height of a lowercase letter is referred to as the X-height or body of type because a lowercase "X" shape easily describes the height. The X-height or body varies from typeface to typeface depending upon its design. It is a visual measurement of type.

Ascenders

This is the portion on letters that rise above the X-height or body of type. The height may vary in some typefaces, some extending beyond the capline, which is the top extent of the typeface capitol letters, others may not.

Descenders

This portion of the letterform falls below the X-height or body of type. This would include such letters as g, j, p, and so on. As with the ascenders, not all may extend to the bottom of the size of type depending upon the style.

Serifs

These are parts of letters that have finishing strokes, are called serifs. Their origins come from the early Romans, who using brushes or chisels, painted or carved over the imperfections of their initial letter strokes. There are many variations of serifs, such as bracketed, rounded, and slab, that not only describe the look of the typeface, but may be associated with a category or classification of type that is presented later in this chapter.

Capital Letters

These are the large characters in an alphabet, and the original form of classical Greek and Latin writing, where only capital letters (also called majuscules) were used.

Lowercase Letters

These are the basically a shortcut deviation of uppercase letters. Known also as minuscule, it requires only one stroke to write, compared to several for an uppercase letter. This obviously isn't important today, but consider the historical development of type. Copying manuscripts and books as done by hand before the invention of wood block printing or printing from movable type, was a long and laborious task which could be shortened by writing with lowercase letters.

The term lowercase comes from the drawers that contained foundry type used to hand set type for relief printing. Being lighter in weight than the drawers that contained the capital letters, they were placed in the lower portion of a wood cabinet that contained the fonts of a particular typeface.

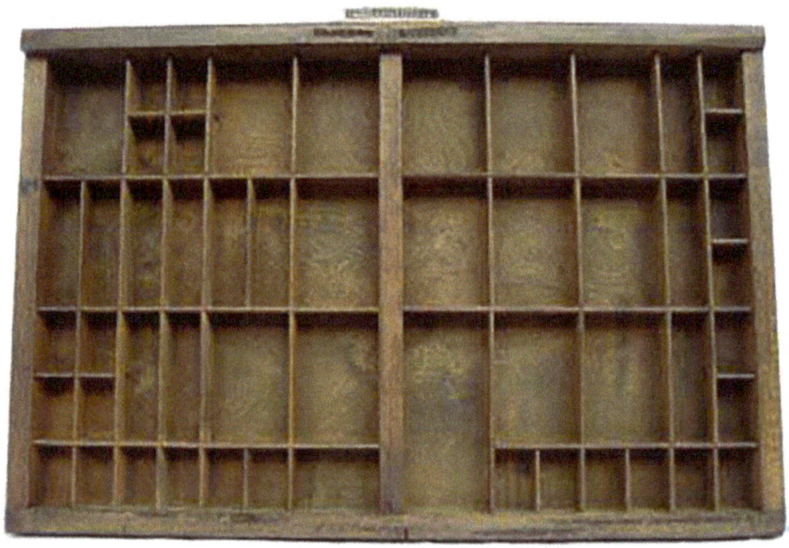

Though not a category of type, often type characters are referred to as either upper case or lower case. The terms come from the location of metal type, known as foundry type, that was used by printers to hand-set type for relief printing. This image shows the compartments in which the characters were organized and kept. Each drawer was a particular font, such as 12 point Bodoni Light. The cabinet would typically contain one typeface with the various sizes and styles. Since the drawers containing the capitol letters were heavier than the drawers containing the minuscule or small letters, they were placed at the top of the cabinets for easier access.

Measuring Type

Measuring type may not seem to be an important skill for a graphic artist. However, it may be that you are asked to design a brochure for a client that has brought in a sample brochure that they like. It then becomes necessary to measure the type for three types of measurement: type size, line spacing, and length. This skill also allows one to specify and select type and its formatting.

Units of Measurement

12 points = 1 Pica

6 picas = 1 inch

72 points - 1 inch

Units of Measurement

Type is measured using points and picas. *Points* are a typographic unit of measurement that originated in the 18th century. There are roughly 72 points in an inch. Points are used as a vertical measurement of type, which includes type size and line spacing. On some occasions it can be included with picas when measuring line length.

Picas are a horizontal measurement used to measure line length, most often column width. The term pica come from a Medieval Latin word for a collection of church rules. The pica originated around 1785, when François-Ambroise "L'éclat" Didot (1730–1804) refined the typographic measuring system.

Type Size

For about 300 hundreds years after Gutenberg, there was no standard system of measurement of type for printers. Type specification was chaotic. By the mid-eighteenth century, the point unit of measurement system was established. In 1886, the United States Type Founders Association adopted it as standard for type measurement.

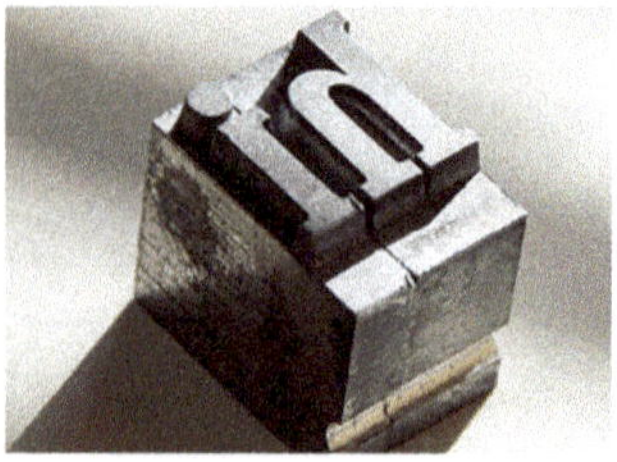

Foundry type. Notice in this example how the ascender of the "h" touches the top of the type metal block but neither reach the bottom. A character with a descender would on the otherhand reach only the bottom.

One would think that type size is measured by the height of a capitol letter within the type sample. That is not the case. Think about foundry type used for relief printing, or that set by a Linotype machine. The raised letterform rests on a block of metal in which the particular character does not cover all of its top surface. So it is the size of the block that is the size of the type.

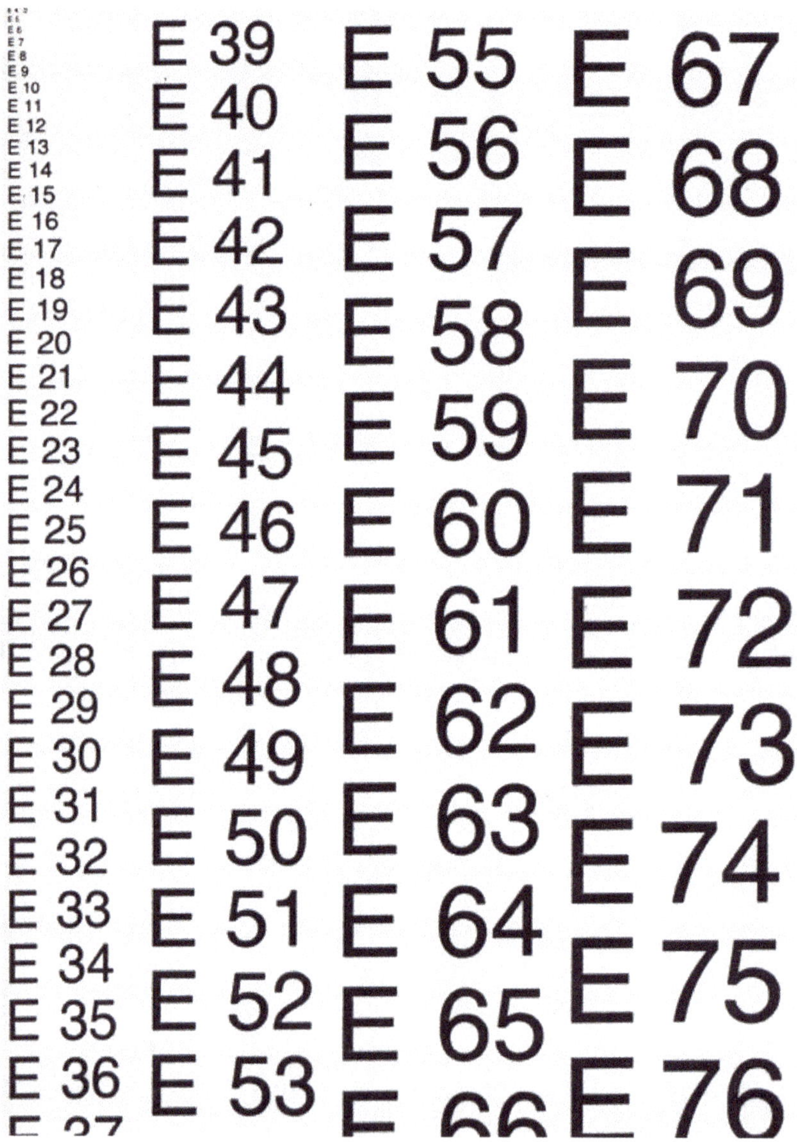

CapE chart used to approximate type size.

In essence, type is measured from the top of the highest ascender in the font to the lowest descender though there is typically a small amount of space at the top and bottom of the entire font.

So how to measure the type? Since it would difficult, if not impractical to find and try to measure letters next to each other that have an ascender and descender, graphic designers often use a Cap-E chart to approximate type size.

The Es on the chart are lined up next to a capitol letter or placed over top if the chart is made of clear plastic to measure size.

E California State
Polytechnic University,
San Luis Obispo

Line Spacing or Leading

This is the additional space added between lines of type. Typically this is about 120% of the size of type, so a type that measures 10 points would have 2 points of space added. This is often a default for auto spacing for page layout programs like Adobe InDesign. The term *leading* can also be used to indicate line spacing. This term has its foundation in lead strips of metal that was placed between the lines of cast metal or foundry type for spacing. Since this is a vertical measurement the unit of measurement is *points*.

To measure line spacing a chart that has sets of several lines with equal spacing is used. The lines are lined up next to the baselines of the type sample. When they match the line spacing for that set of lines, the line spacing is indicated. This method is used since it would be very difficult to measure small sizes as the example below. Additionally, line spacing is specified as the type size plus the additional space. So for an example, line spacing would be 12 points and would be written as 10/12 indicating the type size and line spacing.

Graphic designers work with line spacing for editing purposes to get more or less text into the area being set or to add some openness to the design. Some typefaces by their design require more spacing to be more readable.

California State
Polytechnic University,
San Luis Obispo

Line Length

Much like measuring with a ruler, the line length of set type is measuring the longest line in the sample. Depending upon the type format its set in, not all lines are the same length. Formats will be covered later in *Typesetting Formats*. So actually, one is measuring the column width that the type is set in. Line length is measured in picas and sometimes includes points. As example, 24 and half picas is expressed as 24p6 or 24 picas and 6 points. Remember 12 points equals one pica?

California State
Polytechnic University,
San Luis Obispo

Brass line gauge circa 1920s.

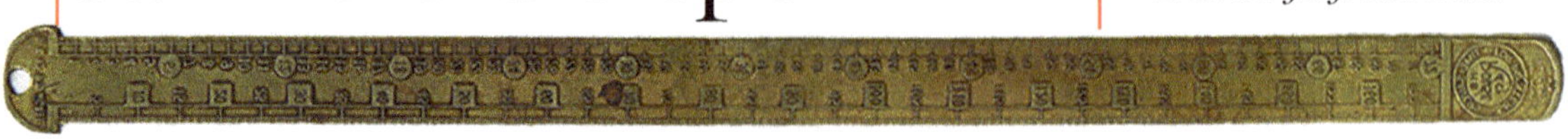

Type Categories

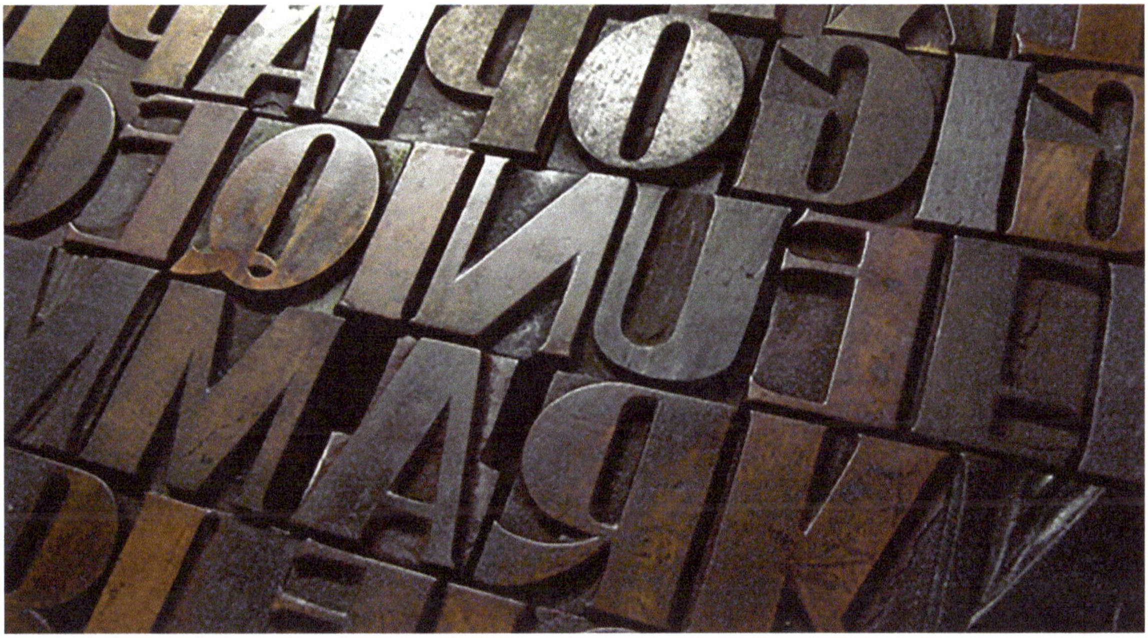

Large wood type was used for big headlines on a newspaper and posters because large metal type had a tendency to develop uneven surfaces, or crack, as it cooled. It also cost half that of metal did.

Depending upon which design book or resource on typography, type is classified or placed into various categories very differently. However, considering type by its use, its common characteristics, and its "personality," one can understand how their subtle differences make a big difference. Knowing the terms and characteristics of these categories can help you in the process of selecting the appropriate type for a project.

Serif/Sans Serif

Serif

You may recall from the section on parts of type, that the serif is an embellishment that not only adds a design element, but aids in the reading of text. Since when we read, our eyes look at primarily the top portion of the lowercase letters, skimming along. The serif acts like a directional-like element that speeds the reading. Most text for reading is set with a serif typeface.

Sans Serif

Sans serif, means without serif. These block or square typefaces are used mostly for display type like headlines, and subheads. The type compliments and distinguishes itself from the serif type used for text.

Display/Text

When selecting type by its use, text or display is the first choice a designer makes.

Text

Text is type mainly used for reading such as in books, magazines, and newspapers. It typically is a serif typeface, 14 point or smaller. It is type, designed to be read.

Display

Display, often called headlines by non-designers, is 14 point and larger and most often a sans serif typeface. It is used for a few words such as headlines and sub-heads or used in basic layouts such as ads because of its initial attraction, and contrast to text.

Type Design

The following is a classification based upon a historical look at type design and the characteristics that each category of each typefaces have in common. These are often very subtle differences in the parts that make up the letters and other glyphs.

A more extensive listing of letter features and characteristics that are used to examine the differences in typefaces and their styles.
- Graphic courtesy of ckgd.net.

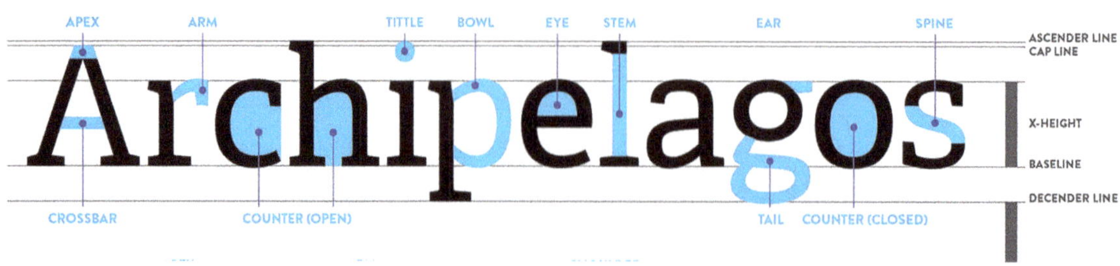

Old Style

Garamond

Times New Roman, Palatino, Garamond and Centaur.

This category, sometimes referred to as Humanist (closely connected to calligraphy and the movement of the hand), includes the first Roman types, originally created between the late 15th and mid 18th centuries, as well as other designs that have similar patterns. The axis of curved strokes is normally inclined to the left in these designs. There tends to be little contrast in the weight of the strokes, and hairlines tend to be on the heavy side. Serifs are almost always bracketed and head serifs are often angled.

Modern

Bodoni

Bodoni, Didot and Onyx

Modern typefaces have a Neoclassical style to them and are distinguishable by their sudden-onset vertical stress and strong contrast. Serifs and horizontals are very thin, almost hairlines. One of the first, and ultimately the most influential typographer, was Giambattista Bodoni, of Parma, Italy.

Transitional

Baskerville

Baskerville, Caslon

The first transitional typefaces came into being and use in the late 1700s and early 1800s, period in history that we now

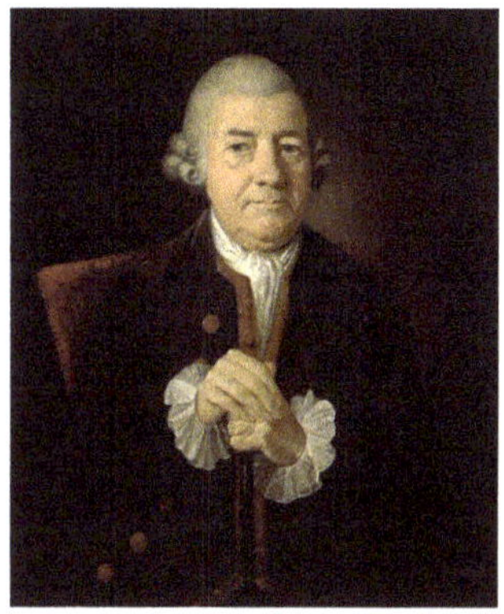

John Baskerville (1706–75) was fifty years old when he came to typesetting and printing, after making a fortune in 'japanned wares,' which is a type of finish that originated as a European imitation of Asian lacquerwork. Baskerville ventured into publishing where he was responsible for every stage in a book's production up to the stage of printing and finishing the sheets. His typefaces, including the one named after him. His typefaces were greatly admired by fellow printer at the time, Benjamin Franklin.

refer to as The Age of Enlightenment, a time that revolution in France, North America and beyond occurred.

John Baskerville, the printer and typographer established this style in the mid 18th century. The design and use of this style, with thinner strokes and subtle character shapes, and sharper serifs than Old Style, was made possible because of the ability to print on a smoother paper that was created using a calendering method. Its conjectured that Baskerville developed a early form of this paper finishing process, though he closely guarded his innovations.

Egyptian

Bookman

Clarendon, Bookman

Following Transitional in the early 1800s was the birth of the Slab Serif, otherwise known as Egyptian, Square Serif, Mechanical or Mécanes. This category of type was inspired by a new wave of advertising, and this style was perfect for billboards, pamphlets, and posters of the day. Until this time, type was designed to serve one purpose—it was designed for primarily for text for books and other publications. With the Industrial Age fostering mechanical applications, such as innovations in printing technology (e.g. the Steam Press, 1814), advertisers in particular were looking for a type that could stand out, and thus was born the display face—type for use at large sizes of short lines of type.

The poet Robert Southey first recorded the word "Egyptian" in connection with the style in 1807. Napoleon had returned from Egypt in 1799, sparking a wave of Egyptomania throughout Europe. Recall the Rosetta Stone?

There is minimal variation of thick and thin strokes for this style. The serifs are heavy with squared-off ends. The typefaces have large x-heights with vertical stress in rounded characters.

Contemporary

Futura

Futura, Arial, Tahoma and Helvetica.

These are typefaces that were designed the last 100 years. A classical example is Futura created by Paul Renner between 1924 and 1926. The geometric sans-serif style is in line with contemporary design at that time period, exemplified by the Bauhaus, believing that modern typeface should express modern models rather than be a rival of a previous design.

Typesetting Formats

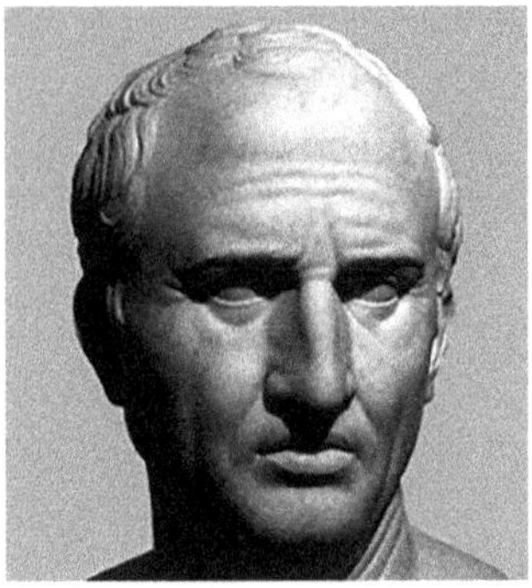

Roman philosopher and politician, Cicero . The type examples on the previous pages uses text known as Lorem ispsum. It is filler type used by designers and graphic artist to do layouts when the final text is not available or yet written. Most layout software, like Adobe InDesign, allow you to place it in place of the final text. The Latin text comes from the book "de Finibus Bonorum et Malorum" (The Extremes of Good and Evil) by Cicero, written in 45 BC. It is a treatise on the theory of ethics, and was very popular during the Renaissance. Lorem ispum has been used by typographers and printers since the 1500s.

Type is typically set in columns or blocks. There are six ways in which the type can be formatted depending upon readability, communication purpose, and editorial considerations. They are flush left, flush right, justified, centered, asymmetrical, and run-around.

Flush Left

In this format, each line of type begins at the left edge of the column of block and ends unevenly breaking most often where a complete word ends. There is little hyphenation with this format so the typography or look of the typesetting is pleasing. It however, has fewer characters per line than justified. It has a causal feel to it and works well for less formal designs. This digital book uses this format for reading matter.

Lorem ipsum dolor sit amet, consectetur adipiscing elit. Nuncnec consectetur neque. In ac dolor elementum, lacinia felis non, consequat nibh. Donec ut placerat neque, ut semper diam. Fusce sit amet dictum felis, in scelerisque neque. Sed ut orci est. Donec at nisi urna. Donec purus nisl, euismod vel felis in, volutpat sodales enim.

Flush Right

Type set just the opposite of flush left is this format. Since people in Western cultures mostly read left to right, and start the next line from the left. This is a format that is not suited to a great deal of text to read. Often it is used as a caption to an image at the right of it, in which the edge of the type lines up visually with the image.

Lorem ipsum dolor sit amet, consectetur adipiscing elit. Nuncnec consectetur neque. In ac dolor elementum, lacinia felis non, consequat nibh. Donec ut placerat neque, ut semper diam. Fusce sit amet dictum felis, in scelerisque neque. Sed ut orci est. Donec at nisi urna. Donec purus nisl, euismod vel felis in, volutpat sodales enim.

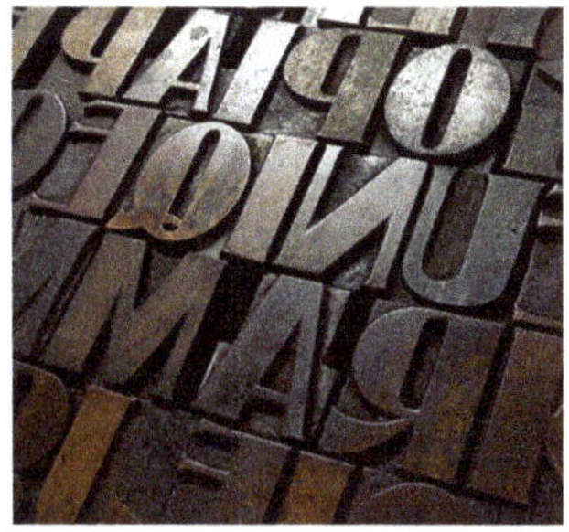

Flush Right format is often used for captions for images where the caption is placed at the left side making that edge flush with the image edge.

Justified

Commonly used for publications such as newspapers and magazines, this format has the most characters per line than any other format. This is important for publications since space for type is limited, so this format provides for more room for advertising. It is a more conservative format than the previous formats described.

Lorem ipsum dolor sit amet, consectetur adipiscing elit. Nuncnec consectetur neque. In ac dolor elementum, lacinia felis non, consequat nibh. Donec ut placerat neque, ut semper diam. Fusce sit amet dictum felis, in scelerisque neque. Sed ut orci est. Donec at nisi urna. Donec purus nisl, euismod vel felis in, volutpat sodales enim.

Centered

Mainly used for headings or display type, this format is only used for a line or two of type because of its readability problem similar to Flush Right. Often a sans serif and even capitol letters are used to provide an impact or design organizational element.

Lorem ipsum dolor sit amet, consectetur adipiscing elit. Nuncnec consectetur neque. In ac dolor elementum, lacinia felis non, consequat nibh.

Asymmetrical

Also a format that presents problems reading much text, it is not commonly used. Most often one would see this in ads or layouts that have an unconventional design. It is more or less random placement of lines and line spacing. In a way, its reminiscence of E. E. Cummings poetry.

Lorem ipsum dolor sit amet, consectetur adipiscing elit.
Nuncnec consectetur neque.
Donec ut placerat neque, ut semper diam.
Fusce sit amet dictum felis, in scelerisque neque.
Donec at nisi urna. Donec purus nisl, euismod vel felis
in, volutpat sodales enim.

Run-around

Run-around, also known as text-wrap is type usually set in another format such as Flush Left or Justified that forms around an image or graphic.

Lorem ipsum dolor sit amet, consectetur adipiscing elit. Nuncnec consectetur neque. In ac dolor elementum, lacinia felis non, consequat nibh. Donec ut placerat neque, ut semper diam. Fusce sit amet dictum felis, in scelerisque neque. Sed ut orci est. Donec at nisi urna. Donec purus nisl, euismod vel felis in, volutpat sodales enim.

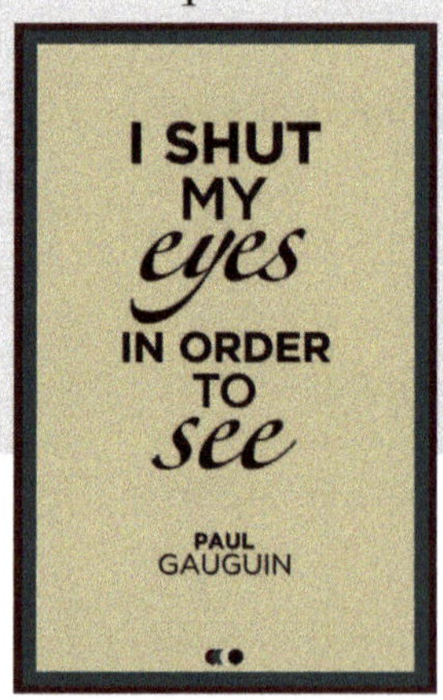

Type Adjustments

The Art of typography is the subtle selections, modifications, and adjustments to typesetting that makes it more than just reading matter, but as a very important graphical element.

Letterspacing/Wordspacing and Tracking

As the terms suggest, this is the space between individual letters and characters; and between words. Type manufacturers design the default settings for these but a designer may wish to increase the amount of space to provide better legibility or lightness to the type, that is its looseness. Often an increase in leading provides additional openness. A drawback to too much space is that it disrupts the relationship between letters so that they no longer form familiar words. Decreasing, or tightening the space may be done to include more text within a block or column of type. With too much tightness, letters start to run together and look like another letter. An “r” and “i” together might look like an “n.” The combination of letterspacing and wordspacing is known as **Tracking**.

Kerning

Kerning is the adjustment of space between two letters—adding or decreasing space to create more visually appealing and readable text. Fonts typically have built-in kerning which adjusts for certain pairs of letters when set next to each other. These are called **Kerned Pairs**. A good example is an “A” and a “W.” Set with monospacing, there would be a unattractive whitespace between the two. Headlines usually benefit from kerning and text set in ALL CAPS almost always requires kerning for best appearance.

A W

Without kerning.

AW

With kerning.

Widows and Orphans, oh my!

The following three are an example of poor typography and should be avoided by adjusting letterspacing or tracking, or by editorial changes.

Widow

A Widow is the last line of a paragraph at the top of the next column or page. The term can also be used to refer simply to an uncomfortably short (e.g. a single word or two very short words) as the final line of a paragraph at the bottom of a column.

Orphan

The first line of a paragraph that is at the bottom of a column of type is called an Orphan. It results in "trapped whitespace" above it which is undesirable.

Rivers

Rivers of white space. This problem occurs when letters are spaced too tightly (wordspacing hasn't changed) or justified type is set in too narrow of a column. The result are lines or cracks that run vertically through the paragraph, caused by a random and unfortunate positioning of word spaces on successive lines.

> Lorem ipsum dolor sit amet, consectetur adipiscing elit. Nuncnec consectetur neque. In ac dolor elementum, lacinia felis non, consequat nibh. Donec ut placerat neque, ut semper diam. Fusce sit amet dictum felis, in scelerisque neque. Sed ut orci est. Donec at nisi urna. Donec purus nisl, euismod vel felis in, volutpat sodales enim.

CHAPTER 5

COMMUNICATION

"What is life? It is the flash of a firefly in the night. It is the breath of a buffalo in the wintertime. It is the little shadow that runs across the grass and looses itself in the sunset."

— Crowfoot
Blackfoot Nation

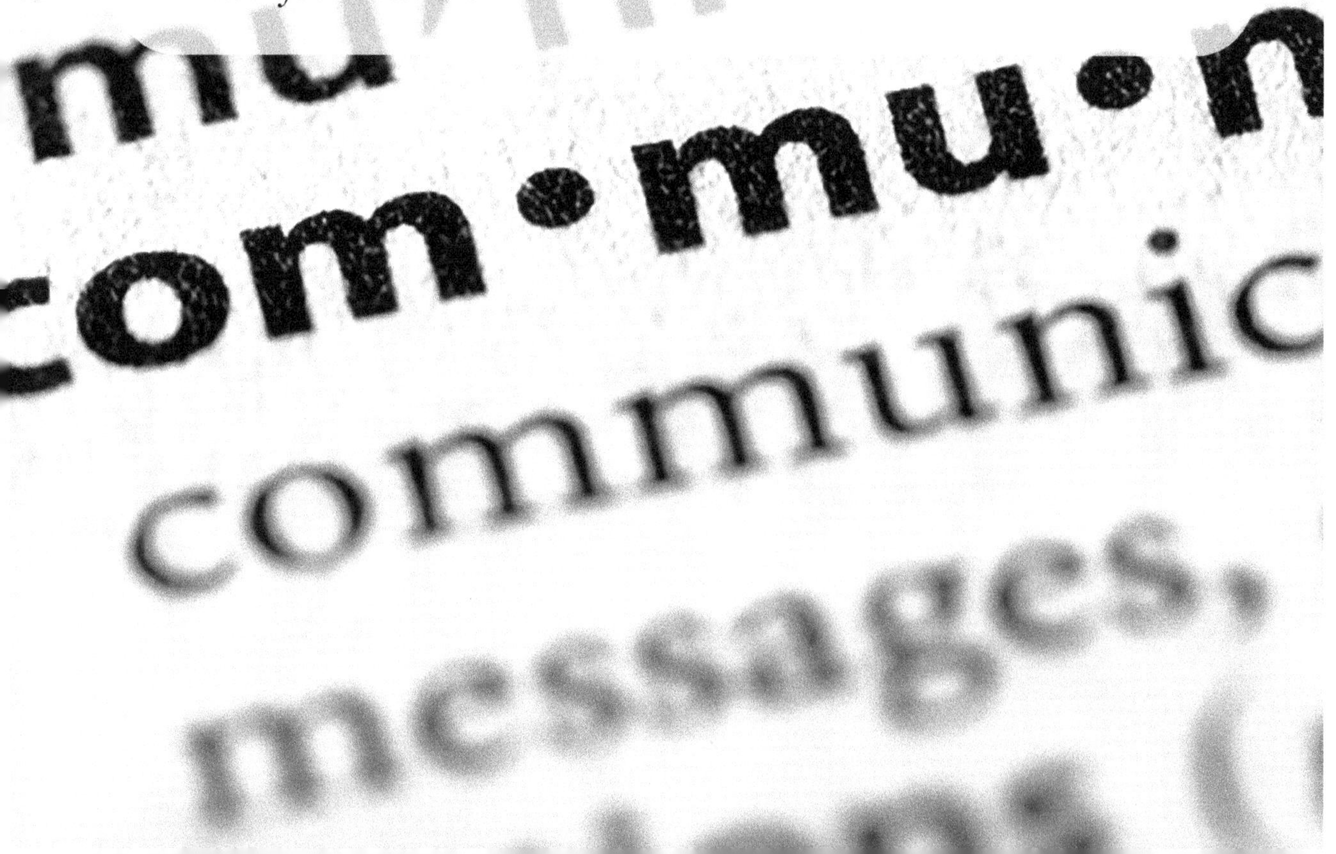

Communication Model

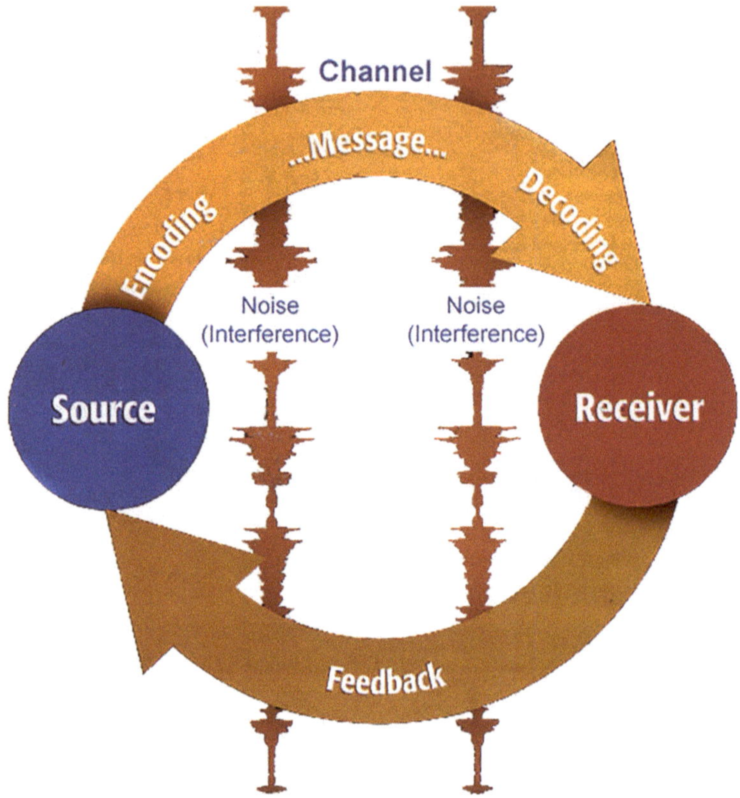

How perceptive is the quote at the start of this chapter by Crowfoot? How connected was he with his environment? And what a clear and precise way of communicating that to us. That in essence is the "product" or objective of graphic communications. It is not the printed poster, the logo, the Web page, rather it is *communication*. Those are just the medium used to communicate in a visual sense, just like speech and writing. To develop the skills to communicate through any medium, one needs to cultivate their perception of the world. They need to improve their use of the five senses to clearly "see" and process the stimuli to fully understand.

For the graphic artist in particular, this is very important. It allows one to clearly define the "design problem" and arrive at creative solutions. It is the first step in the process of creating graphic products that communicate effectively and efficiently.

Perception ⟶ Selection ⟶ Production

Without true perception the following two steps in the process will lack direction and communicative value.

Perception for the graphic artist comes in two forms, perception of the world, as has been briefly described above, and perception of the needs of the client. We'll first begin by looking at the process of perception and the barriers that limit, distort, or prevent perception. You will see how this is an integral part of the communication model. Later, perception of the client's needs will be covered in preparation for the chapter, *Design Process*. Remember communication is the product of graphic communications. All that is done both in the creative sense and in production, should be focused on this goal. To effectively and efficiently produce communication, one needs to understand the fundamental processes that occur. It can be explained by examining a communication model. In this model you can recognize the source and the receiver. The source is the person or organization that is communicating to another person or organization. It is the ability of a system, whether it is through speech, use of Web pages, or publishing a magazine to communicate information to the end user that determines how complete the communication is.

Communication, too often does not fully happen, if at all. Here is a reference to a movie in which communication is an important element within the movie. "What we got here, is failure to communicate."
— from the movie Cool Hand Luke, starring Paul Newman

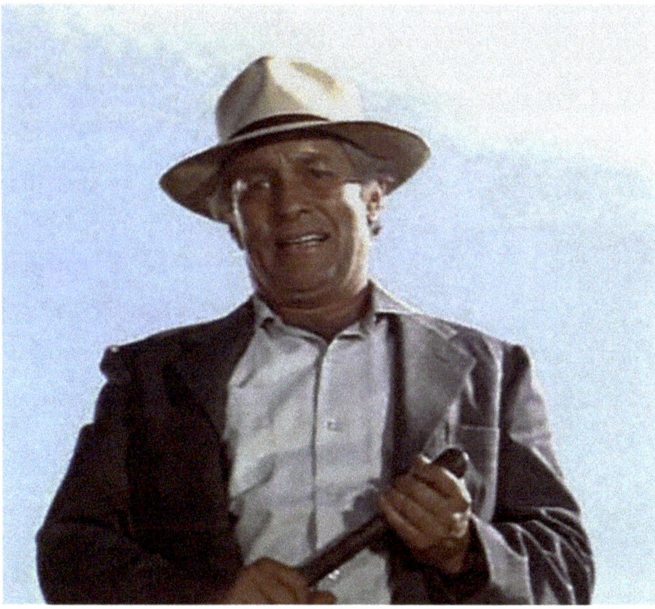

The communication starts by first encoding the message to be communicated. If speaking to an audience the speaker encodes the message using a language which has structure and organization such as words, sentences, and inflections. A channel or media is used to carry that message. In this example, it is speaking using their voice. At the receiver end, the message is decoded. It is heard, recognized, and understood. Feedback is important to communication to determine to what degree it has occurred. The people in the audience falling asleep or a standing ovation are obvious examples of feedback.

What you as a person, an artist, or graphic designer need to understand is that lessened or failure to communicate may occur due to interferences in two areas, physical and mental. These will be discussed later in - *Interferences*.

The channel or media used to carry the message also affects how communication takes place. Marshall McLuhan, universally regarded as the father of communications and media studies and prophet of the information age said,"The medium is the message." What he meant was that the medium used to communicate a message embeds itself in the message creating a symbiotic relationship that influences how the message is perceived.

Consider the movie you watched in a theatre which is projected onto a screen. A few months later you watched the same movie that you downloaded from Netflix and watched it on your flat screen TV. Did it have the same look and feel? Did the story have the same impact? Where the emotions you felt the same? Was it visually the same?

For a designer, the subtle difference between a coated paper and uncoated paper will provide a different "message" as an example.

Perception

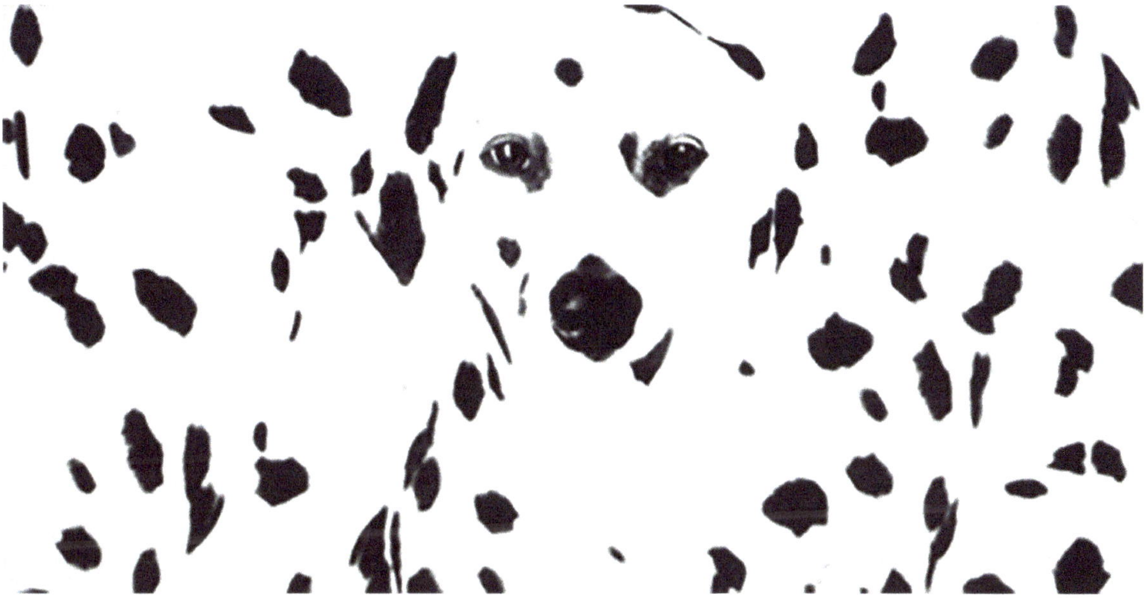

Anais Nin said, " We don't see things as they are, we see them as we are." We perceive our world not in terms of absolutes but rather as changing contextual relationships. When we look at an event, for example, we are constantly engaged in judging one aspect of it against another aspect or another event. A car is going fast because another is going slow or because it moves past a relatively stationary object. An object is big because another one is smaller. The beam from the same flashlight looks pitifully dim in the midday sun but bright and powerful in a dark room.

At first glance, one sees just random spots of black until association to past experiences and memories of images seen are made and a recognition of a simple image of a Dalmatian is seen.

"Can't see the forest for the trees." *See next page.*

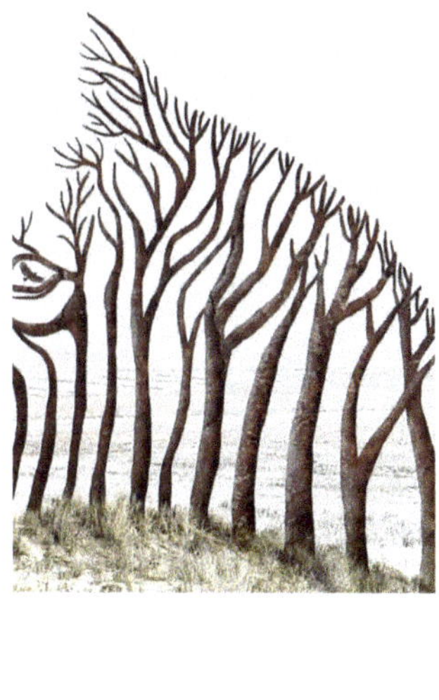

How can we ever make sense of our multiple views of a changing world of sensations? We tend to put up shields to perception to help prevent overload. We all develop habitual ways of seeing and hearing that makes us focus on and notice only a small portion of what actually is there. We screen out most of the sensations that reach our eyes, ears, and other senses; and stabilize and simplify as much as possible what we do perceive.

We then place an understanding or meaning to what it is that we are experiencing. The perception process looks like this:

Stimuli ⟶ Recognition ⟶ Understanding

According to researchers Dr. L.D. Rosenblum, Dr. Harold Stolovitch, and Dr Erica Keeps, our senses processes at the same time, the following percentages of use as compared to our other senses.

83.0% – Sight

11.0% – Hearing

03.5% – Smell

01.5% – Touch

01.0% – Taste

Surrealism photography by Luisa Azevedo.

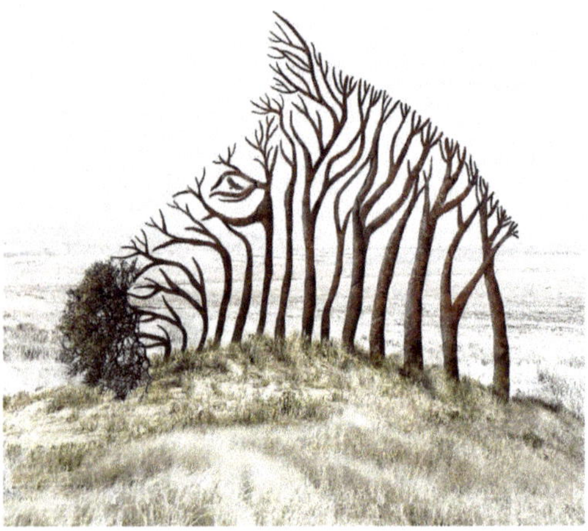

Dr. Stolovitch and Dr. Keeps used the following examples to help us understand this better. Imagine you're in an open field. How far can you see? About 50 miles. How far can you hear? Maybe a mile or two. How about smell? 10-20 yards, assuming that the wind is not blowing. How about touch? Just an arm's length. Taste? A couple of inches.

Interferences

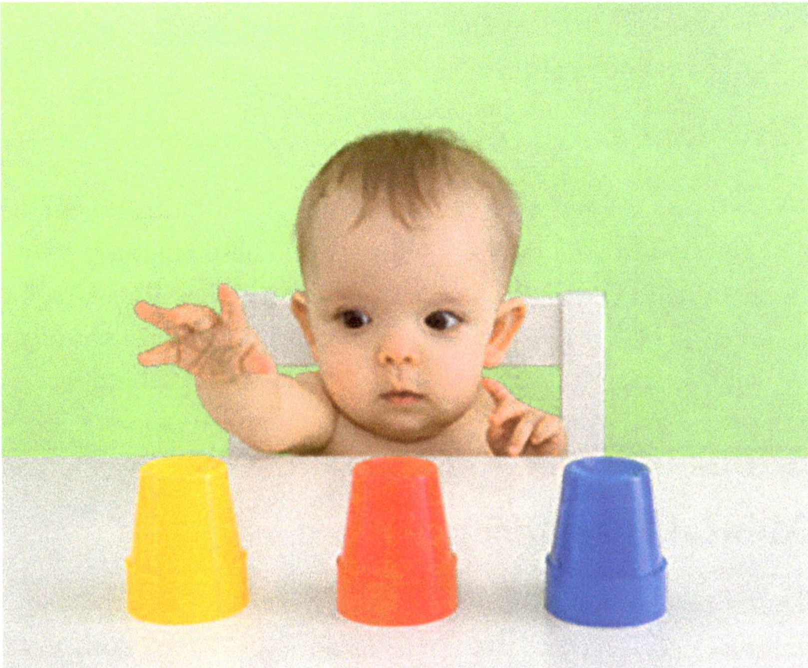

As a child we were very curious about our new world. All sights, sounds, smells, tastes, and the things we felt were all new to us. "Grabby hands" wanted to explore everything. And as our mind developed, we then became to associate stimuli with things and events— mom's voice, the smell of food cooking, the comforting blanket.

It's this investigation of things without inhibitions that is true perception. Now unfortunately, through the demands of society, family, education, and other forces, the unbridled "play" and inquiry is quashed, redirected, and diminished— relegated to "playtime." Historically, for many creative people this has not been the case, and they, ironically often are considered at the fringe of society, not fitting the norm. Their art, music, and inventions are a result of this curiosity and perception.

Though certainly not necessary to be a Rembrandt, Edison, or Beethoven, to be creative as a designer or artist one needs to understand the various interferences that present themselves to effective and efficient communication and thereby be able to lessen or eliminate them.

Physical Interferences

These types of inferences occur between the stimuli and our recognition of that stimuli by our senses. These are fairly easy to understand and include such things as barriers like walls, distance, and the environment such as fog. A person's disability, such as poor eye-sight or an illness like a cold where one can't smell are other examples of physical interferences. Can you think of more?

Mental Interferences

This is an area you have more control over, provided you are willing to perceive and place true meaning on what your senses have recognized. Anthony J. Dangelo said, "Your mind is like a parachute. It only works if it is open." These inferences then, occur between recognition and understanding. Let's look at a number of these in more detail.

Visual Interpretation

When we see things we usually understand what is the image and non-image, or more commonly, what is the subject and what is not. A horse standing in a field is the subject, while the field is the background. We determine this because of the difference in colors, detail; and our experience seeing horses and fields in the past.

In the graphics field this image/non-image is known as *figure/ground*. Consider three forms of figure-ground relationship: *Simple figure-ground, Figure-ground reversal, and Figure-ground* ambiguity. The latter providing the most interference.

Simple Figure-ground This is the most common of the things we see where the figure is positive and generally active, and the ground is generally negative and passive.

Eagle Mountain Capital

Courtesy of LogoMoose.com

Figure-ground Reversal In this relationship both the figure and ground can have interchangeable roles. Shapes form in the space between figures and create a visual inversion. Negative space often becomes positive and positive becomes negative. This type of visual interpretation makes for some interesting design possibilities.

BLACK CAT

Courtesy of Peter Vasvari

Figure-ground Ambiguity Obviously this is a concern and certainly represents an interference to communication. One can't determine visually which is the figure and which the ground. There are no or few visual clues, combined with a lack of experience, it's difficult to decipher the image. No feature dominates another.

Classic examples of Figure-ground Ambiguity. Do you see the Eskimo and Indian Chief and the old woman and young lady? (Below)

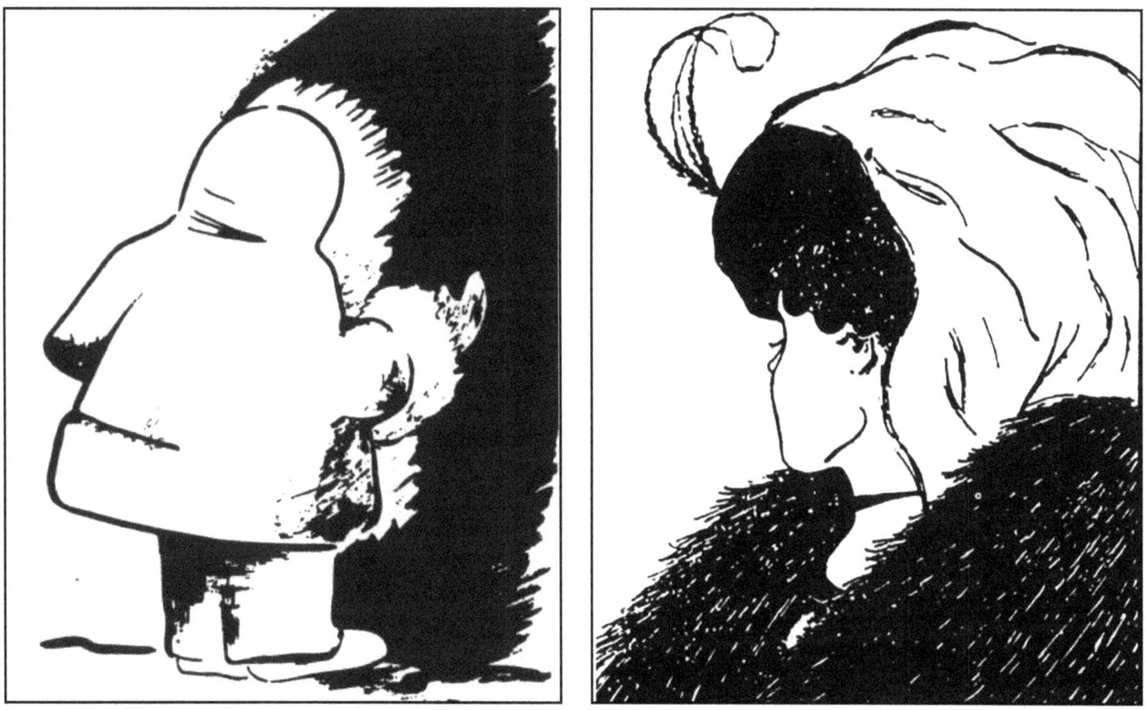

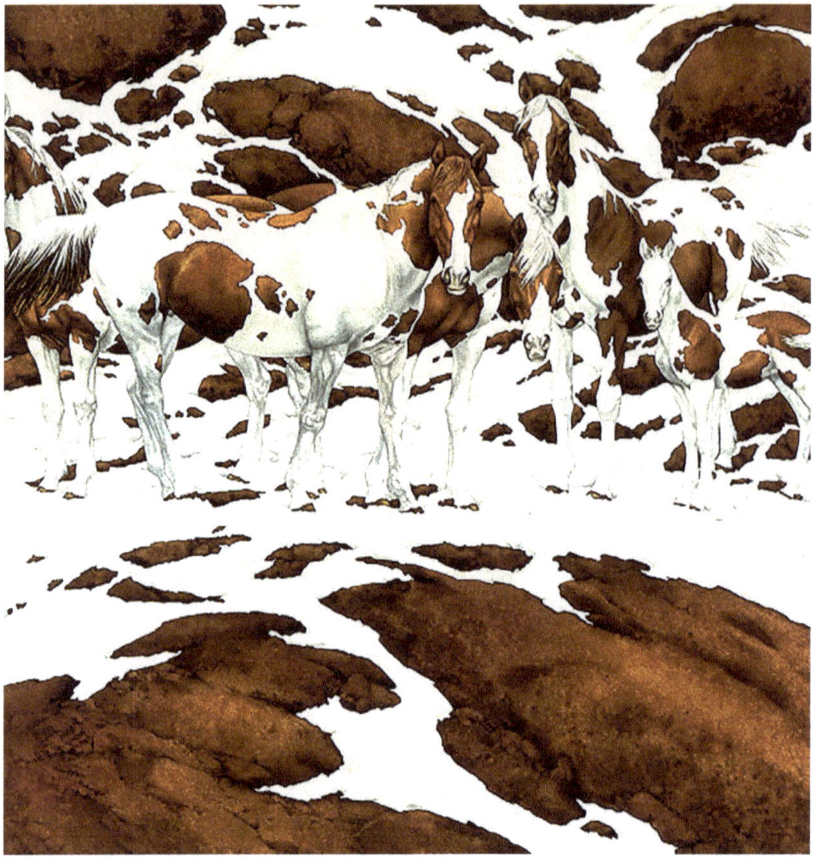

"Pintos" by Bev Doolittle. In this painting of pintos, the artist uses a figure-ground ambiguity technique to create this painting, a style she calls "camouflage art." How many horses can you find? —Courtesy of Bev Doolittle

Knowledge/Experience

As we grow from a baby to an adult we experience many things and acquire knowledge through those experiences and also through more formal means such as family and school. Interference to communication occurs when we lack the knowledge or experience to understand something.

здравствуйте, какдела?

In this example, even when we recognize this as writing, and hear the words, we don't have the knowledge or experience to read it nor understand it unless you know the language. Curious? In Russian it means, "Hi, how are you?

Time

What did you have for dinner last night? Last week? Last year on this date? As time goes by we loose the moment and what we know, and remember— it fades away. Even after a short period of time our perception of what we experienced changes, looses detail, and becomes mixed with other experiences. Those fond memories of the one special family campout you had, most likely include experiences from several different times, and with embellishments. Time then is an interference, so immediacy of communicating becomes a priority.

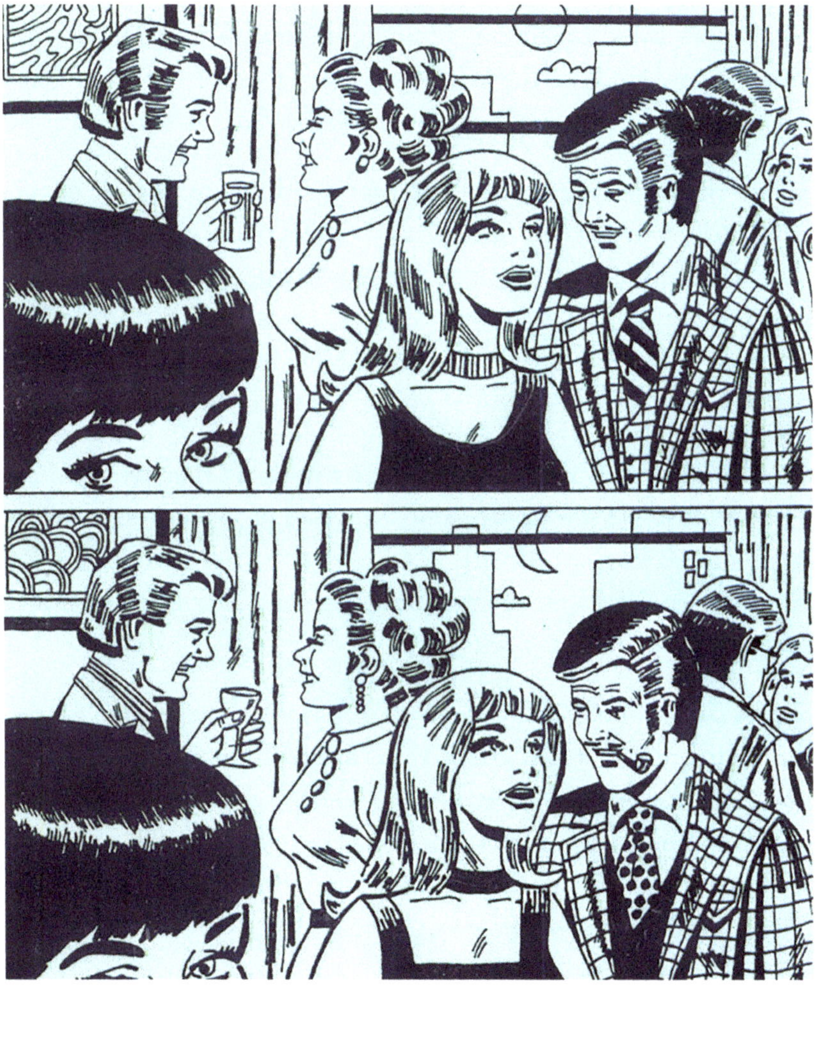

Test your ability to identify things and remember them for a period of time. Give yourself 60 seconds to look at both of these pictures. Identify the differences you see but don't write them down. When the time is up, go to the next page or turn away from this page. Write down as many differences that you remember. How well did you do?

Mental Capacity

Much like the RAM of a computer, humans can only intake and hold so much stimulus at one time. It is not mental capacity in the sense of understanding and making decisions for ourself, but rather the amount of information our brains can acquire at one time and understand. In our modern world we would be overwhelmed if much of it, the less important is not filtered out.

What one finds in communicating that we can recall the first part of it and some of the last part, but the mid-portion tends to be more difficult to remember since some of it has been "tossed out" because there isn't anymore memory room left in the brain. *Try this exercise on the next page before reading on.*

How far did you get in the first column, down to "FEN" or "PIV"? Did you recall "LEM" and "PUR"? How about the second column? Were you able to get further down the list? Did you remember "BIG" and "HAT"? Was the third column even easier? Certainly the last must have been easy. I would bet you were able to recall all of the words in that column.

So why did it get progressively easier to recall the "words"? They all are written in the same font, all are in capitols, and have vowels and consonants. Obviously the first column contains "words" that for the first part are either not English words or are unconventional.

The second column contains words that we have known since an early age. The third are familiar as well, but looking closer, you may have noticed that they are the names of animals. In fact the animals are all mammals. Lastly, the final column is also familiar to us but there is much more that allows you to recall that entire list of words.

SER	RED	CAT	A
GUB	HOUSE	HORSE	BOY
DAL	ROAD	DOG	WENT
FEN	PHONE	PIG	TO
PIV	AIR	MOUSE	THE
MUR	WRONG	DEER	STORE
CAG	HIS	BEAR	TO
BOR	PHOTO	ZEBRA	BUY
LEM	BIG	RAT	SOME
PUR	HAT	LION	CANDY

Starting at the left, recite to yourself several times the words. Hide this table and then recite back the words. How well did you do? Now do the same for each of the other columns. Were you better each new time? Why?

Looking back at the examples, notice that structure and organization is progressively applied to them. In the first column at least we understand that the glyphs (characters) are used for writing and have sounds. They even have a basic format to them. Next are English words and then a category of words associated with animals. And then lastly, a sentence structure is applied to the words.

Organization and structure, much like the objective for a graphic designer to organize and structure layouts to provide communication with the least interferences. In the *Chapter 6 -Design Process: Principles and Elements of Design,* techniques and methods that create organization and structure in design will be covered.

As mentioned earlier, because our mental capacity is limited, we recall the first part of information and then a smaller portion of it at the end, but have difficulty recalling information

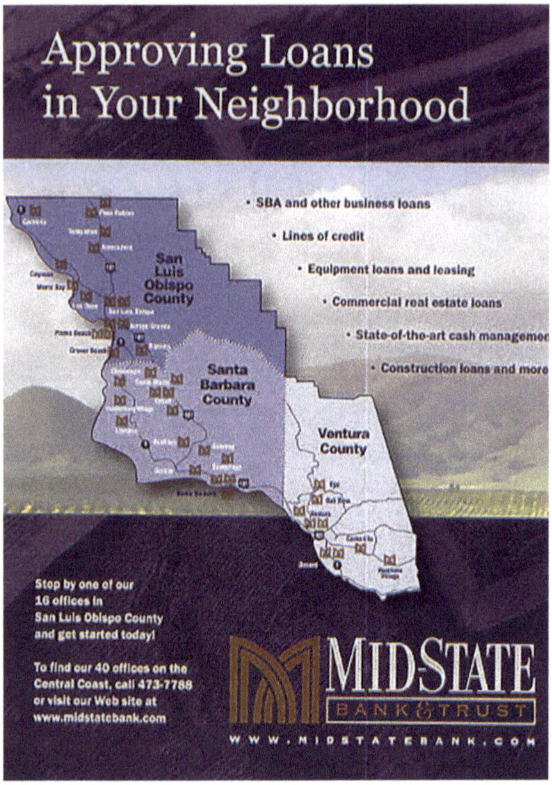

in the middle. Something to consider when holding meetings, developing lessons, and in creating design layouts. Put the most important information up front where it will be remembered, that important agenda item, the lesson objective, that advertising message. Then, at the end, leave a "stamp" to be taken away, the action to take, a summary of things learned, the company logo.

Notice in the ad for a bank at the left, that the most important information is at the beginning of the eye-movement throughout the design. "Approving Loans in Your Neighborhood." Next our eye follows down the map where secondary information is placed—the least remembered. Finally the last visual we see is the logo. The visual "stamp" that connects "Approving Loans" with Mid-State Bank.

Human Tendencies

We as humans want answers to things. We want to know what's out there—crossing the oceans to new continents, rocketing to the moon, diving into the abyss. Solving these mysteries we categorize, classify, organize, and standardize things. We then assimilate them as facts to the point where they are assumed without truly perceiving them.

On smaller, everyday situations our brain automatically adds, modifies, or substitutes information as we process things that are common, assumed. This "pigeon holing" occasionally presents a problem and causes

What's wrong with this this line?

miscommunication or incorrectness, often embarrassing as this example at right demonstrates. Certainly an interference to be wary of. This is a good reason to have someone proof your work. They won't "mentally correct" your work like you would.

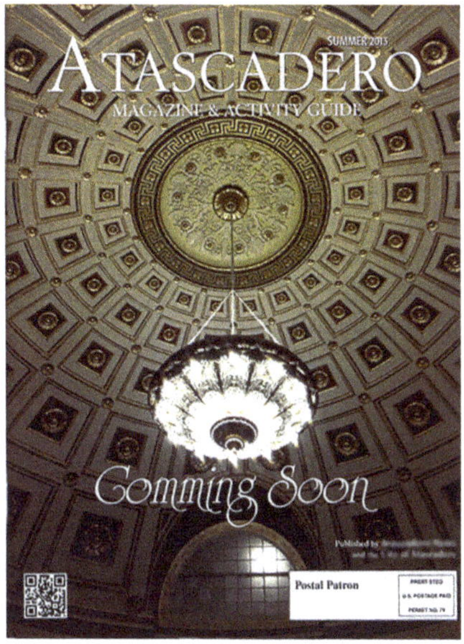

Oops!

Of course all typos in this book were purposely put into the book for those looking for some.

Brain Development/Deterioration

As we grow our brains develop and as we age, often we tend to loose our ability to process information either through a refusal to perceive things as they are, "that's how I've always done it," or because of, unfortunately, diseases like Alzheimer's and dementia. Understanding the audience you are designing for relative to brain development and deterioration will allow for better communication with them.

An article in U.S. News & World Report titled "Inside The Teen Brain," by Shannon Brownie, outlines some of the dynamic developments taking place in the young adult brain.

"...one of the last parts [of the brain] to mature is in charge of making sound judgments and calming unruly emotions. Indeed, the brain inside a teenager's skull is closer to a child's brain than an adult's. Still being forged are the connections between neurons that affect not only emotional skills but also physical and mental abilities [such as organizing multiple tasks or grasping abstract ideas."

"His prefrontal cortex, where judgments are formed, is practically asleep at the wheel. At the same time, his limbic system, where raw emotions such as anger are generated, is entering a stage of development in which it goes into hyperdrive. [This inability to perform "executive functions"] include the brain's ability to handle ambiguous information and make decisions, to coordinate signals in different regions of the brain, and tamp down or prolong emotions generated in the limbic system."

Additionally, "One of the last steps in making an adult brain is the coating of nerves in white matter, fatty cells that spiral around the shaft of nerves . . . known as myelin, that acts like insulation on an electrical cord. It know appears that brains don't finish myelinating until the early 20s. Nerves myelinate in girls earlier than in boys, which may help explain why teenage girls seem more emotionally mature than boys, whose myelin levels may not equal girl's until age 30."

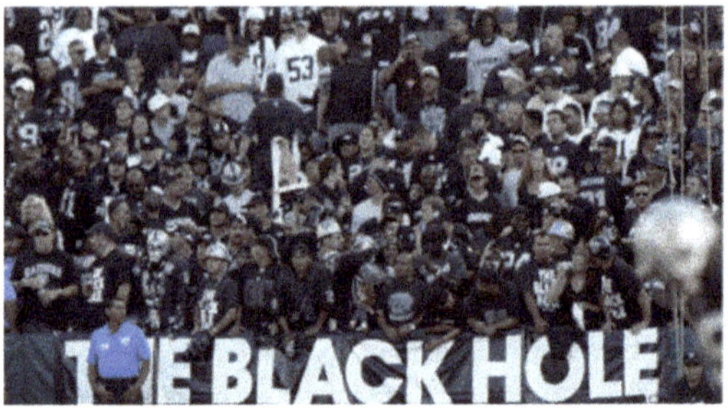

Some societal interferences may simply be caused by commonality or peer pressure.

Societal

Where we live, our culture, ethnic background, regional traditions, religious beliefs and more, influence us regarding the world about us which often interferes with our perception of it. Someone living in the South opinion of grits is most likely different than someone living in California. The food tastes the same, its that it is more commonplace and palatable in Georgia and Alabama than in California because of societal influences, traditions, and so forth.

Other more dramatic and sometimes instant change in things cause societal interference to our perception. Consider World War II and the attack on Pearl Harbor and how our opinion of the Japanese people with the culture of beautiful Art, enchanting music, mystic Mount Fuji, Bonsai trees, delicious sushi changed on December 7th, 1941. This consternation caused America to send thousands of American citizens to concentration camps and alter our perception of Japanese for quite some time.

Contrived

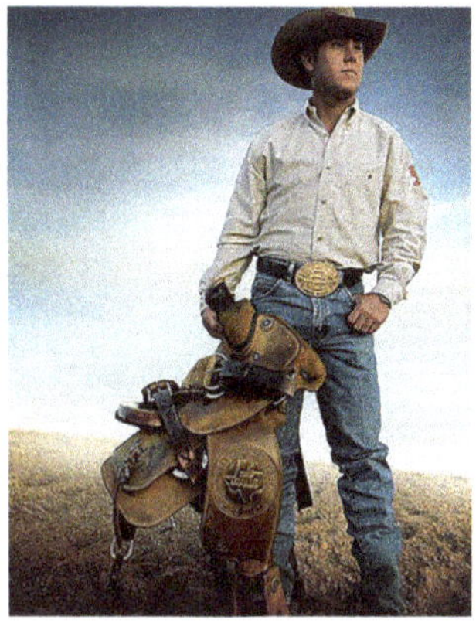

These interferences are caused by marketing and advertising whose purpose is to inform, persuade, or direct us. In other words, to alter our perception in such a way as to be favorable to the message and act accordingly. What? You buy those Levis because they fit right. Do they? Don't you know cowboys wear Wrangler jeans? And you don't?

Marketing is the action or business of promoting and selling products or services, including market research and advertising. Its importance to business success and more is reflected when The Harvard Business Review says in the article, *The Ultimate Marketing Machine*, "In the past decade, what marketers do to engage customers has changed almost beyond recognition. With the possible exception of information technology, we can't think of another discipline that has evolved so quickly. Tools and strategies that were cutting-edge just a few years ago are fast becoming obsolete, and new approaches are appearing every day. Marketers today are awash in customer data, and most are finding narrow ways to use that information—to, say, improve the targeting of messages. Knowing what an individual consumer is doing where and when is now table stakes."

Advertising is key and crucial. On a big scale, think of the cost and impact of a spot aired during the Super Bowl. The average national 30-second spot costs $3.5 million. Must be a reason—to influence you, to interfere with your perception.

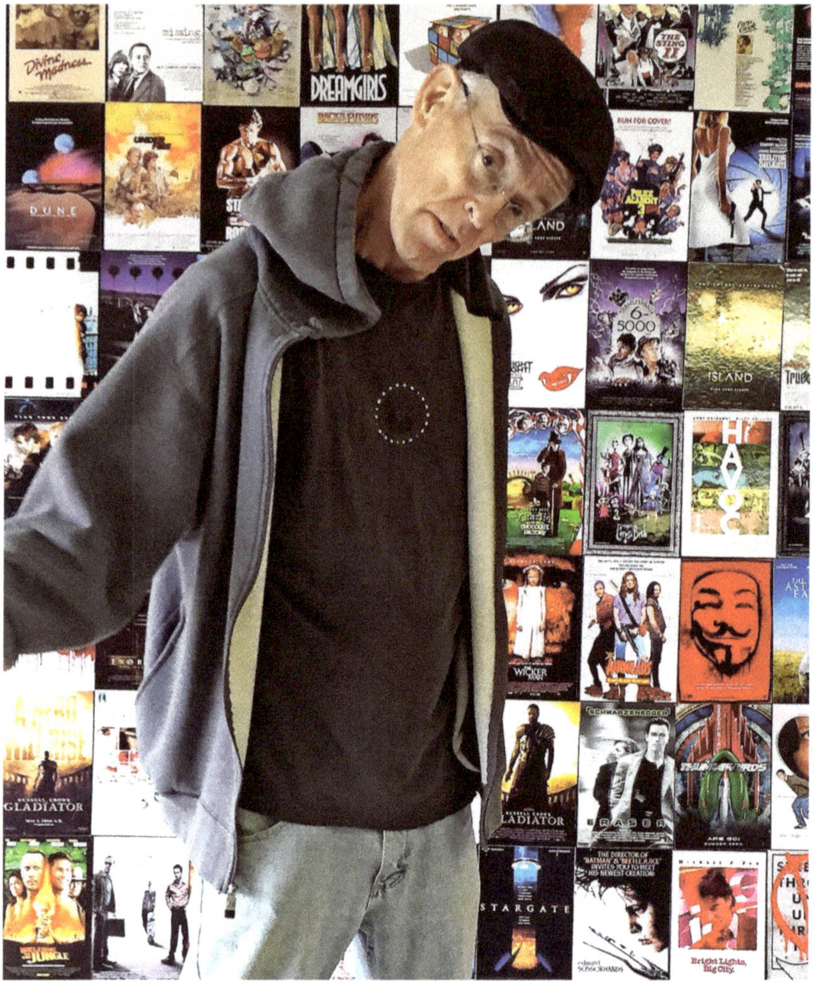

Jeffrey Bacon, creative director with recogniable movie posters he designed along with his design partners and production teams.

The concept of communication and the process of design are very much interrelated and connected. Jeffrey Bacon, with partners started a design business in the LA area creating and producing print and other media products primarily for the film industry. As creative director, Jeffrey designed a number of items including movie posters. Over his many years as a designer, he has created a number of Jeff-isms— a philosophy of communication and design concepts. Three of his 30 Jeff-ism are listed here.

Jeff-ism #1: What's the Big Idea?
Concept is King. Identifying the primary need is crucial to providing a solution. Jeff says that most clients "want the problem to go away." Provide the solution by knowing what the big idea is.

Jeff-ism #7: Go for the sevens
Jeff learned this from George Lucas who explained how he crafts his films based upon the audience asking "what does one seven year old say to another seven year old?" Substitute 17 year olds, 27 year olds, etc.

Jeff-ism #10: "Good is the enemy of great. What is the worst piece you are showing? Your "Bag of Courage" should contain work that is either really rough or pristinely polished.

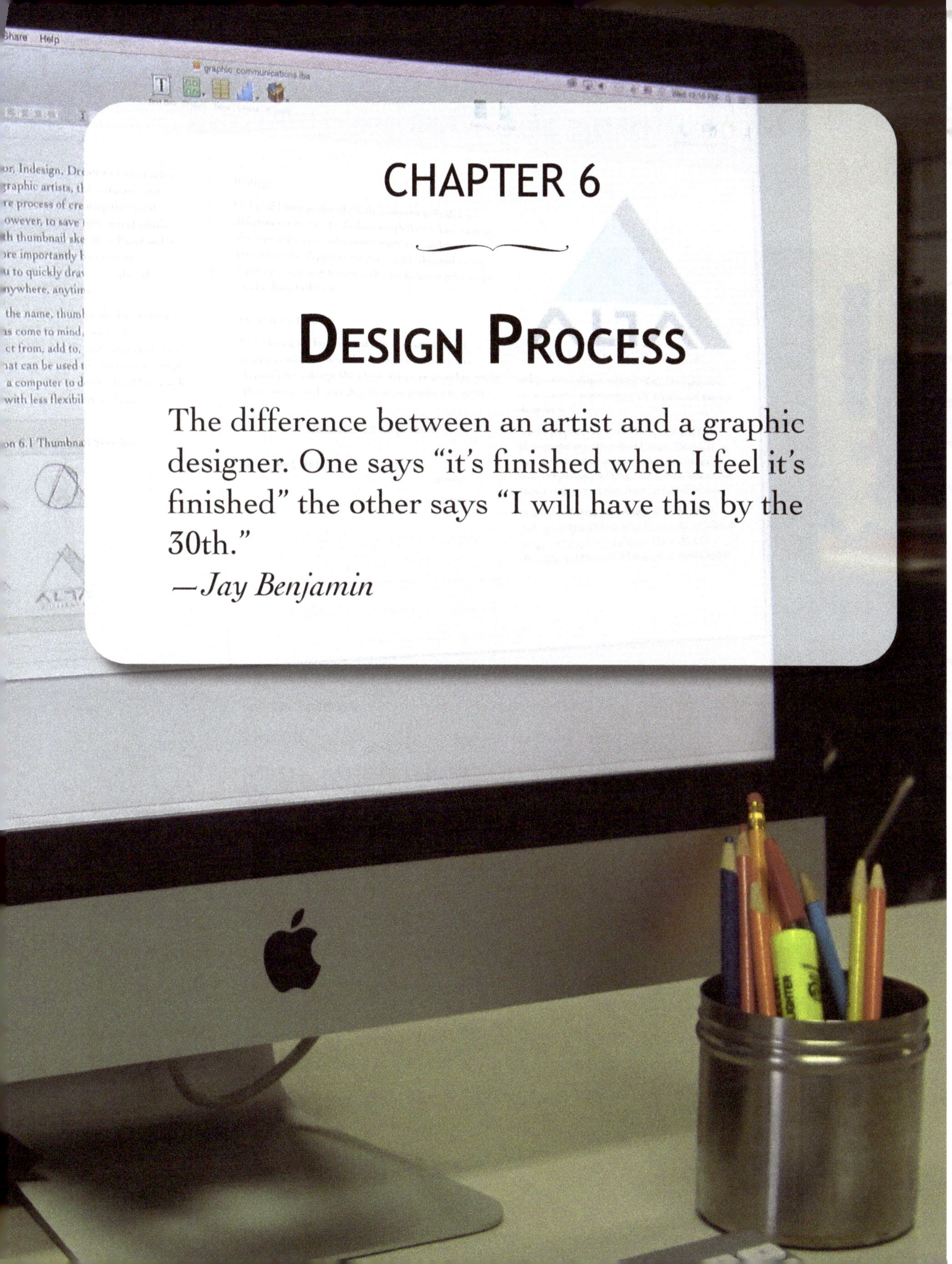

CHAPTER 6

Design Process

The difference between an artist and a graphic designer. One says "it's finished when I feel it's finished" the other says "I will have this by the 30th."

—*Jay Benjamin*

Determining the Design Problem

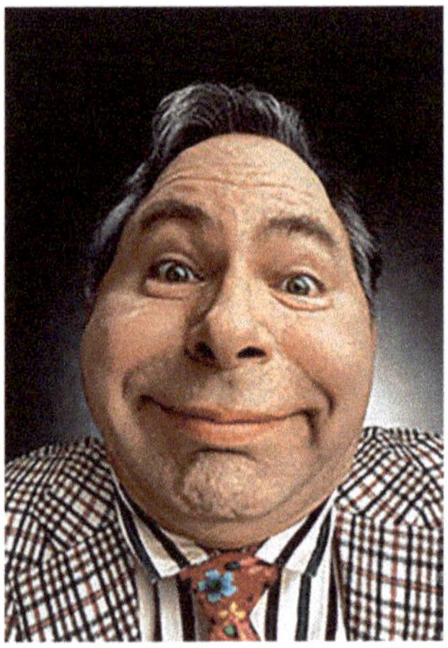

The design process begins by first gathering information. Reflecting upon the chapter on *Perception*, and the need to be open-minded and not assuming things, the more factual and accurate information one can obtain, the more resources are available to draw on to create the design. To begin with, a designer needs to know about the client and what it is they wish to communicate. Also, of importance is understanding who the audience will be and what overall image is to be portrayed in the finished product.

As one determines the design problem, and eventually the solution, reference your research and understanding of what is needed by the client to the communication model which was described in *Chapter 5 Communication*.

Client Profile or Creative Brief

For print shops, design studios, and individual freelance graphic artists, it is essential to obtain some general information at the first meeting such as: the name of the business or organization, where they are located, and contact information. Next is to find out more ancillary, but certainly valuable information. This includes what products or services they sell or provide. It is a perfect opportunity to use examples of these items as inspiration for conceptualizing. Parts that make up the product, tools used, fabric, colors— all fair game.

Is the client's business or organization large or small, mom and pop or corporate giant? Dealing with the owner directly is undoubtedly different than dealing with a middle management person.

Example of Fictitious Client

Alta California is a respected architectural firm located in the downtown financial district of San Francisco. There are three "principles" and a staff of 15 architects, designers, and support staff. They were founded in 1985 by John Smith who remains as the CEO of the company. The name of the firm comes from the name of the first newspaper in central California- The Alta California. Their focus on architecture design is eco-friendly and sustainable single and multiple family housing. They have received many awards for their designs including the prestigious SIA Architectural Design Award. Primary competition for Alta California are D-Scheme Studio, Modulus, and Group 41 Incorporated, which are located in the Bay Area. Alta California's clients include individual and development companies looking for innovative 21st century design with a "green" theme.

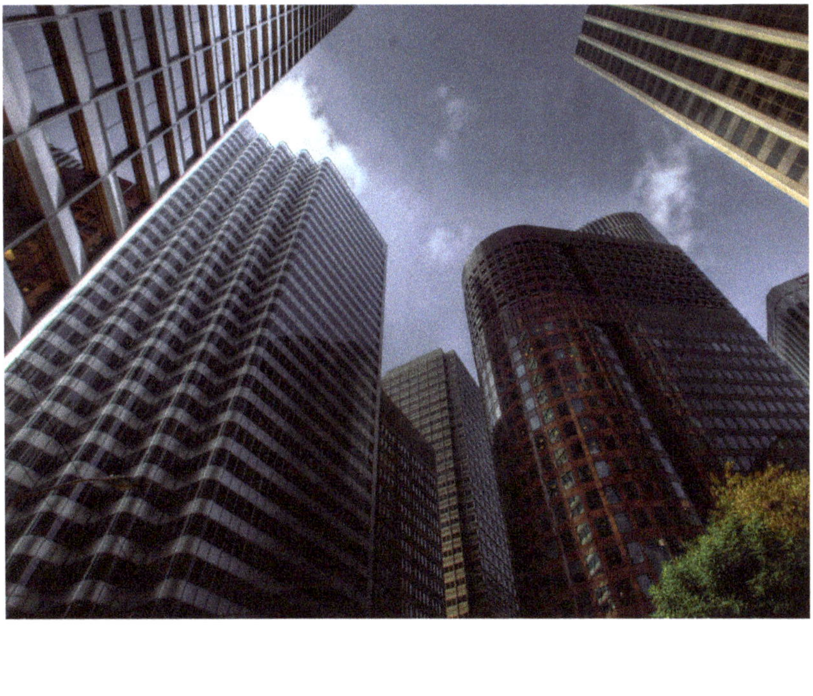

What image do they wish to portray? In other words, how do they wish their customers and associates to view them? Professional, reliable, family-owned, great customer service, quality products, and friendly may describe them.

Who are their competitors, both locally and elsewhere? What advantages or disadvantages does the competition have? And what does their print and digital media look like? Colors, type, images may provide design themes that are common to that industry or organization type.

Message

What is to be communicated? What is the purpose? Is it to inform, such as of an upcoming concert, persuade people of how special the concert will be, or to direct them to purchase tickets for the concert. Refining what the message is, will help focus the design process. Communication is the product.

Is the message to have mass distribution, such as a television commercial, or specifically targeted like individualized and personalized mailings?

Target Market to Audience

To whom, is the message targeted? For those in the marketing field this is very important and at the center of their work. Likewise it is also important for the graphic artist. What are the demographics of the market the client wishes to focus on? Gender, age, income, education level, ethnicity, are only a few of the statistics to gather.

Where is the audience located? No longer does the audience (customer) need to be located close by. It is widely accepted that for most products and services there is a global economy and the client wishes to participate, for example by having an online store.

Even more specifically, a designer may need to determine the likes and dislikes of the audience and how receptive they are to the message, with perhaps the ultimate goal of them taking action, such as making a purchase. What are their wants and needs?

Production

Will the product be printed or digital, or perhaps both in which perhaps layout and elements can be re-purposed? What materials will be used, such as paper, which comes in many colors, finishes, weights, grades, sizes, and quality? What format (dimensions) may be used— standard, or customized? What colors are to be used, standard ink color or spot color for printing, specific RGB color for digital media? Are there technical production requirements? Who will do what and who is responsible? What is most important: speed, quality, or cost? And of course, when is the deadline for it to be done?

Product Image

How will the design function? Will it be primarily type or image driven? Are there certain graphical elements to be included such as icon, symbols, or a logo? What meaning will be associated with the product? Is it a sign that means what it says, or does it stand for something else as a symbol. Or perhaps it is an icon that represents what the source of the image is or is it a metaphor with an open ended interpretation?

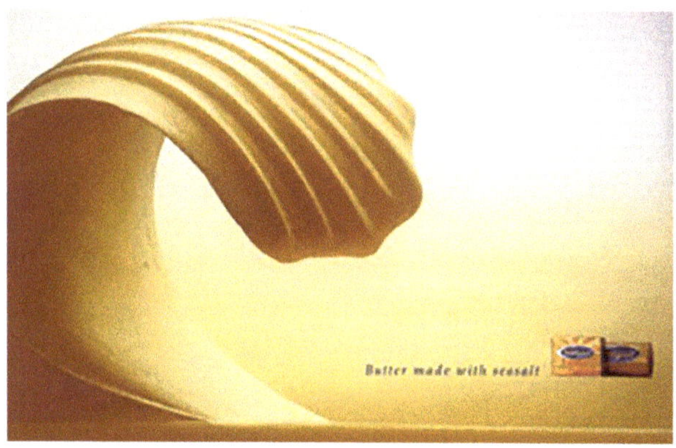

Metaphors use objects, images, or concepts that are directly related to the message. Note how the wave relates to the motto for this product, "Butter made with seasalt." —http://www.innovationinpractice.com/

Coming up with a Design

That white sheet of paper or that blank window on the computer screen is staring you in the face. Where to start, what to do? On-demand creativity isn't reality. Well if one has started the design process by gather information and resources as outlined in the last section, then most likely the creative juices are beginning to flow.

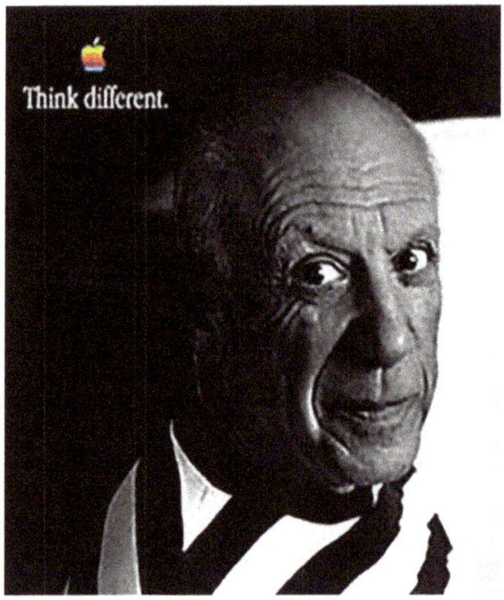

Great design concept for Apple suggesting their "Think Different" philosophy, like the famous people in a series of posters, separates them from their competition.

But what is it, to be creative? It's seeing and doing things differently than has been done in the past. It's putting a different spin on things, looking at things with a clear and often different perception and understanding. It's taking a number of related and unrelated things and assembling them in a fashion to provide a new and fresh understanding or vision of something. It's that old but useful adage, "Think outside of the box." Clint Runge, Co-Founder of the design firm, Archrival takes this concept further saying, "I try not to think outside of the box anymore, but on its edge, its corners, its flap, and under its bar code."

But where to start? Let's look at a few "tools" that will help. Since we've looked at perception and identifying the design problem already in this book you already have skills and resources to begin coming up with a design, but there's more that can help.

Diversity

When possible, work with others or get other's opinions. We all have different strengths and weaknesses, as well as vastly broad and varied experiences. This diversity provides vision beyond what one has and allows those helping or working as a team to describe and bounce ideas off one another with their unique perspective, which often sparks other ideas. A crucible of creative energy!

Perspective

And speaking of perspective, look at things from a different, even unusual viewpoint. As example, here are some assignments from John Baldessari of CalArts, Post Studio Art course: Describe the visual verbally and the verbal visually. Photograph backs of things, underneaths of things, extreme foreshortening, uncharacteristic views.

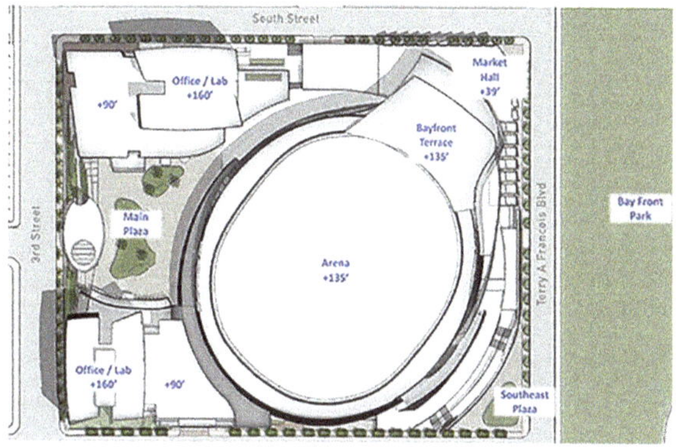

Early architectural concept rendering of the Golden State Warriors new stadium in San Francisco. This perspective unfortunately resembles a sketch of something one might find in their bathroom. Oops!

Association

Make a list of things associated with the design problem. Things with similar names, colors, textures, sounds, processes and so on. How do they relate or not? Why are they different or analogous? How can one be juxtaposed or combined with the other? Build a "Mood Board" of these.

As example, let's assume you are designing for a client that has a business that has the word *horse* as part of it's name. Now what does that conjure up? Shown on the following page are just a few things that are associated with horse. Can you think of more? Certainly many different associations that allow the creative juices to flow.

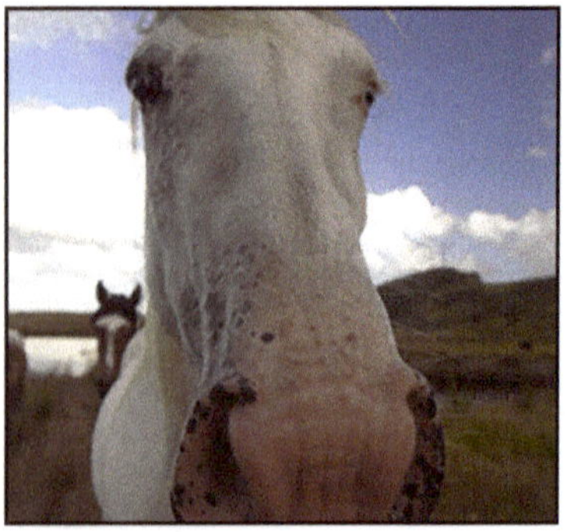
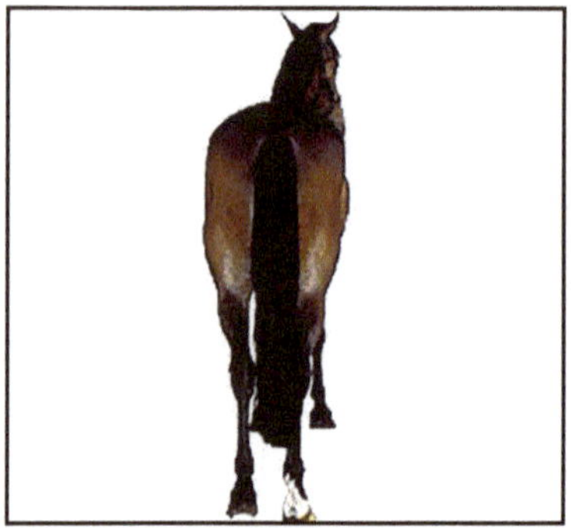
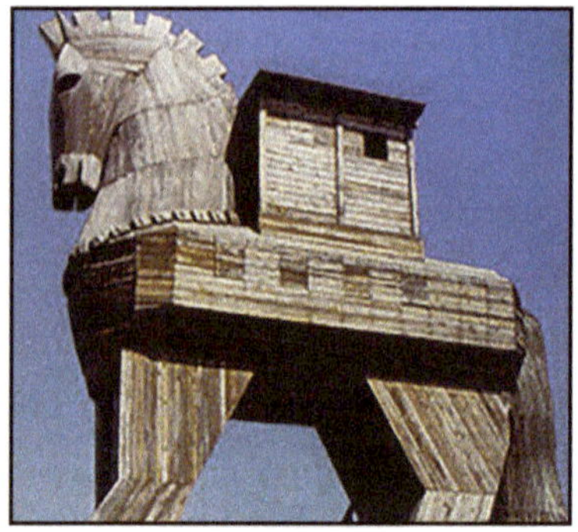
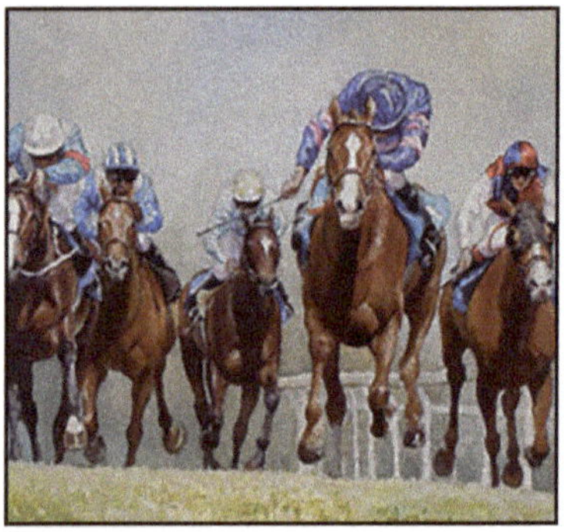
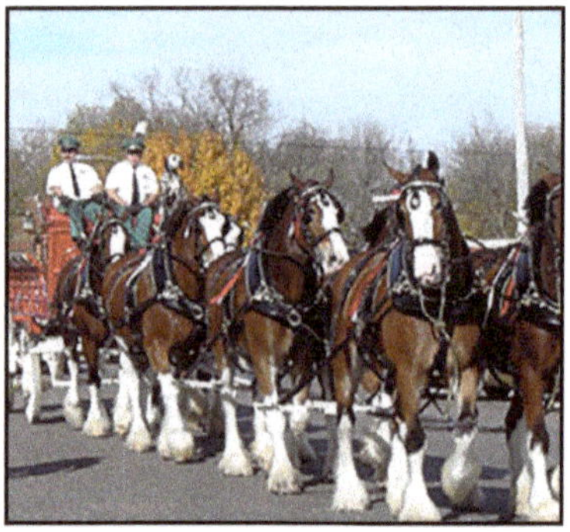
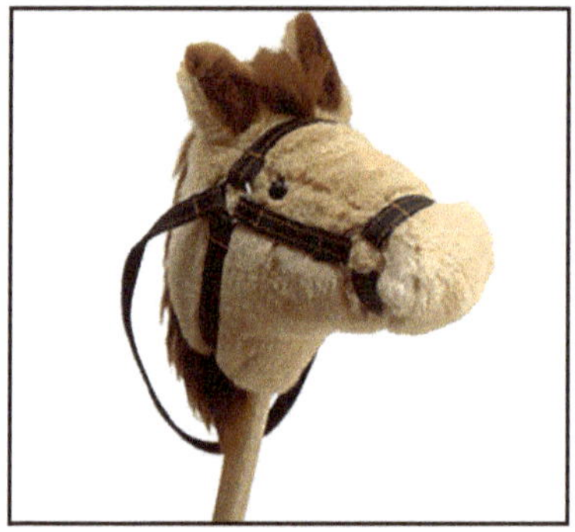
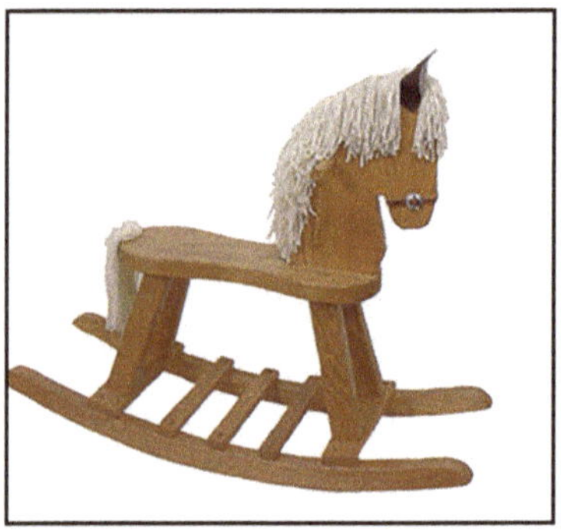
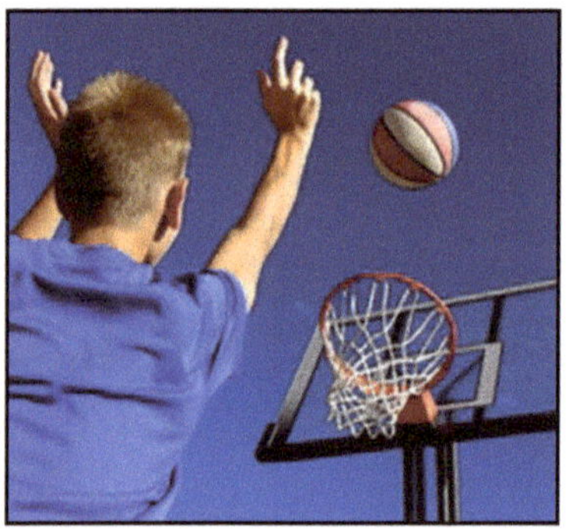
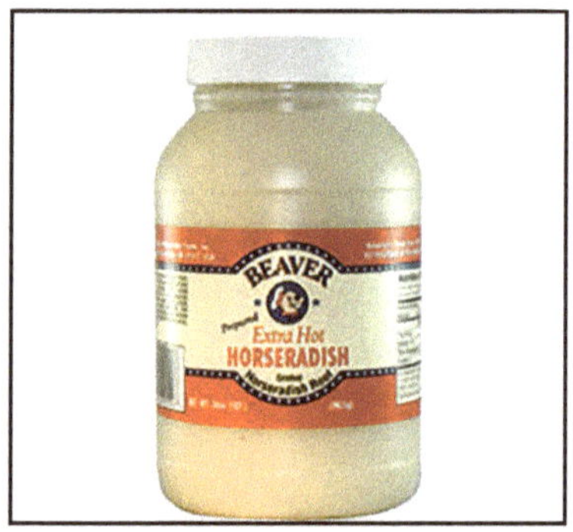
BEAVER
Extra Hot
HORSERADISH
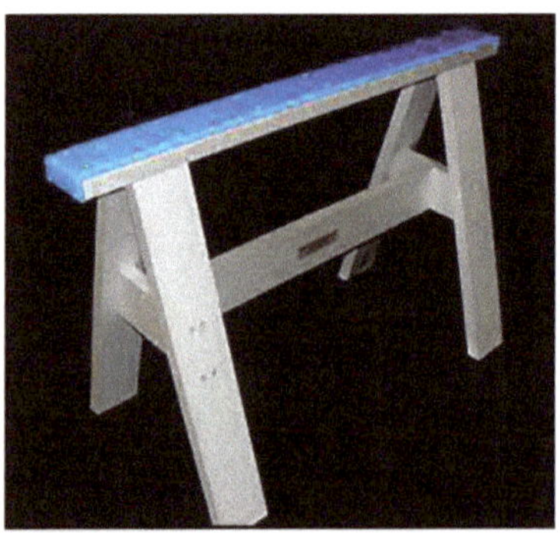
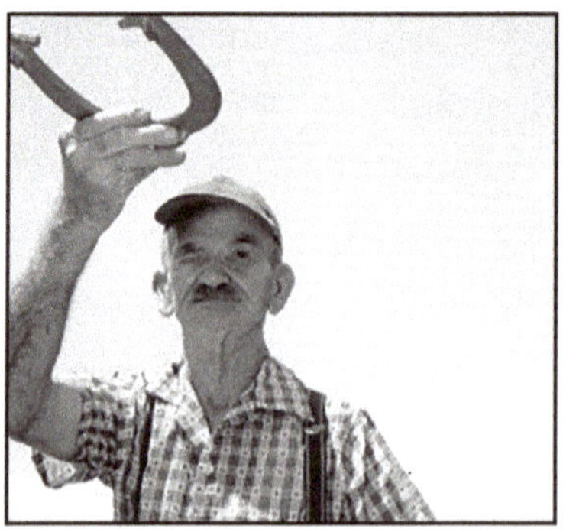
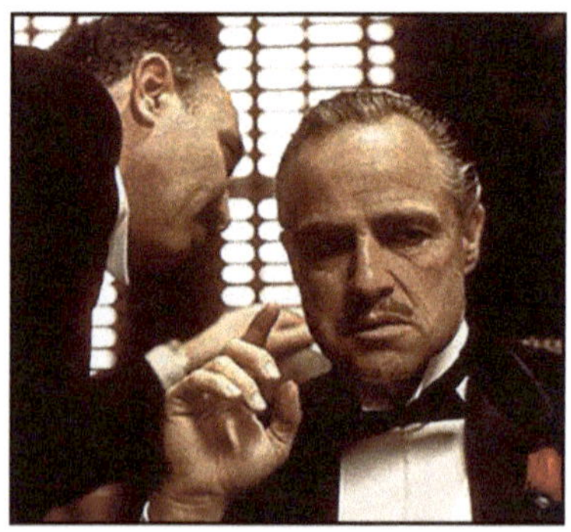

Mood Board

As described earlier, a mood or inspiration board is a great way to assemble and view a number of images, colors, textures, and typefaces that will aid you in the creation of your design.

Through the next few pages, we'll follow steps in which a typical graphic artist or design studio might do to design a logo and related products for the fictitious company *Alta California*, an architectural firm. As previously described, the process would begin by developing a client profile followed by a mood board. The mood board at this time may even be shown to the client for comment and input.

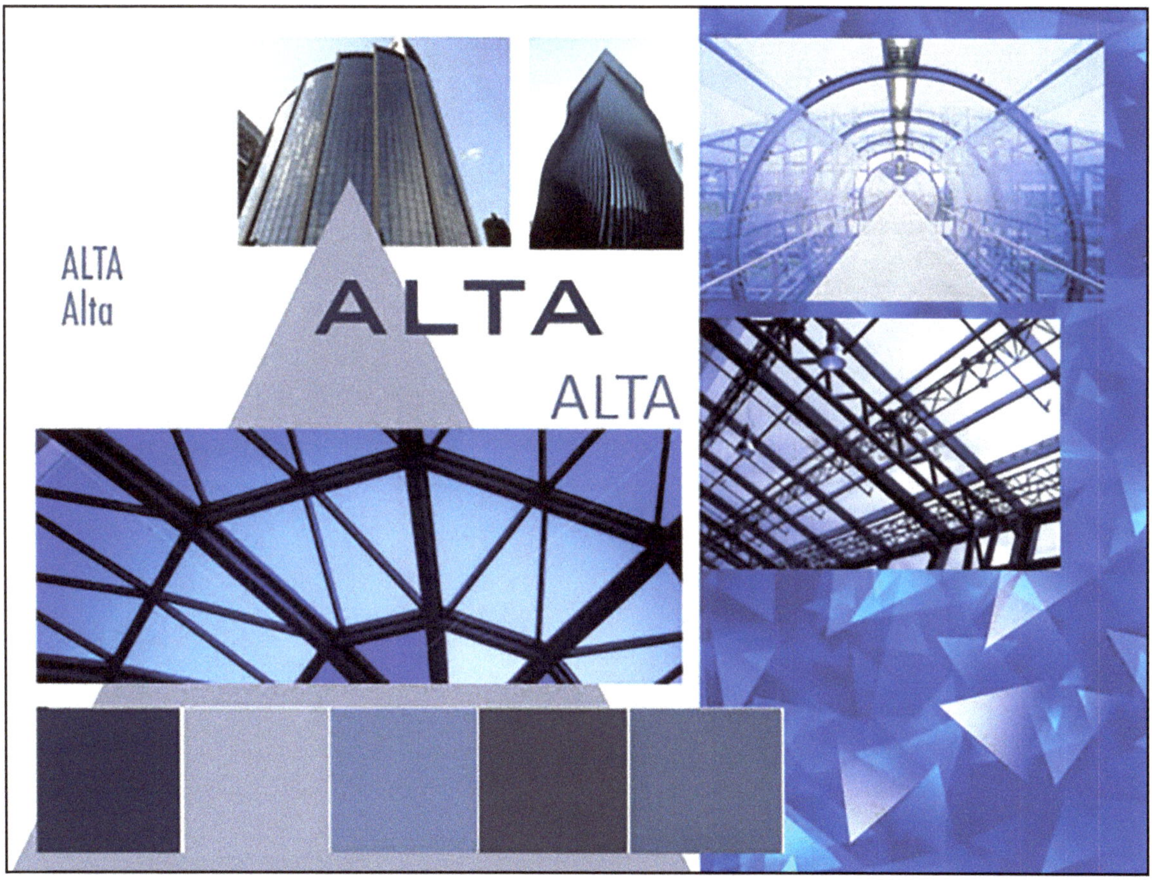

Steps of Design

Traditionally there have been four steps of design: thumbnails, rough, comprehensive, and artwork. All has blurred with the switch to the computer and graphics software programs in the mid-1980s to create designs and layouts. The comprehensive and artwork basically are the same thing now with the graphics file being both whether it is a Photoshop, Illustrator, InDesign, or other graphics file. For some graphic artists, the computer and software covers the entire process of creating the visual design.

Thumbnails

It is suggested however, to save time and of course money, by beginning with thumbnail sketches. Paper and a pencil cost little, but more importantly by creating thumbnails it allows you to quickly draw a number of sketches pretty much anywhere, anytime.

These are small, hence the name, thumbnails, sketches. By drawing a number of them as ideas come to mind, one is able to compare, contrast, select from, add to, and generally have a wide variety of ideas that can be used to construct an initial design concept. Using a computer to do this would be much more time consuming with less flexibility and ease.

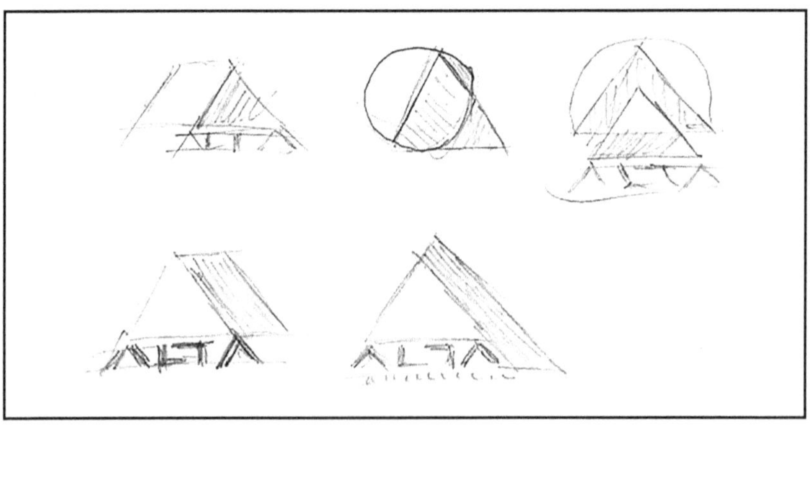

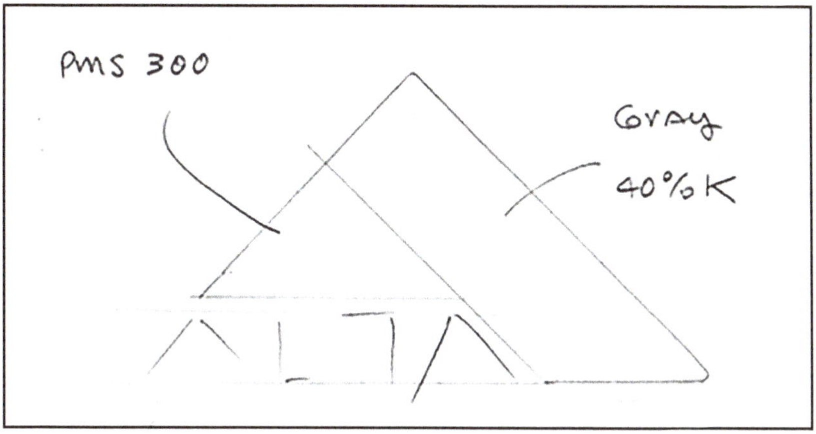

Rough

One could go directly to the computer to finalize the design or create an intermediary rough sketch. The rough is also a pencil sketch but is drawn more accurately and proportionally. Typefaces may be roughly sketched, colors, type specification, images indicated, and other pertinent information can be described on it.

Graphics File

Considering the final use and type of image or layout, computer software is used to create the necessary files. Typically for a design like a logo, a *draw program* like Adobe Illustrator is used since the design often is graphical in nature with geometric shapes and solid colors. Draw programs create scalable images without loss of quality and maintain sharp detail.

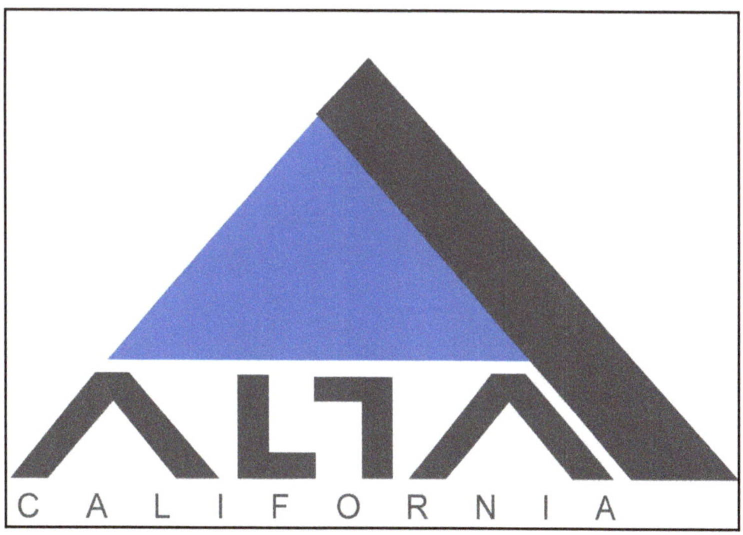

A *paint program*, like Adobe Photoshop, is used for photographic or continuous-tone images. The images can have a number of adjustments made to them using paint tools and adjustment processes including color, lightness/darkness and the use of filters for embellishment and artistic reasons.

A *layout or desktop publishing program* like Adobe InDesign or QuarkXPress is used to assemble a number of images and graphics into a layout working with *Principles and Elements of Design* when creating layouts.

Graphics Software Programs

Adobe Illustrator

The industry-standard vector graphics software is used by millions of designers and artists to create everything from gorgeous web and mobile graphics to logos, icons, book illustrations, product packaging, and billboards.

Adobe Photoshop

The world's best imaging and graphic design software is at the core of just about every creative project, from photo editing and compositing to digital painting, animation, and graphic design.

Adobe InDesign

InDesign is the industry-leading layout and page design software for print and digital media. It's everything you need to create and publish books, digital magazines, eBooks, posters, interactive PDFs, and more.

Quark QuarkXpress

More than a print layout software, QuarkXpress now can transform your print designs into modern web pages with Flex Layouts that enable users to deliver responsive web design without coding.

Principles and Elements of Design

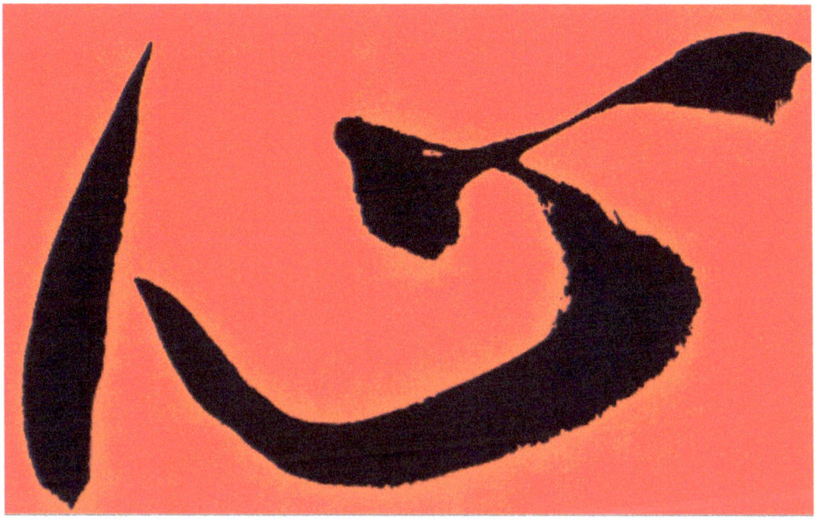

It is fitting that the Japanese character for expressing the idea of PREPARATION should also stand for heart, mind, and soul. Because only when the three come together in a single purpose can excellence in any task be achieved. This is a great example of Unity which is a Principle of Design.

We can make an analogy to the construction of a house. Think of the *Elements of Design* as the two by fours, nails, screws, roofing, concrete, and paint that the house will be built from. The *Principles of Design* are the floor plans, permits, zoning ordinances, and building code that describes how the house can and should be built. Though the elements of design are constant, the principles (rules) on the other hand often are bent or broken. The principles are there to establish a traditional and effective way to create design. When necessary to create a desired effect then, they may be deviated from, just know them first!

Elements of Design

Point

A point is a location. It visually is not there. Its a position on a design layout or X and Y coordinates on the viewport of a web page.

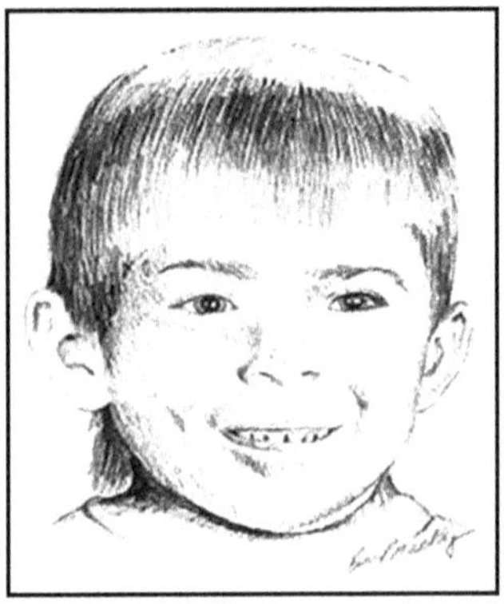

Line

A line is an element characterized by length and direction, a vector. Lines may be thick, thin, dotted, vary in width, have color, and other attributes. They make up most drawings and illustrations.

Shape

A shape is a closed line, defined by its perimeter. Shapes are geometric like a rectangle or may be organic.

Texture

Texture is the surface appearance of a shape that refers to a tactile material. Texture adds interest and realism.

Color

Color is the response of the eye to differing wavelengths of light defined by— **hue**, **saturation** and **value**.

Space

The distance around and/or the area between design objects or elements.

Principles of Design

Depending upon the design book or course you are taking, different lists of principles may be included. The following is a rather comprehensive list of principles divided into two categories: primary and support principles. It should be noted that no principle is utilized by itself within a design and layout, but rather a number of principles often interrelated to each other are in effect manipulating the elements of the design. The principles provide a good foundation for making design decisions.

Primary Principles

Unity

Unity is the prime principle and objective of all design. All other principles serve to reach this end. It is the control of variety in a design focusing the various elements in a design such as type, photographs, graphics, illustrations through choice and location within the layout. It refers to the coherence of the whole, the sense that all of the parts are working together to achieve a common result; a harmony of all the parts.

In a way, this principle is similar to Gestalt psychology theory of the human minds ability to acquire and maintain meaningful perceptions in an apparently chaotic world. "The whole is greater than the sum of its parts."

Variety

A complementary principle to unity, variety provides visual interest to what would be ordinary and bland. The delicate balance between these first two principles provides exciting and creative design.

Hierarchy

One of the primary tasks of a designer is to manage the visual hierarchical structure of a layout, the arranged order. Through organization, positioning, and identifying the most important part of the design, the second, and so forth, a visual path (or eye movement) can be establish. In addition to that, the information is organized in a manner to provide the most effective communication. Its like the road signs that take you to that vacation destination.

Dominance

Dominance is the influence of one design element over another one. You may begin to see how principles of design are interrelated. Dominance of elements over other ones provides a hierarchy of elements. The use of the support principle, emphasis is used to create dominance.

Proportion

Proportion refers to the size relationship of elements or their parts. The height and width of a rectangle, as an example may have a 2 to 4 relationship. It may also refer to the relationship proportionally of one element to another such as a 2" circle to a 6" circle. This principle is important in many types of product designs such as publications since common format and material sizes will have set proportional ratios.

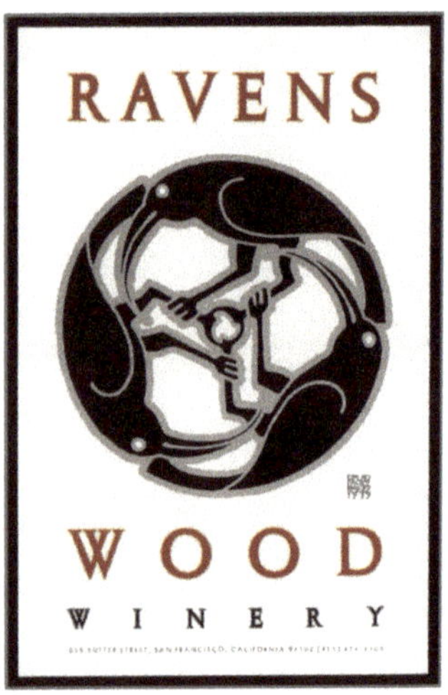

Overall, this poster design has symmetrical balance, while the center element has radial balance. —Ravens Wood Winery

Balance

Balance is the visual weight distribution of elements within a design. There are two main forms of balance— Symmetrical and Asymmetrical. For some designs, a Radial or Crystallographic balance is used.

Symmetrical

In this type of balance, elements of equal or close to equal visual weight and or number are placed on either side of a center vertical axis. It is conservative in nature with the eye-movement top to bottom or bottom to top.

Asymmetrical

"Heavy" visual weight on one side of a layout is balanced by visual weight that is more detailed, has more elements, bolder color. The fulcrum is more towards the heavy element. Eye

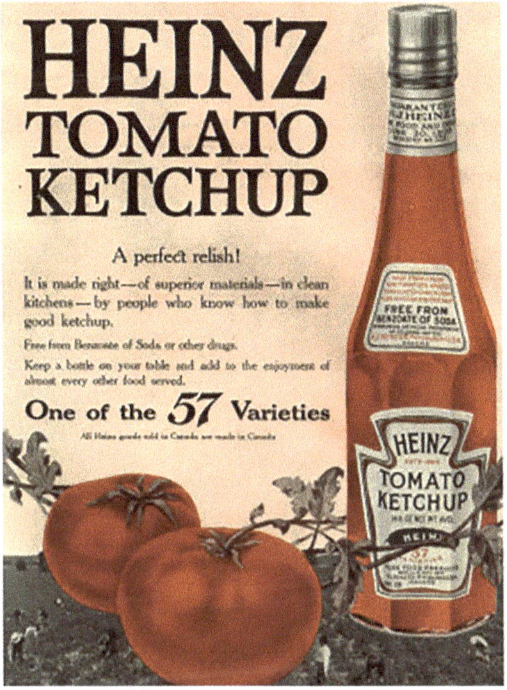

Early ad layout using Asymmetrical balance. Notice how the large bottle "weight" is offset by the number of smaller "weight" images.

movement is more fluid and not necessarily top to bottom but rather more side to side and informal.

Radial

This form of balance involves the arrangement of elements that radiate from the center of the layout—circular and concentric.

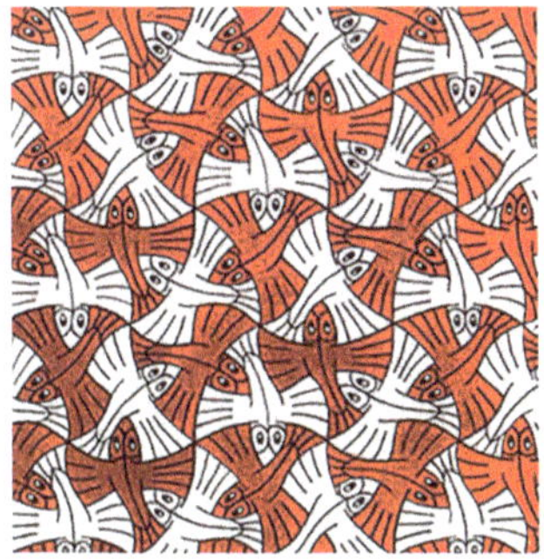

Crystallographic Balance.
— Flying Fish by M. C. Escher

Crystallographic

Not commonly used, Crystallographic balance, also know as mosaic balance, is repeating elements of equal weight with an even distribution of elements within a layout. There is no focal point and everything has equal emphasis.

Support Principles

Scale

Scale refers to the size of elements within a composition either referred to as a comparison (that one is larger than that one) or measured in units. Scale can be used to create variety and emphasis in a design and help establish visual hierarchy.

Emphasis

Emphasis provides a focal point for the viewer by giving prominence to an element or group of elements. Humans tend to be attracted to color over black and white, large over small, many over few, and complex over simple. Choice of type, color, scale and other attributes can provide emphasis by which within a layout, can provide dominance which in turn provide hierarchy and eye-movement.

Rhythm

Much like music where sound and absence of sound provide the melody and syncopation, so does the placement of images and their spacing as well as visual emphasis provide the composition.

Eye Movement

This is the prescribed path that the viewer follows through a

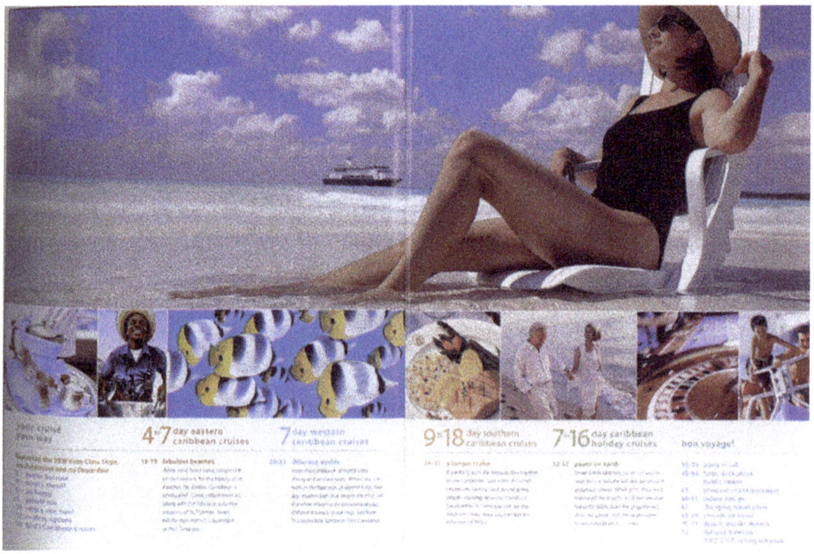

In this magazine layout, the eye movement is first from the woman's face down along her legs to the series of pictures and headings—left to right.

layout. As described previously, the three Principles: emphasis, dominance, and hierarchy, are utilized to create the "sign posts" to follow. Can you make a correlation with "mental capacity" that was described in *Chapter 5- Communication?*

Proximity

This principle refers to the placement of elements together and apart and the relative size and distance between them. Elements that are close to each other suggest a commonality whereas, those that are separated imply being unassociated.

Repetition

Repetition is the placement of elements in a regular pattern either related or juxtaposed. The repeated elements may vary in size, shape to provide variety and unity.

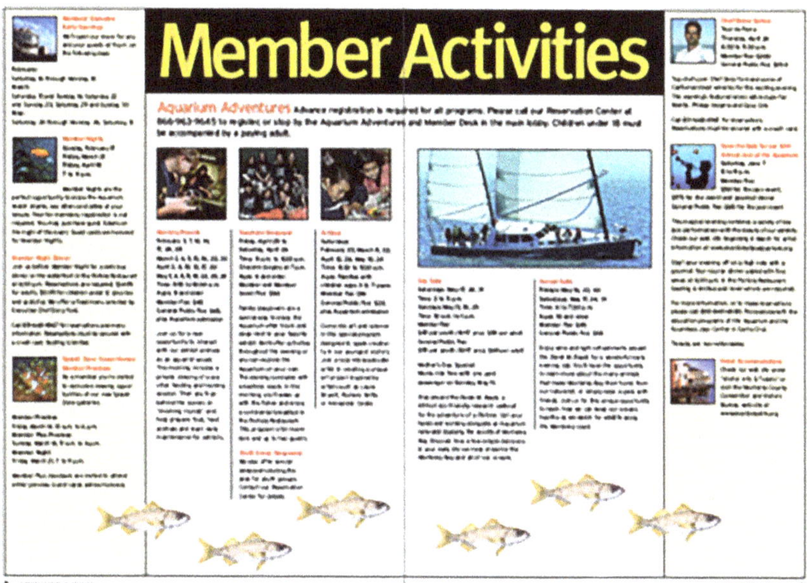

Notice how the captions and content have proximity *to the pictures they are describing. Not only are the fish repeated but the pictures have the same sizes and shape except the ship. Headings and colors are also repeated,* repetition.

Creating Layouts

Creating layouts is the process of positioning images, text, and graphics that provide the visuals to be printed or digital product. Depending upon the product to be created, particular and often traditional structure to the layout is desired or required, such as size, number of columns, or type of folding. Setting up a desktop publishing program, such as Adobe InDesign, to create a layout, will include some basic information such as the dimensions, margins, number of columns, and space between columns. Furthermore, one may add guide lines that will also aid in positioning the various elements.

To begin the layout process one should take several steps before even opening the layout software. As you learned in *Chapter 6- Determining the Design Problem,* the first step in creating designs is to learn about the customer or client and determine what their needs are and what particular set of requirements they may have. Next work up thumbnail sketches of layouts to visualize and make some basic layout decisions. A rough sketch may also be made that may include notation of colors,

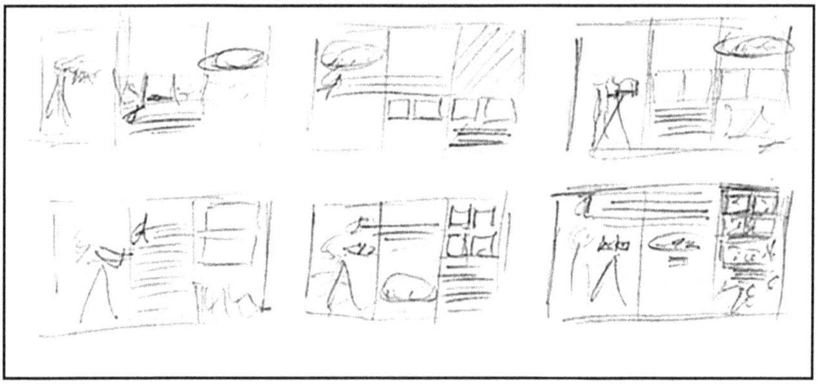

Thumbnail sketches for a design of a brochure.

typefaces, images, and formatting. Furthermore, if the product is to be more than a single page, such as a brochure or certainly for any publication, a dummy is a handy tool. A dummy is simply a sheet of paper (for publications, may be many sheets), that have a rough sketch of elements to be found on the assorted parts, folded if necessary. The dummy allows you to look at the relationship of the panels or pages that make up the product. More will be discussed about the use of a dummy in the following section, *Publication Design*.

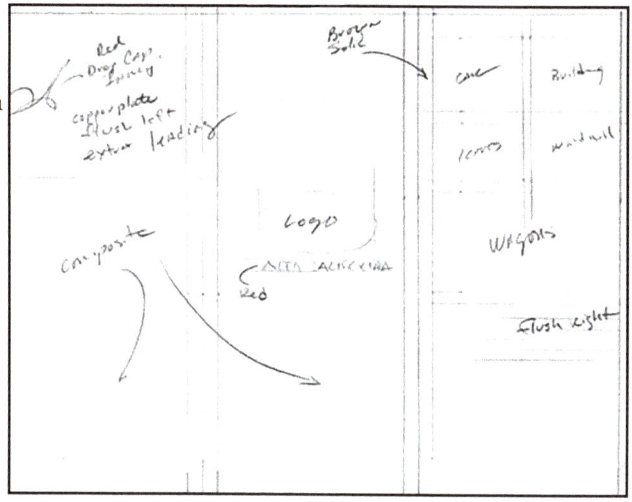

A detailed rough *with notations.*

When using desktop publishing software like Adobe InDesign or QuarkXPress to do layouts, initially various measurements and parameters are set as mentioned earlier in this section. This process goes more smoothly if you have created a rough with specifications.

Grid

A grid subdivides a page vertically and horizontally into margins, columns, inter-column spaces, lines of type, and spaces between blocks of type and images. These subdivisions form the basis of a modular and systematic approach to the layout, particularly for multi-page documents. This combination of margins, columns, gutters, and guidelines help establish a grid. A grid aids in the placement of the elements on the layout pro-

Note how the Grid on the previous page provides unity and structure to this brochure design.

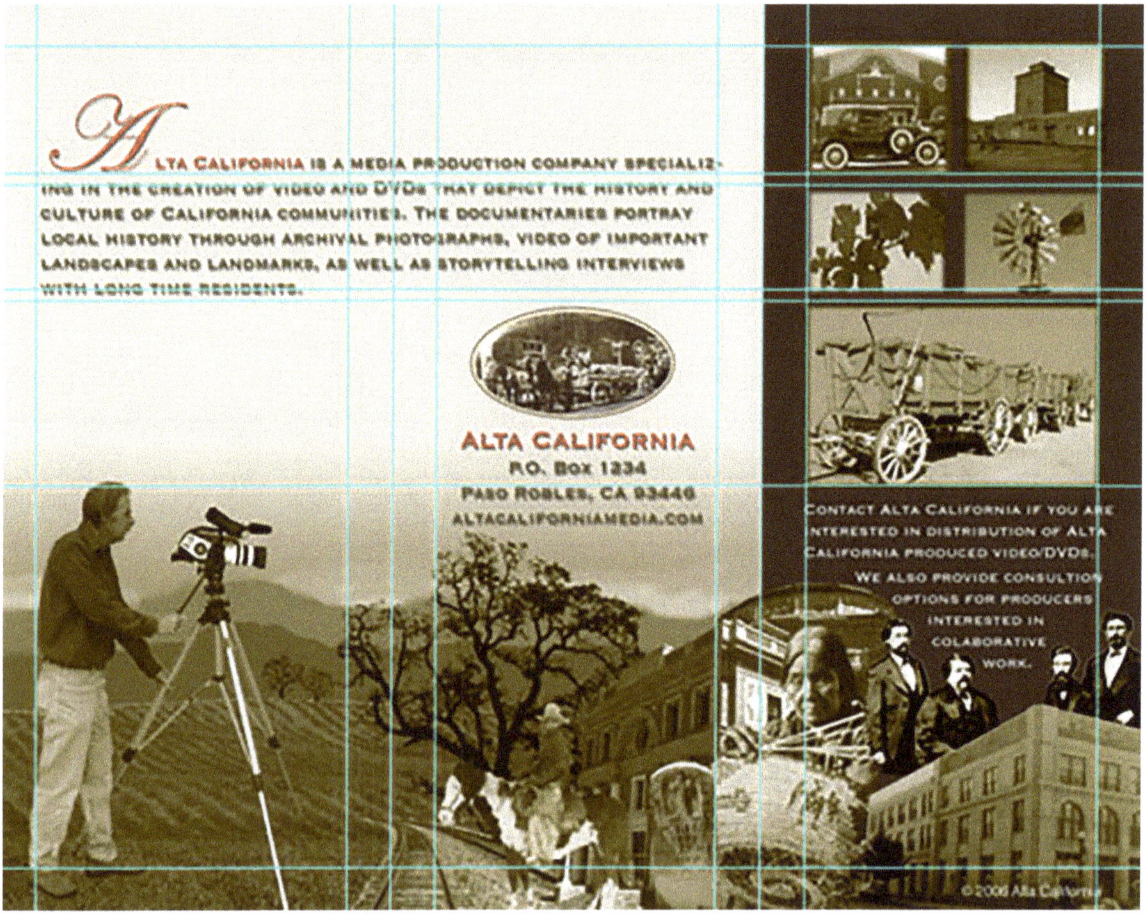

viding structure, precision, and consistency—essential to good design. Overall a grid provides repeatability, composition, and communication.

The repeatability of a grid makes similar pages in a multi-page design have the same structure and gives multiple single designs, such as packaging for a line of teas of different flavors a common look.

The precepts of composition are inherited in the aesthetics and conventions of "schools" dating back to classical Rome. These ridged confines of a grid need to be considered a "rule of thumb" and be massaged and even broken to meet the ultimate goal of the design.

Communication of the message then, is a positive aspect of using the grid. Readers find given elements in the same place, and designers use composition and placement of elements within a grid to guide readers to important elements and information. Th grid eliminates the idle variations which may be considered clever but merely impose themselves between the reader and the message.

Though "graphic design" nor "grids" were talked about until the mid-twentieth century, designers or their predecessors have been utilizing some form of structure to organize content, proportion, space, and form before then. Prior to typesetting and printing there were texts available to read, primarily religious materials, laid out by scribes using calligraphy, often in more than one column, with lettering that was arranged left, with color and variations in letter size used for emphasis.

With the invention of printing from movable type by Johann Gutenberg, circa 1437, the manuscript format was assimilated but with a new wrinkle, justified type. This typesetting format, symmetrical in balance, would exist as page layout

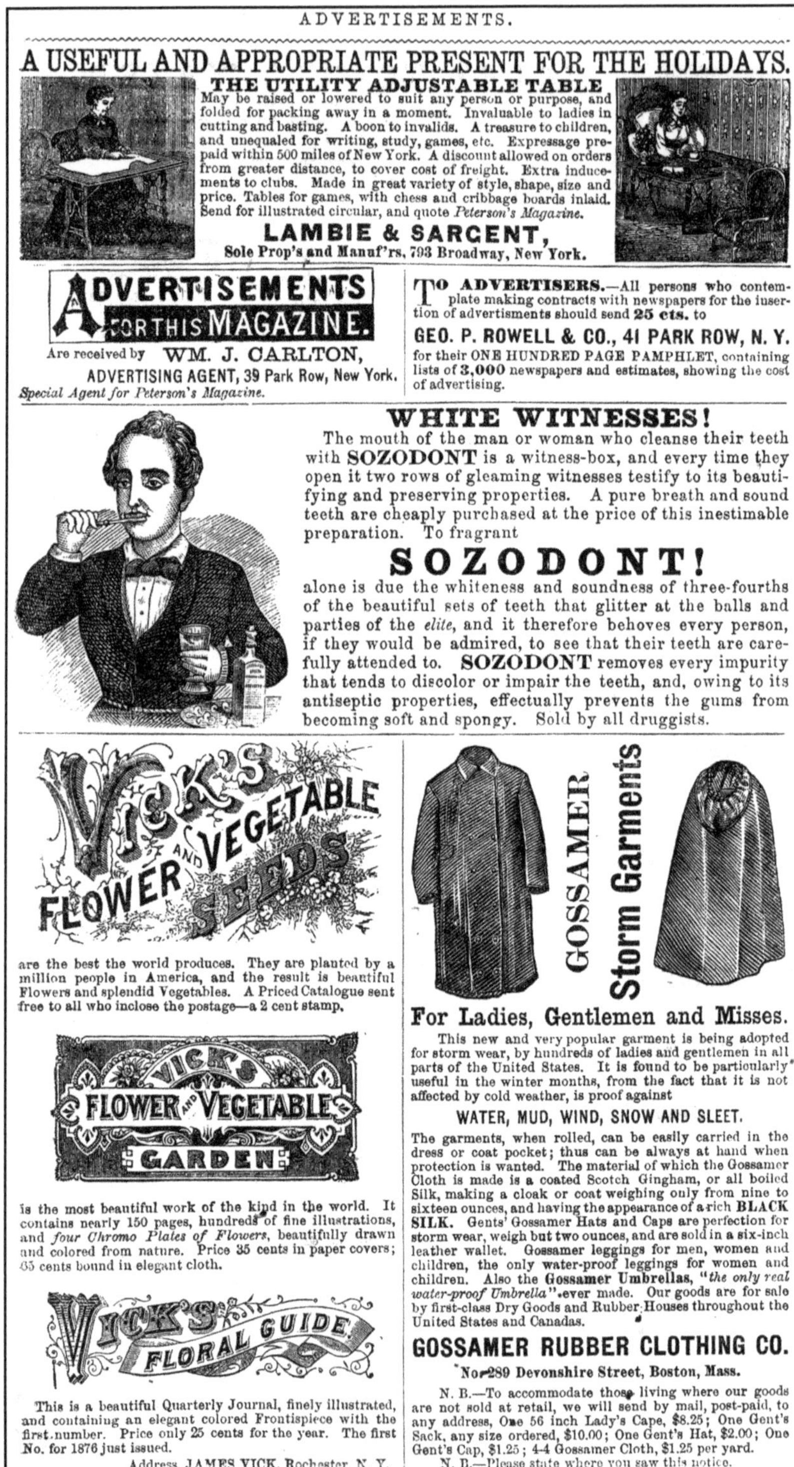

ADVERTISEMENTS.

A USEFUL AND APPROPRIATE PRESENT FOR THE HOLIDAYS.

THE UTILITY ADJUSTABLE TABLE

May be raised or lowered to suit any person or purpose, and folded for packing away in a moment. Invaluable to ladies in cutting and basting. A boon to invalids. A treasure to children, and unequaled for writing, study, games, etc. Expressage prepaid within 500 miles of New York. A discount allowed on orders from greater distance, to cover cost of freight. Extra inducements to clubs. Made in great variety of style, shape, size and price. Tables for games, with chess and cribbage boards inlaid. Send for illustrated circular, and quote *Peterson's Magazine.*

LAMBIE & SARGENT,
Sole Prop's and Manuf'rs, 793 Broadway, New York.

ADVERTISEMENTS FOR THIS MAGAZINE.
Are received by WM. J. CARLTON,
ADVERTISING AGENT, 39 Park Row, New York.
Special Agent for Peterson's Magazine.

TO ADVERTISERS.—All persons who contemplate making contracts with newspapers for the insertion of advertisments should send **25 cts.** to

GEO. P. ROWELL & CO., 41 PARK ROW, N. Y.

for their ONE HUNDRED PAGE PAMPHLET, containing lists of **3,000** newspapers and estimates, showing the cost of advertising.

WHITE WITNESSES!

The mouth of the man or woman who cleanse their teeth with **SOZODONT** is a witness-box, and every time they open it two rows of gleaming witnesses testify to its beautifying and preserving properties. A pure breath and sound teeth are cheaply purchased at the price of this inestimable preparation. To fragrant

SOZODONT!

alone is due the whiteness and soundness of three-fourths of the beautiful sets of teeth that glitter at the balls and parties of the *elite*, and it therefore behoves every person, if they would be admired, to see that their teeth are carefully attended to. **SOZODONT** removes every impurity that tends to discolor or impair the teeth, and, owing to its antiseptic properties, effectually prevents the gums from becoming soft and spongy. Sold by all druggists.

VICK'S FLOWER AND VEGETABLE SEEDS

are the best the world produces. They are planted by a million people in America, and the result is beautiful Flowers and splendid Vegetables. A Priced Catalogue sent free to all who inclose the postage—a 2 cent stamp.

VICK'S FLOWER AND VEGETABLE GARDEN

is the most beautiful work of the kind in the world. It contains nearly 150 pages, hundreds of fine illustrations, and *four Chromo Plates of Flowers*, beautifully drawn and colored from nature. Price 35 cents in paper covers; 65 cents bound in elegant cloth.

VICK'S FLORAL GUIDE

This is a beautiful Quarterly Journal, finely illustrated, and containing an elegant colored Frontispiece with the first number. Price only 25 cents for the year. The first No. for 1876 just issued.

Address, JAMES VICK, Rochester, N. Y.

GOSSAMER Storm Garments

For Ladies, Gentlemen and Misses.

This new and very popular garment is being adopted for storm wear, by hundreds of ladies and gentlemen in all parts of the United States. It is found to be particularly useful in the winter months, from the fact that it is not affected by cold weather, is proof against

WATER, MUD, WIND, SNOW AND SLEET.

The garments, when rolled, can be easily carried in the dress or coat pocket; thus can be always at hand when protection is wanted. The material of which the Gossamer Cloth is made is a coated Scotch Gingham, or all boiled Silk, making a cloak or coat weighing only from nine to sixteen ounces, and having the appearance of a rich **BLACK SILK.** Gents' Gossamer Hats and Caps are perfection for storm wear, weigh but two ounces, and are sold in a six-inch leather wallet. Gossamer leggings for men, women and children, the only water-proof leggings for women and children. Also the **Gossamer Umbrellas,** "*the only real water-proof Umbrella*" ever made. Our goods are for sale by first-class Dry Goods and Rubber Houses throughout the United States and Canadas.

GOSSAMER RUBBER CLOTHING CO.
No. 289 Devonshire Street, Boston, Mass.

N. B.—To accommodate those living where our goods are not sold at retail, we will send by mail, post-paid, to any address, One 56 inch Lady's Cape, $8.25; One Gent's Sack, any size ordered, $10.00; One Gent's Hat, $2.00; One Gent's Cap, $1.25; 4-4 Gossamer Cloth, $1.25 per yard.

N. B.—Please state where you saw this notice.

This 19th century ad is an example of the eclectic layout of competing content and advertisements that were common at this time.

structure until the 20th century, which at that time was primarily was for the printing of books. The Industrial Revolution marked the beginning of mass production of things, including printing, which flourished to meet the demands to produce publications and other products to communicate diverse messages to an increasingly literate people. Graphic design evolved, to make sense out of designs that had many elements competing for attention. *(See the ad on the previous page)*

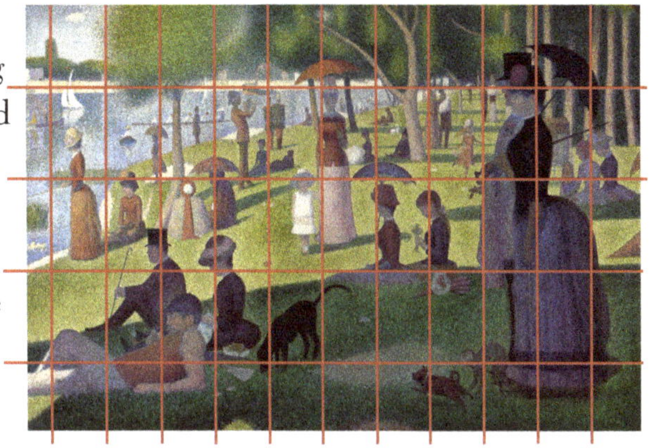

A Sunday on La Grande Jatte, Georges Seurat, 1884. Note how the elements in the painting align to this grind.

The early twentieth-century art movements—futurism, dadaism, surrealism, constructivism, and expressionism—would influence the further development of the grid. Visual space

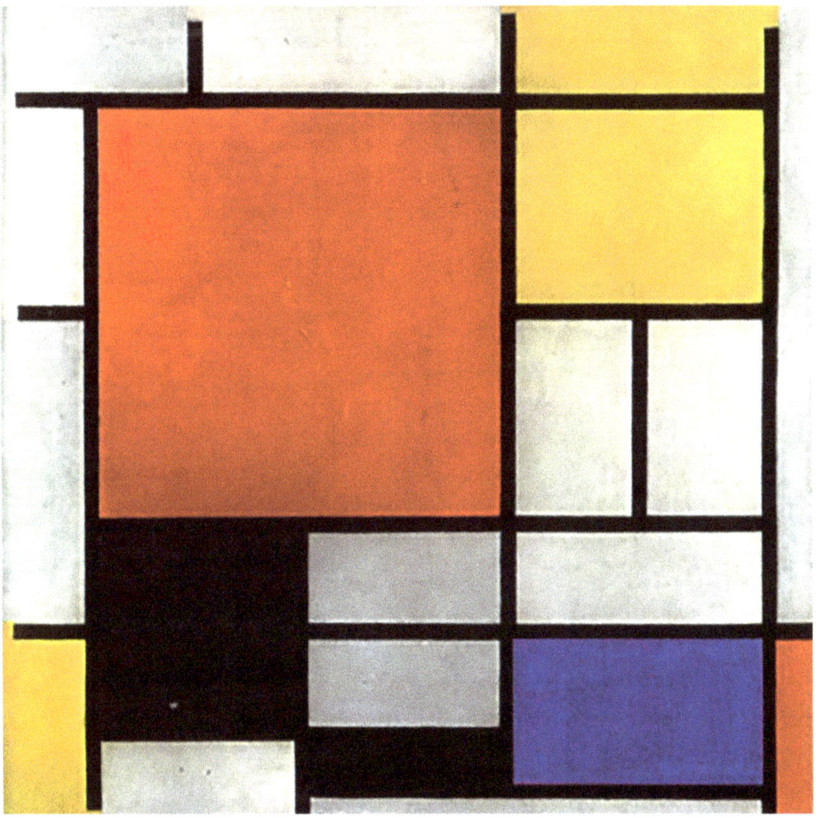

In this classic composition, Red Yellow Blue and Black, 1921, by Piet Mondrian, one can see the influence of the Bauhaus and its design concepts of structure and order.

would become a dynamic component in typographic layout by this influence.

In 1919, The Bauhaus, a German word meaning "house of building", was a school founded in Weimar, Germany by architect Walter Gropius. The school emerged out of late-19th-century desires to reunite the applied arts and manufacturing. The Bauhaus is responsible for design solutions utilizing the grid that became popular in the 1920s.

Following the Bauhaus concepts of design evolved the Swiss Style which can be defined as, "an authentic pursue for simplicity – the beauty in the underlines of a purpose, not beauty as a purpose in itself." This style perpetuated the principle "form follows function" and became a mantra for design in the 1930s. Swiss style is all about using less, so instead of adding more elements to work with, they prefer to remove as much as possible. The core of these ideas were first presented in the book "Grid Systems in Graphic Design," by Josef Müller-Brockmann, a graphic designer and teacher, which helped to spread the knowledge about the grids. These concepts and use of grid design, heavily influences designers to this day.

Proportion and Page Layout

A grid typically establishes the area in which most of the elements in a layout are positioned. This is referred to as the live matter in publications. This area and the dimensions of the layout have proportional relationships of their height and width and to each other.

Historically, a proportion that has been used in the design of many things from the Great Pyramids, to Greek, architecture, Medieval church design, and even the painting Mona Lisa, is the **Golden Section**. The proportional ratio is roughly 1.618

or the number Phi. It can be derived with a number of geometric constructions, each of which divides a line segment at the unique point where the ratio of the whole of the line to the largest segment is the same ratio as the large segment is to the small segment.

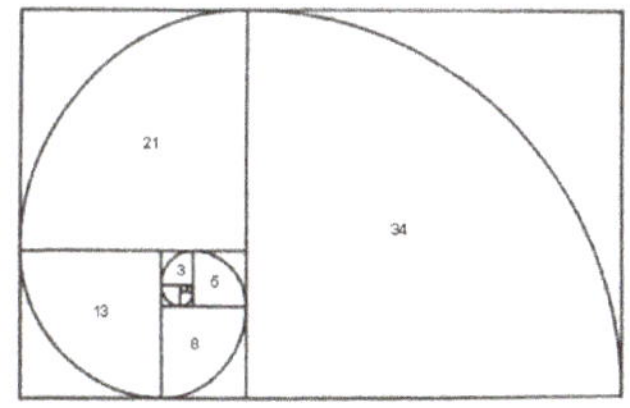

Fibonacci spiral.

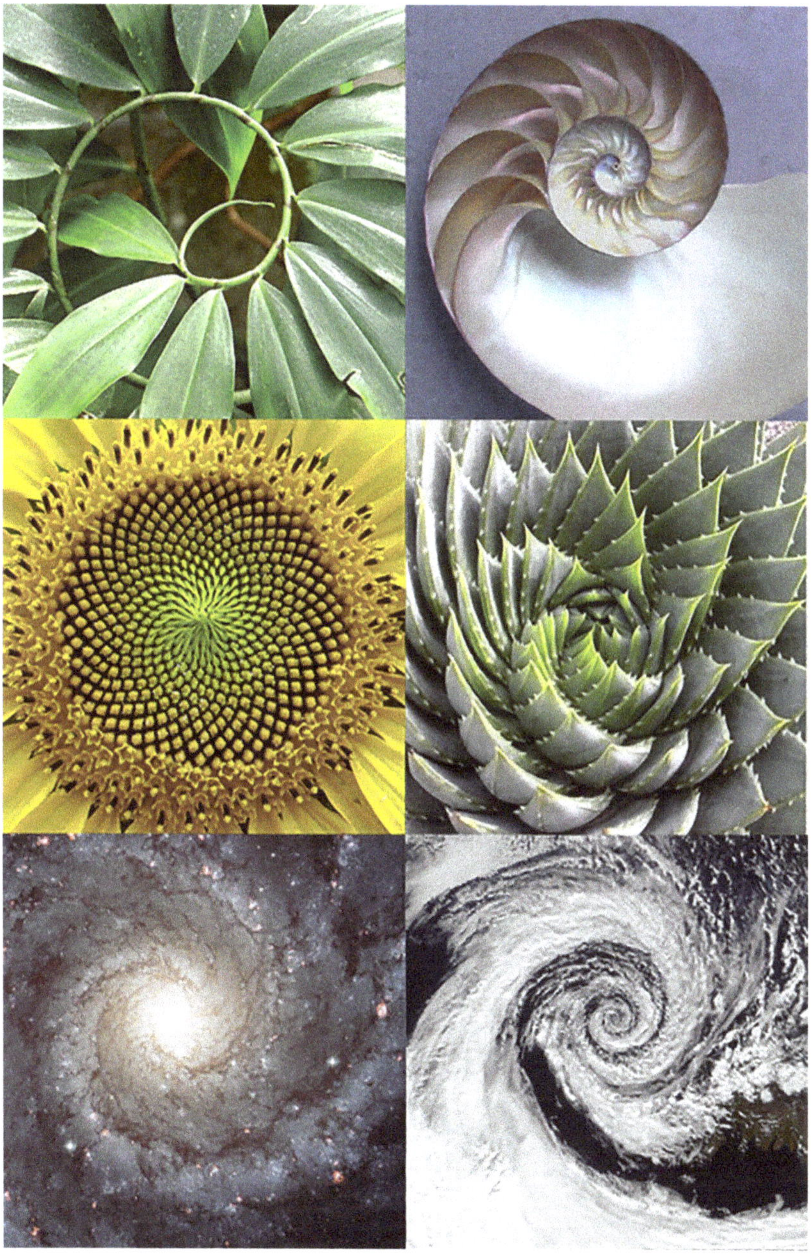

The spiral structure found in nature.

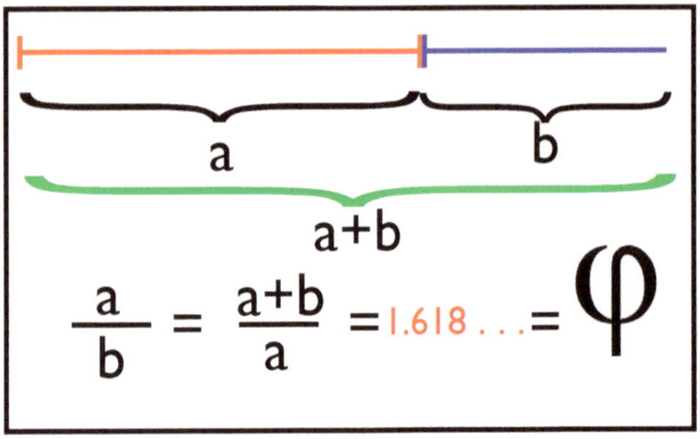

Golden Section- proportion.

The the Fibonacci sequence of numbers (units), closely replicates the golden section or golden ratio. The Fibonacci sequence is first described in the book "Liber Abaci" (1202), by Leonardo Bonacci, known as Fibonacci. The sequence is 0, 1, 1, 2, 3, 5, 8, 13, 21 and so on. The Fibonacci sequence is closely related to the Golden Section and becomes closer to the ratio, the higher

Red – Vertical height of base at ground level : Top of first level : Top of second floor

Blue – Vertical height of base of second level : Top of second level : Top of third level

Green – Horizontal width of outside of left top section : Inside of top right section : Outside of top right section

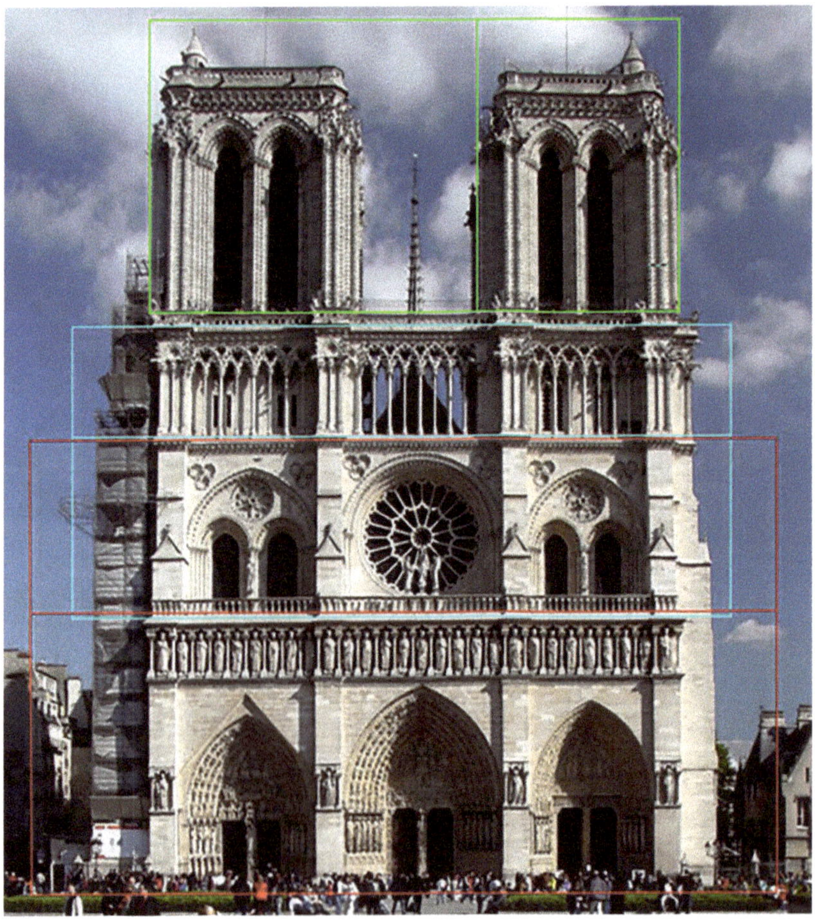

Notre Dame in Paris, which was built between 1163 and 1250 AD.

the numbers. It is frequently found in nature as well in human design. No wonder that this ratio is so comforting to humankind and makes it a strong consideration to use when creating design and layout.

Other Common Proportional Ratios

Classical Proportions

Also know as the Tschichold, Van de Graaf, or Golden Canon this ratio was discovered by Van de Graaf when researching the design of medieval manuscripts and incunabula. The canon was popularized by renown type designer, Jan Tschichold in his book, "The Form of the Book." Classical Proportions of 2:3 work well to define the margins and live matter of a book page.

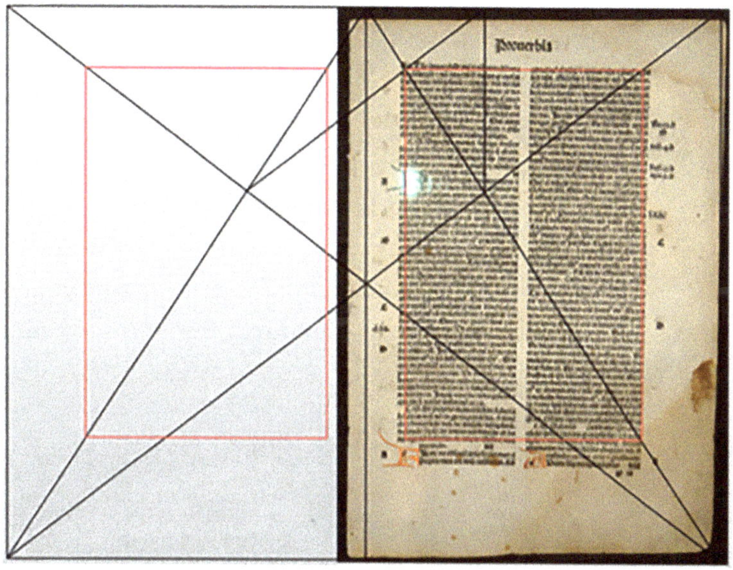

Turning the live matter sideways revels that it is the width of the page.

Silver Ratio

This ratio is related to the ISO standard for paper which are common to European countries and many other parts of the

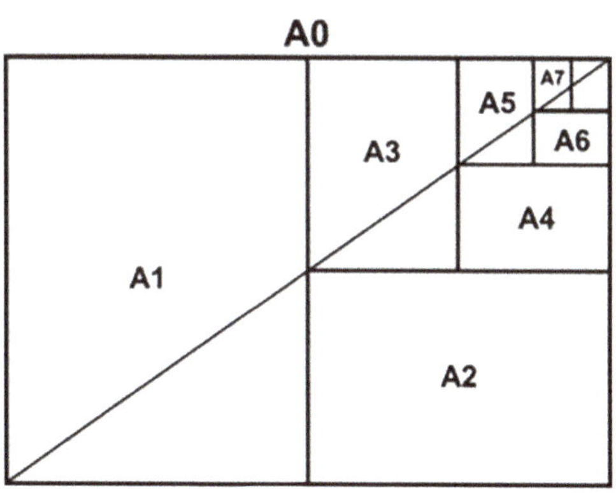

The ISO Paper Standards provide an efficient use of paper cut from larger sheets.

world. It is based on the aspect ratio of √2 or 1:1.4142. The base A0 size of paper is defined as having an area of 1 m2 with dimensions of 841 by 1,189 millimeters (33.1 in × 46.8 in). Smaller sheets of paper are therefore can efficiently be cut from larger ones with no waste.

Photographic Aspect

Common photo sizes are 4 X 6, 6 X 9, and 8 X 12 which have a ratio of 1:1.5.

Computer Monitors

Obviously, important to Web design, currently the most common monitor resolution in pixels is 1920 X 1080 with a 16:9 or 1.78 ratio. A few years ago, a 1024 X 768 monitor was the standard, 4:3 or a 1.33 ratio. The iPad is 3:4 or 4:3 1.33 ratio.

Television

It has been some time since the once standard 4 X 3 ratio TV screen was replaced by the wide screen with a 16 X 9 ratio.

In Review

Using a grid for structure and understanding the aesthetics and utilitarian virtues of the varied proportions described, will aid one in creating pleasing and effective layouts.

Publication Design

Publication design is simply an extension of creating layouts, whereby the product is multi-faceted and three-dimensional. Products include common items such as books, magazines, newspapers, and newsletters. All of these have multiple pages that are printed on both sides and most often are bound in some fashion. Graphic designers not only create layouts for each page using Principles of Design, but also must consider production requirements and various special techniques. They also must incorporate common publication format and style specifications.

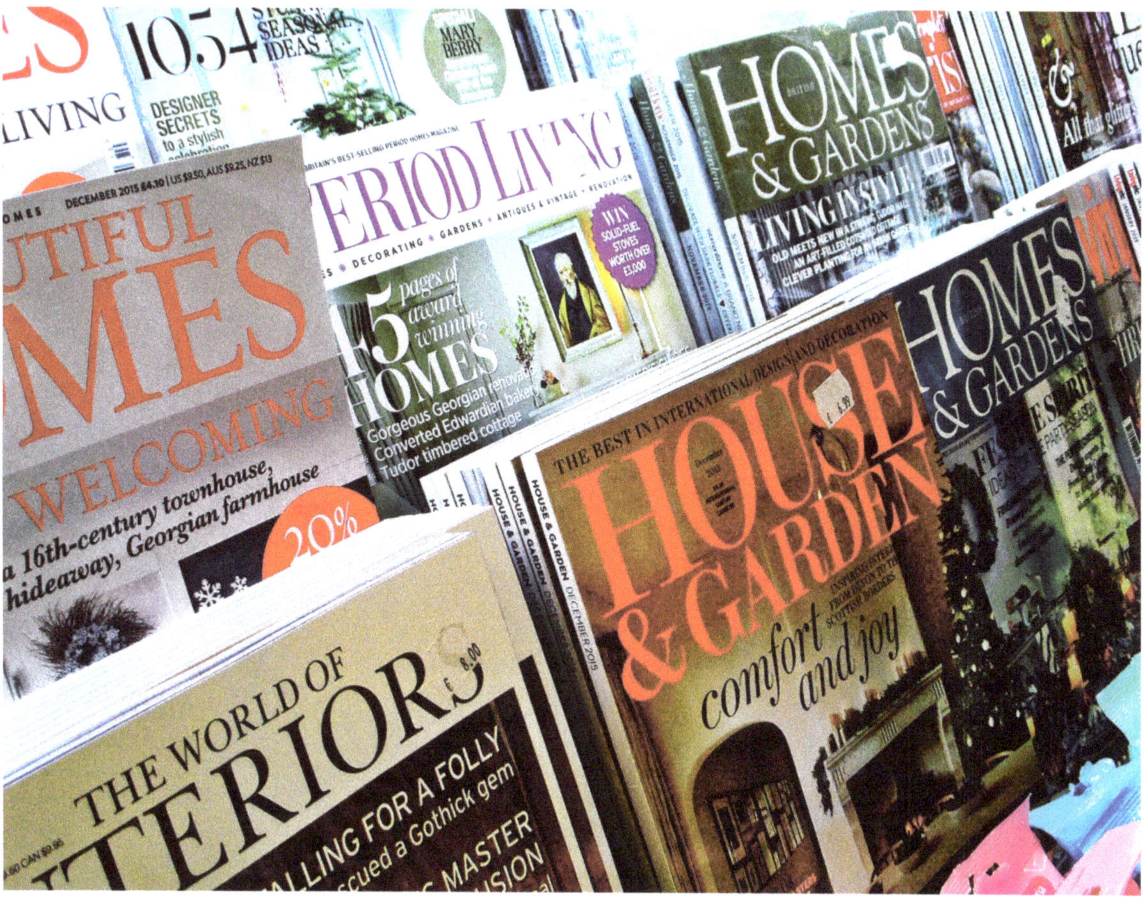

Format

A publication's format refers to it's physical dimensions. These sizes are determined by common practice, use, basis paper size *(see Chapter 7 - Paper- Specifying Paper)* used in printing, and printing equipment ability.

Books

For mass **market books**, they must be at least 4-1/4" x 7" to fit on racks used to display and sell them.

Trade paperbacks, are often in the 5-1/2" x 8-1/2" to 6" x 9" range. This page proportion of 2:3 has long been considered ideal for a book page.

Manuals and workbooks are larger and, depending on the printing equipment being used to produce them, are in the 8" x 10" to 8-1/2" x 11" range.

Novels are produced in different sizes but 5-1/2" x 8-1/2" is the most popular size, though 5-1/4" x 8" is also common.

General nonfiction titles typically are 6" x 9," or those that have sidebars or pull quotes, are 7" x 10".

Magazines

8 3/8" x 10 7/8" is the most economical and common magazine page size. Most press and bindery equipment is designed to produce this size efficiently and with minimum paper waste. Heatset web offset printing and text grade of paper for sheet fed presses which has a basis size of 25" x 38" suit this size well. Oversize and undersize magazines can be produced but their cost per square inch is almost always higher. Most often, the paper used is a coated stock finish that has a gloss, satin, or matte finish.

Newspapers

For most United States and Canadian newspapers, the **Broadsheet** newspaper page size, 11.75" x 21.5 is the largest of the various newspaper formats and is characterized by long vertical pages. The New York Times, USA Today and The Wall Street Journal are all examples of broadsheet. The term derives from types of popular prints – usually just of a single sheet – sold on the streets and containing various types of matter, from ballads to political satire. The first broadsheet newspaper was the *Dutch Courante*, published in 1618.

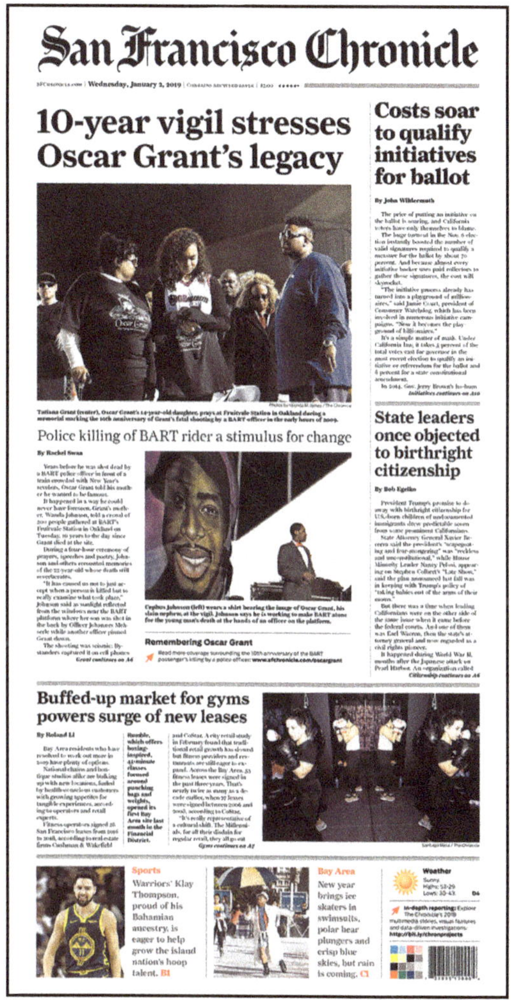

San Francisco Chronicle

Wednesday, January 2, 2019

10-year vigil stresses Oscar Grant's legacy

Costs soar to qualify initiatives for ballot

Police killing of BART rider a stimulus for change

State leaders once objected to birthright citizenship

Remembering Oscar Grant

Buffed-up market for gyms powers surge of new leases

Sports

Warriors' Klay Thompson, proud of his Bahamian ancestry, is eager to help grow the island nation's hoop talent. B1

Bay Area

New year brings ice skaters in swimsuits, polar bear plungers and crisp blue skies, but rain is coming. C1

Weather

At the Newseum website are posted daily the front pages of over 780 newspapers from around the world. This is a great resource to look at design of publications.
— http://www.newseum.org/todays-frontpages/

The **Berliner** format is used by many European newspapers, including; The *Guardian* in the UK, *Expresso* in Portugal, and The *University Observer* in Ireland. It is 12.40" x 18.50."

A third format is the **tabloid** which is 17" x 11." The term "tabloid" has become synonymous with down-market newspapers and some small-format papers sometimes called "compact" newspapers .

Newsletters

Newsletters are small versions of a newspaper with typically localized content. These may be of a single sided sheet or multi-page that may be bound together by being stapled.

> Regardless of the type of publication, recognition of its format is the first step in its design.

Style

The style of a publication refers to its look and feel. It is its visual design. The publication styling is created in two areas: **Overhead graphics** — those which remain in place on most pages and for every issue, such as running footers with page numbers, and **Editorial graphics** — those that pertain specifically to the editorial content like stories and associated images and graphics that change issue to issue.

The Principles of Design: Unity, Variety, and Repetition are essential to quality design.

Production Considerations

In addition to format, the printing production requirements and other considerations certainly can dictate its design.

Paper

As you will see in *Chapter 7 Paper*, paper is manufactured using different materials in many different sizes, colors, textures (finish), thicknesses, and forms (roll or sheet). Depending on the type of publication, printing equipment and process used, paper choice is a very important early design decision. One example is the choice of the grade of paper to be used.

Newspapers use newsprint which is relatively inexpensive, produced in rolls for use on web presses, and has a rather porous surface since it is uncoated. For a designer, this means that type with thin strokes won't reproduce well and photographs will be printed using halftones with low resolution (typically 85 or 100 lines per inch) providing a low quality image. Magazines on the other hand often are printed on paper that has a coated or smooth finish that allows for finer detail and higher quality image reproduction.

Imposition

Since publications are multi-page and pages are printed on both sides, they are often printed with multiple pages on each side of a sheet of paper. Depending upon the page size of the publication and the press capability, 4, 8, or even 16 pages

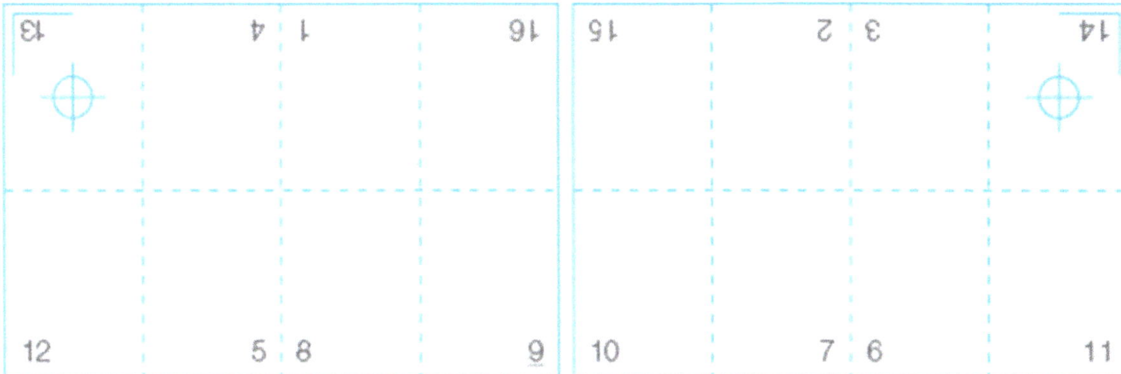

This diagram shows the imposition for a 16-page signature whereas eight pages are printed on each side of the paper. Note the pairs of pages printed next to each other total one more than the number of pages in the signature, in this case, 17!

may be printed on each side. This results in a section of the publication called a **signature**. The signatures after printed are folded, gathered together, and bound.

Depending upon the type of binding, they will either set one within each (saddle stitch binding), or side by side (for side stitch and perfect binding).

This requires an understanding of the relationship and placement of these pages when printed and their location in the publication. Typically a dummy, which is a folded paper miniature of a signature that is numbered, aids in understanding the imposition. An imposition layout may also be a diagram.

Either method provides the scheme for page imposition when creating printing plates and also aids the designer in knowing about design opportunities, such as running an image across a spread, and possible production restrictions or difficulties.

Spreads

There two kinds of **spreads**, reader spreads and printer spreads. A **reader spread** are the two pages a reader sees such a page 4 and 5. Obviously the first and last pages of a publication are singletons. A designer will use design techniques such as horizontal lines, pictures of people that "look" towards the other page, and repeated color or shapes to tie the individual pages visually together.

A **printer spread** are the adjoining pages as they are printed. Notice in the previous illustration that 1 and 16, 2 and 15, etc., are such. Interesting enough, these combinations add up to one more than the total numbers of pages if it is a saddle-stitched publication. The designer should also be aware of what pages are printed on each side of the sheet. A small budget may necessitate printing a second color only on one side (certainly an option). Knowing what pages will have color the designer can plan the design to take appropriate advantage.

Page Layouts

You learned in the previous section, *Creating Layouts,* about the use of various proportional layouts, some having historical beginnings. You also learned how designers utilize the grid to organize and structure layout to position the visual elements. Taking this a step further, let's examine some common layouts used for publications.

First of all, the area contained within the margins of a layout is called the **live matter.** This is where most of the images and text is placed. Not to say that a design can't have elements outside it, in fact this often results in an unordinary and more exciting design.

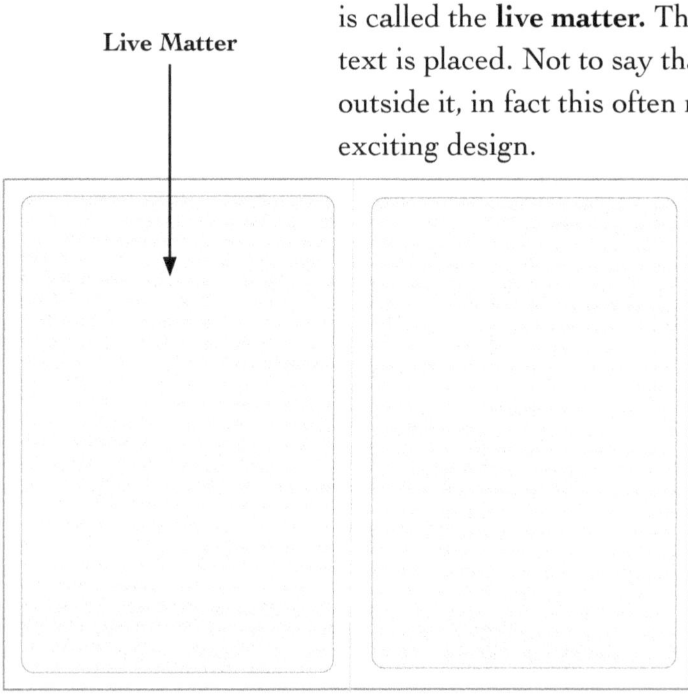

Magazines

Magazines tend to have very thin margins providing as much "real estate" as possible for content and more importantly, advertising.

Books

Traditional margins for a book are described as arbitrary for the head, foot at two times the head, the back (next to the spine or gutter) at .75 of the head, and the fore (at the outside of the page) as two times the back. These are mirrored pages for a spread which is a common layout used to avoid any show through from the other side of the page, especially if printed using the relief printing method which also may cause a slightly raised image.

Another layout for books is when the layout is repeated and has an asymmetrical or informal balance to it as opposed to a symmetrical or formal balance. With this layout, the paper used would have to be thick enough to prevent any show through, though being printed using lithography would present less a chance of that.

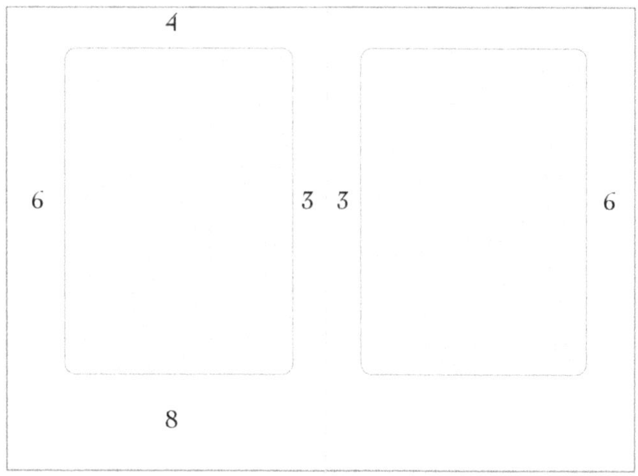

Basic Layout Terms

Mentioned in this section and the previous one *"Creating Layouts,"* there are some common terms used to describe the basic structure of a layout, some more specific to publications. These include margins, gutter, folio, leaf, retro, verso, and spread.

Margins

This is the space between the live matter and edge of the paper. The various proportional relationships of the head, foot, fore, and back may vary as we have just seen.

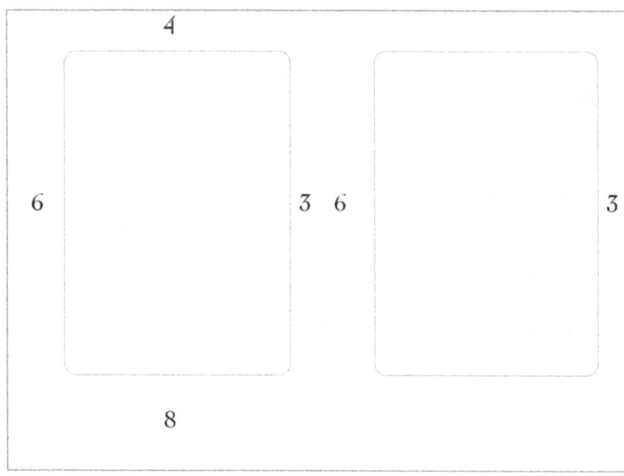

Note, similar proportional measurements in these examples of book page layout, however the position of the live matter, not only as a production consideration, but as a different style choice.

Gutter

This is the location or space where the publication is bound. It is sometimes referred to as the spine, which may also indicate the center point of the outside cover. The gutter is also a similar term that often indicates the space between columns, more properly termed, **column gutter**.

Folio, Leafs, and Sides

Traditionally a **folio,** Latin *folium* (leaf), refers to the sheet of paper that is a book or pamphlet made up of one or more full sheets of paper, on each sheet of which four pages of text are printed, two on each side. Each of these pages may be called a leaf. A folio often also is the page number.

The first page or leaf a reader views is a **recto**, the next or page on back of it, is the **verso**.

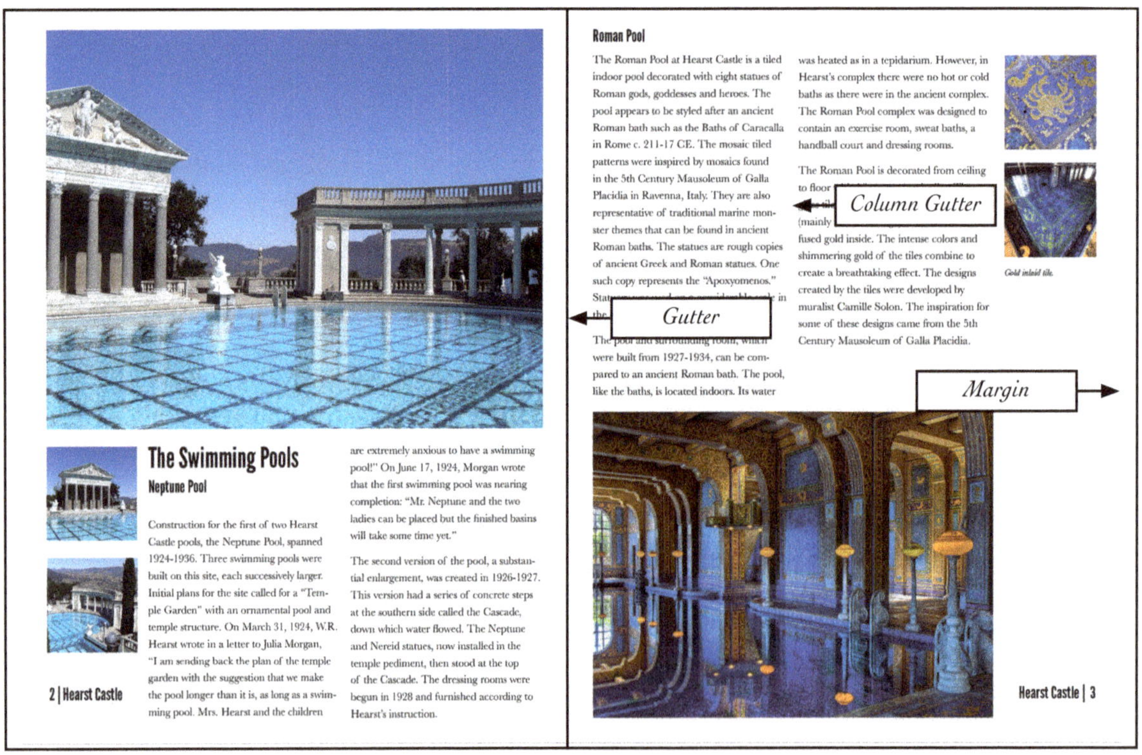

Spreads

More of a visual description than a technical one, a spread refers to the two pages that are next to each other. As described previously in this section, this is an area of design important to the designer to "cross the gutter." Note in the illustration how horizontal lines and use of color bind the two pages into one.

Publication Visual Elements

There are a number of visual elements common to publications, and then some specific to some publication types. These can be categorized into two areas, text and graphical.

Text Elements

Headlines are display type, we saw in *Chapter 4-Typography*, that they are set in 14 point or larger size and typically in a

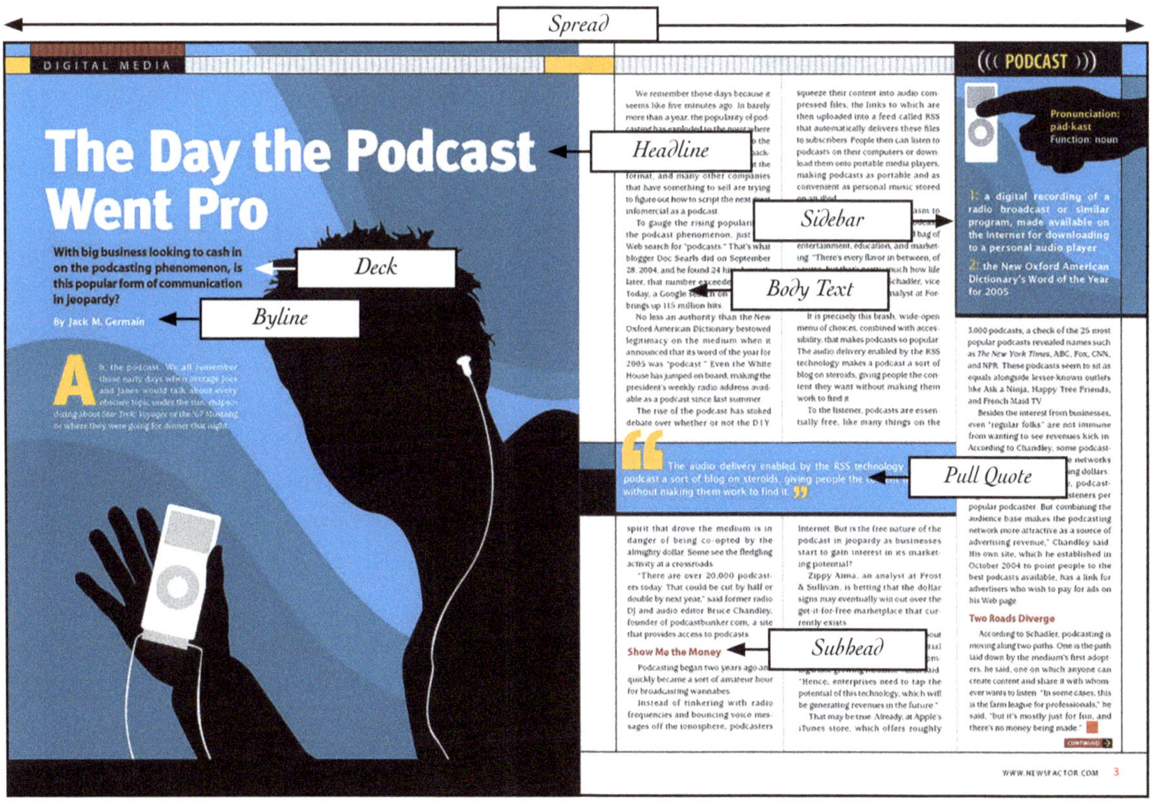

sans serif typeface. Headlines typically are used as a title for an article, feature, or story.

Subheads usually are set in a sans serif typeface that often is the same as headlines set at a smaller size and in a style from the same type family. Subheads help to organize information within the article or story.

Body text is the main reading matter usually set 14 point or smaller— and in a serif typeface for readability.

A **Byline** is set with the author's name, i.e. By John Smith. Note the capitol "B" in By.

Captions are text that describes an image or illustration. Set in a smaller size type, it is distinguished from other type used in some manner, such as being set in italic.

A **kicker** is a short phrase label or short paragraph set above the head. A **deck** is set below it.

Pull quotes are text taken from the main story with embellished styling often with variations of color and size. They are attention getting to take the reader into the story.

A **Sidebar** is a short story that relates to the main story often set in a different font.

Text Editing

A **drop cap** is the first letter of the first word in an opening or transitional paragraph that is much larger than the paragraph text, often two lines of type or more. It says, "hey, this is the start of something."

Paragraph spacing may be added to the beginning or end of a paragraph or both. This provides some definition between paragraphs and opens up the text layout.

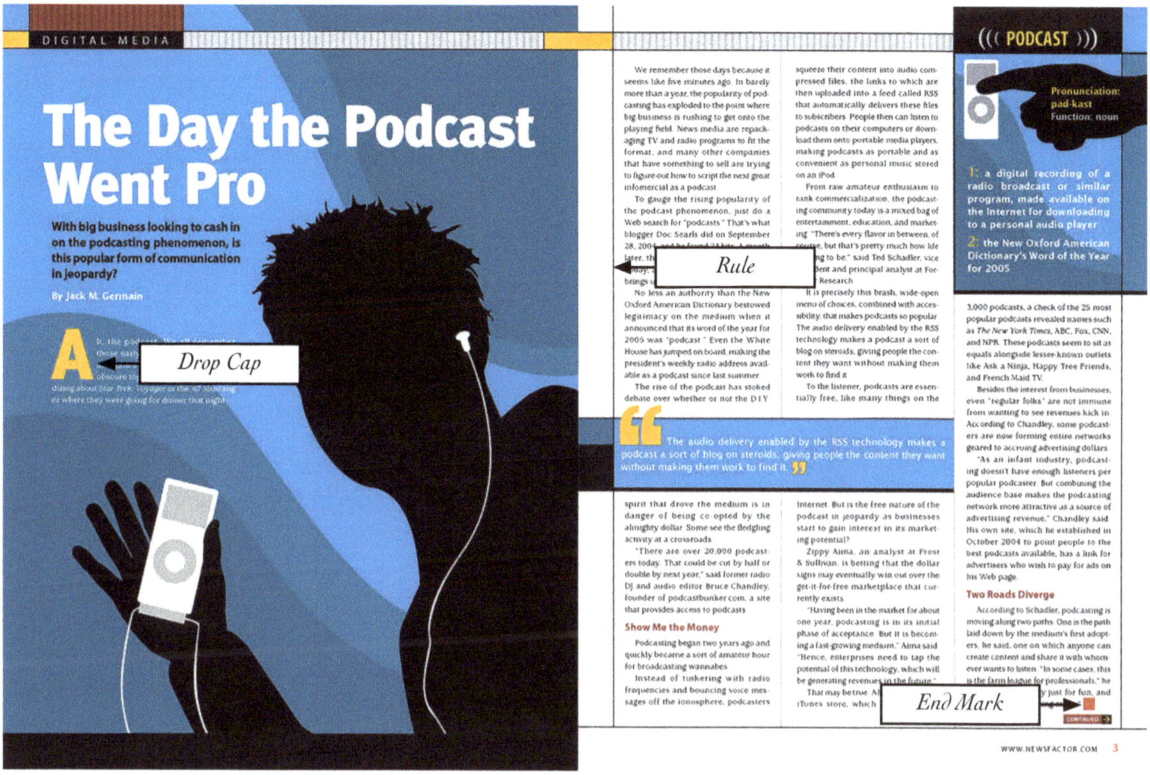

Graphical Elements

Rules are lines that help separate and organize content. As we saw earlier, they also provide a visual eye-movement path.

End marks are a graphical image that says, "this is the end of the story."

Other image enhancements may also include effects like drop shadows, tints, gradients, and special effects like mezzotint.

Special Production Techniques

There are a number of production techniques that can enhance a layout and the finished product. Knowing what they are and what their production requirements are provides a designer options.

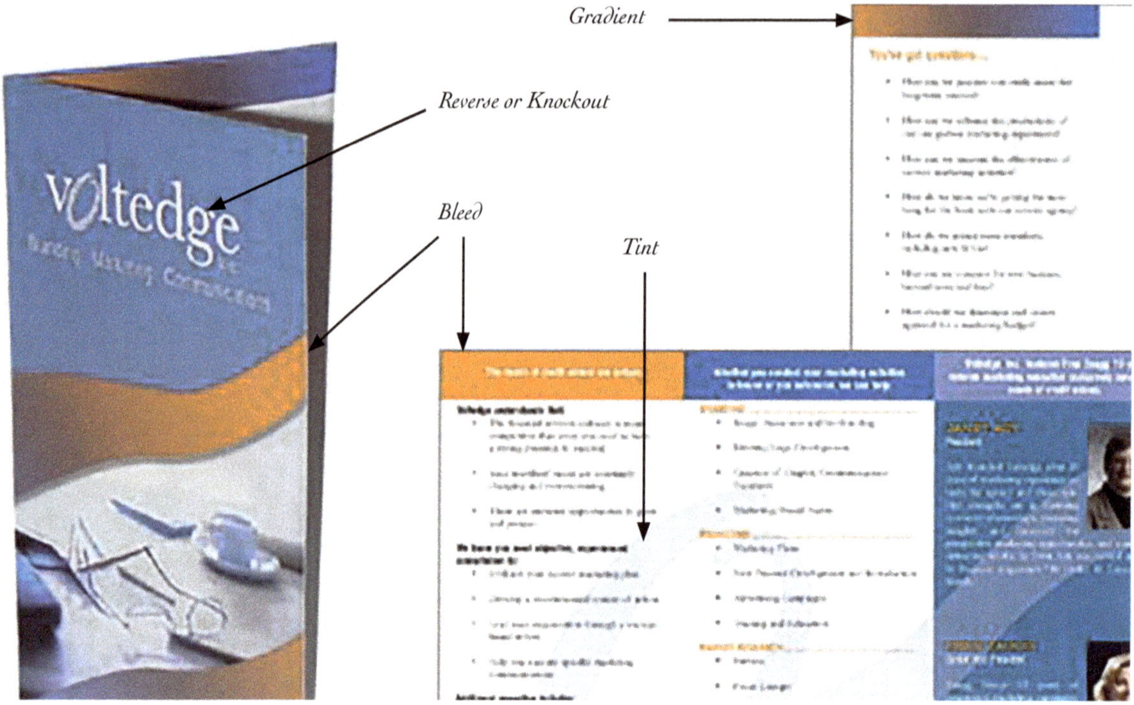

This brochure contains several techniques. Images bleed off on all four sides, and a gradient is used along with a tinted version of the company logo.

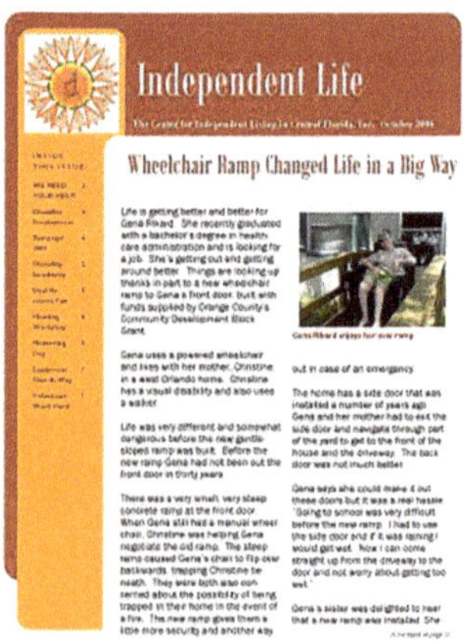

The name of the newsletter is simply the paper showing through.

A **bleed** is when an image or area of ink runs beyond the perimeter of at least one side of a printed sheet. Creating a bleed for a layout requires that the printed item be printed on a larger sheet of paper that will be trimmed down to size. This is required because otherwise the ink would build up on the edges of the paper causing difficulties in printing. The consequences are that the cost of paper for the oversized sheet will be more and an additional finishing cost for the trim. When creating layouts using software, such a design in Adobe InDesign or other desktop publishing software, one has an option to add a bleed line to aid in positioning the elements that bleed.

Reverse or knock out is when a area of text or graphic isn't printed with ink which allows the paper to show as the image. No need to print white, which would require an opaque lithographic ink that may not be very effective.

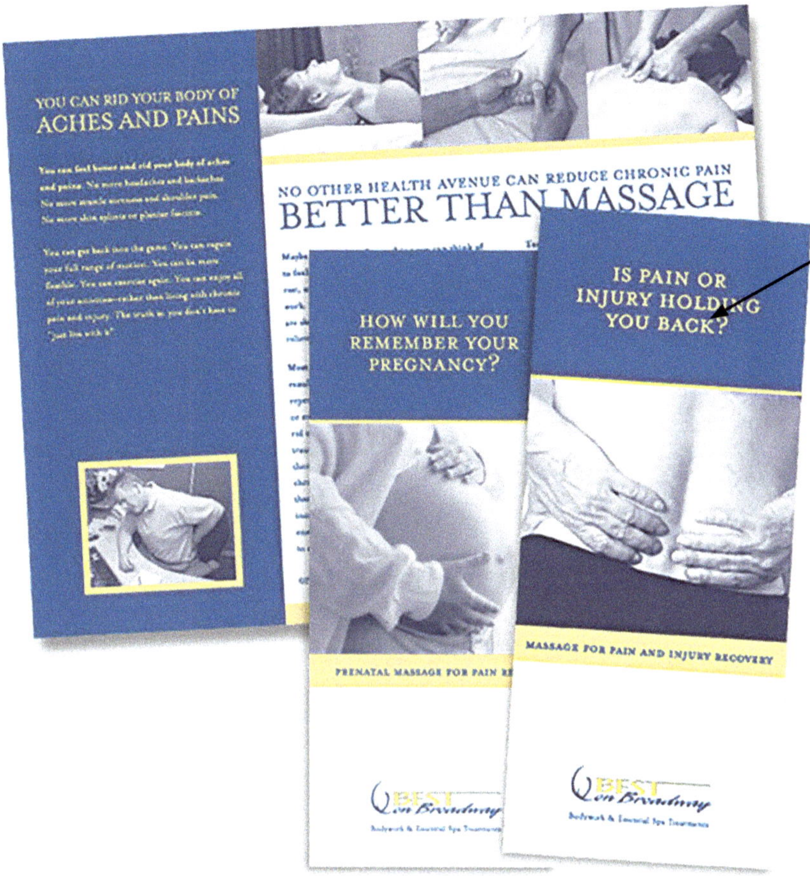

This brochure is printed in yellow and blue. The type on the solid areas of blue has trapping applied to print yellow type and not green.

Similar to reverse or knockout, is a technique known as **trapping**. In essence since lithographic inks are transparent they can't be printed one on top of another without them creating a third color. As example a blue area that has yellow type would instead result in green type. To print the yellow type, first the area is a knockout of the blue. Then the yellow is printed.

Since the registration, or alignment of the two colors is critical, trapping is used. In the process, the blue is "chocked," made more constricted, and the yellow is "spread," made more expanded so the colors overlap slightly. Page layout software have the ability to generate files that have trapping described.

Logo Design

Creating a logo design is one of the most difficult tasks for a graphic designer. An effective logo embodies the essence of a business, organization, or other entity with often very few visual elements. In fact the most recognizable logos like MacDonald's, Nike, and Apple have only one or two shapes. They are, however, instantly identified and associated with the company they represent. Even altered with parts missing, we still can recognize many logos.

This strong identifying association of a logo is called **branding,** which may be part of an overall branding scheme. This certainly is the ultimate goal of a designer when designing a logo.

To maintain and further develop branding of a logo to its company, product, or service, organizations frequently modify or change their logos to be more contemporary, not only in the latest design styles, but connect with their clients because they've changed what they do or provide.

Familiar to all of us, Facebook changed, though only slightly, the typeface used for their logotype (logo that is entirely type) for the first time since they launched in 2004.

Another recent logo change, this in 2011, was done by Starbucks. Simplified and more stylized than previous logos, the name Starbucks Coffee was even eliminated. The reason for the type removal was Starbucks' move into other areas of marketing and sale of other products, not just coffee.

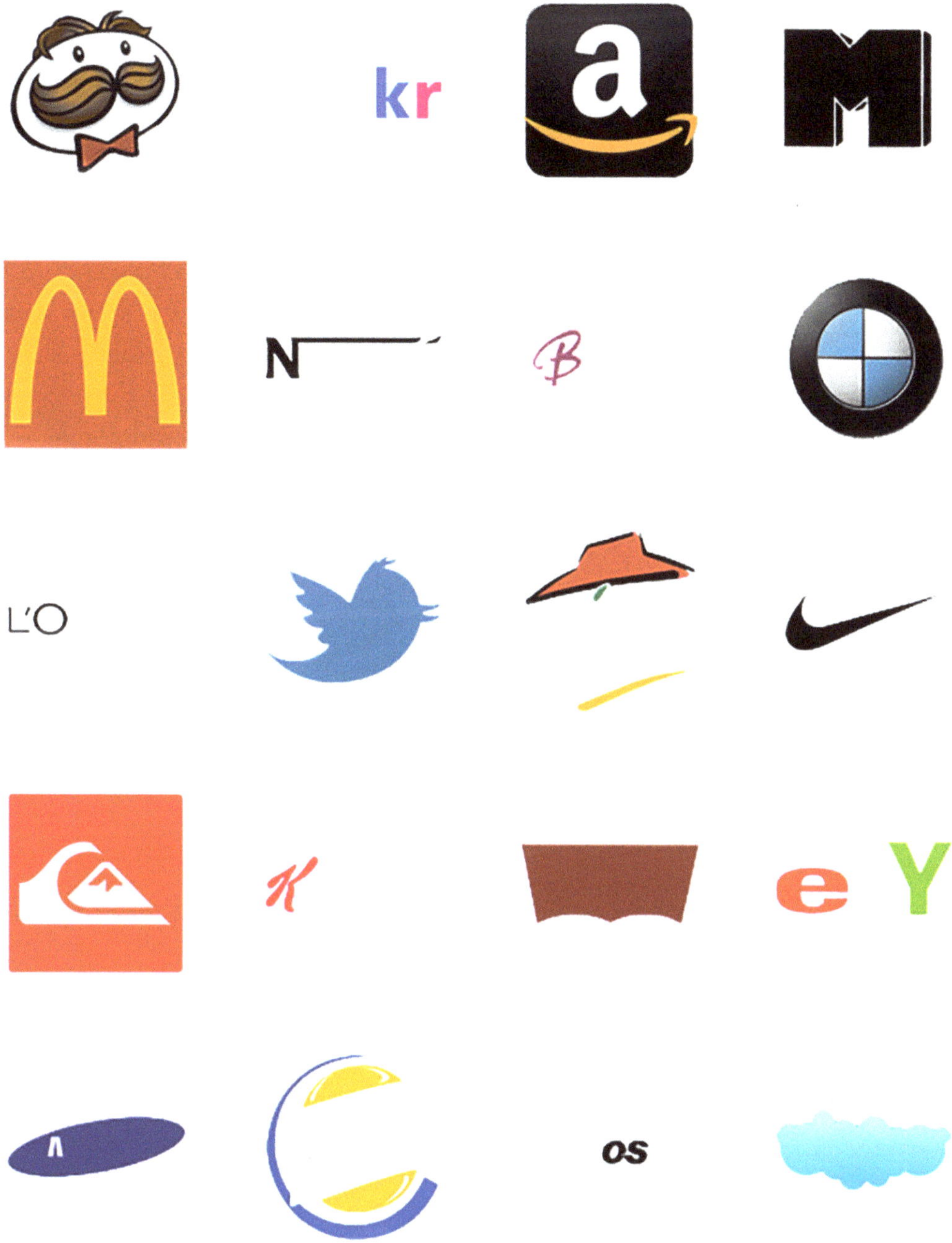

How many of these logos do you recognize even with parts missing and changes?
—Logos Quiz by Atico Mobile S. I.

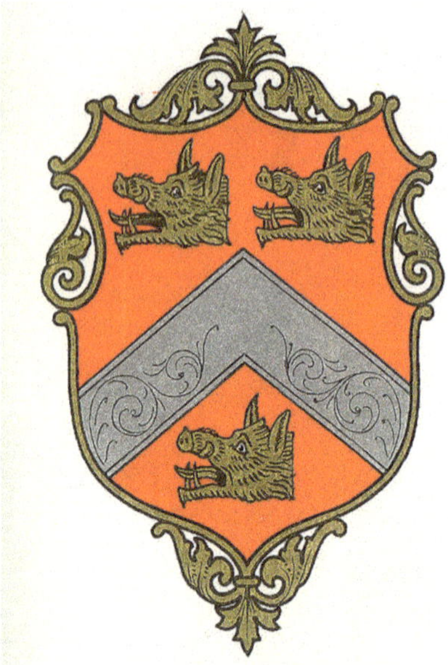

A coat of arms for the Bradley family.

Historical Perspective

Logos have their predecessors, going back as far as the use of brands to identify property whether animal or even human.

Soon to follow would be stamps (relief printing?) pressed on the bottom of pottery to indicate the maker of the bowl, vase, or other item. Certainly with the development of religions, would be symbols that are identified with them. Iconic in nature, these powerful "logos" are constructed of shapes and images that strongly represent the beliefs of their followers.

From the 12th century onwards through medieval times, heraldic designs, known as coat of arms, were used to identify the status and property of the nobility in Europe. A coat of arms consists of several parts: the shield, the mantling, the helm, the wreath, charges, and the crest (note that not all arms have crests). A "blazon of arms" is a simple system of code words to denote colors, placement, and styling of a coat of arms.

Another historical "logo" is a maker's mark that is typically used with hallmarks on precious metals. The stamped marks indicate various information.

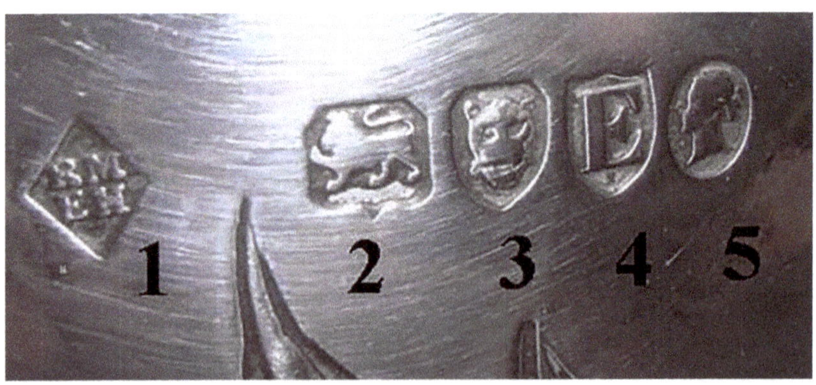

Stamps on this silver punchbowl indicate: 1- Maker's Mark- the maker, 2. Lion Passant- Sterling Silver, 3. Assay Office, 4. Date, and 5. Monarch's Head- duty paid. —courtesy of Wheathills

1971 **1987** **1992** **2011–Present**

The evolution of Starbucks® logo. Note how it has been simplified and that the word coffee has been removed as they moved into selling additional products in addition to coffee.

With the beginning of the 20th century, logos became a very important part of doing business. The commercial world was growing exponentially and with the introduction of color printing, the advertising industry pushed logos to the extent that they become essential for companies.

The Importance of Shapes

Shapes have an endless variety of characteristics, each communicating different messages to your audience and are important building blocks in the visual grammar of a designer.

The affect of shapes can be obvious or subtle and certainly add to or detract from the communication of a design, strengthening or weakening the unity of it. There are three basic types of shapes: Geometric, Nature/organic, and Abstract.

The new Facebook® logo, bottom, opts for a slimmer, more modern font than the original. It changes the double-story "a" from the original 2005 logo and adds a tail to the lowercase "b."

Geometric

Geometric shapes are what most people think of as shapes. Circles, squares, triangles, diamond— are made up of regular patterns that are easily recognizable. This regularity suggests organization and efficiency. They are symmetrical and that has regularity and a structured look and feel suggests order, organization, and efficiency.

Circles

Circles have no beginning or end. They represent the eternal whole and in every culture there are typically forms representing the sun, the earth, the moon, and other celestial objects. Circles are also found in familiar objects such as wheels, balls, and fruit. They suggested well-roundedness and completeness.

Squares and Rectangles

Squares and rectangles are stable. They're familiar and trusted shapes that suggest honesty, conformity, peacefulness, solidity, security, and equality. They represent order, mathematics, rationality, and formality— but can be boring.

Triangles

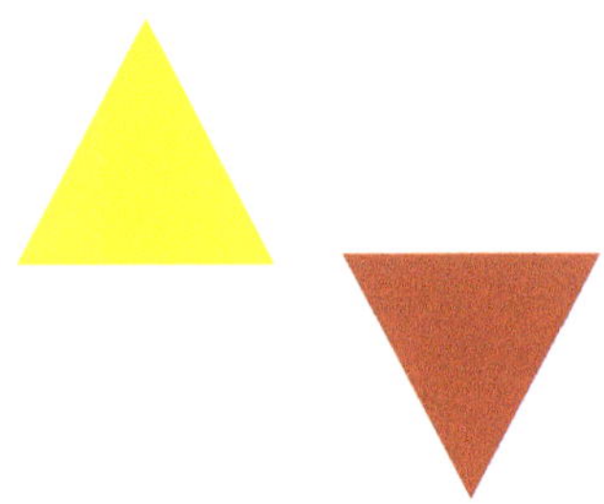

Triangles can be stable when sitting on their base or unstable when not. They have energy and power and are stable or unstable dynamically that suggest either conflict or steady strength. They are symmetrically balanced and can be a symbol for law, science, and religion. We see the shape in pyramids, arrows, and pennants.

Spirals

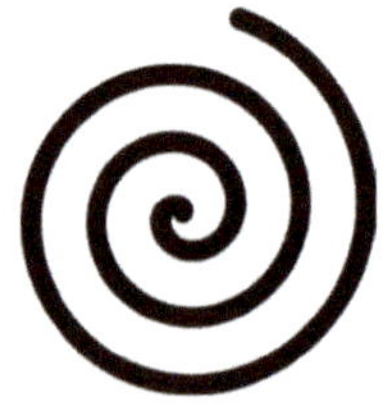

Spirals are expressions of creativity. They are a natural growth pattern for many organisms. Spirals convey ideas of fertility, birth, death, expansion, and transformation. They are cycles of time, life, and the seasons and are a common shape in religious and mystical symbolism.

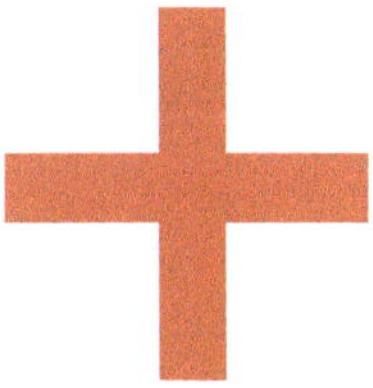

Crosses

Crosses symbolize spirituality and healing, such as Christianity and healthcare. The four points may suggest things such as north, south, east, and west, or the classical elements earth, water, air, and fire as examples.

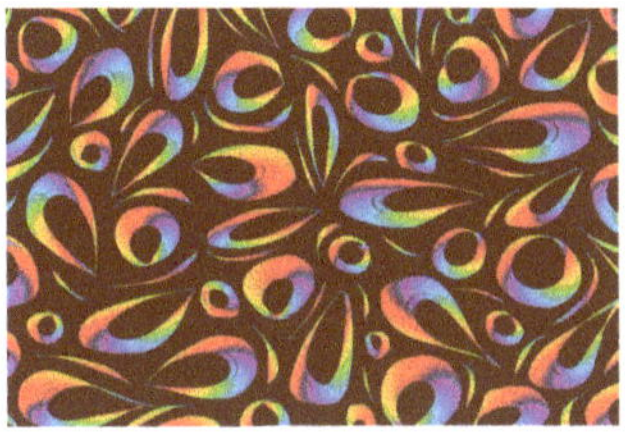

Natural/Organic

These shapes are those that often represent things found in nature and are free flowing, less symmetrical and have an innate harmony and visual interest. They represent such things such as leaves, rocks, and clouds.

Abstract

Abstract shapes have a recognizable form, but are not real. They are simplified and stylized shapes of recognizable forms, often based on organic shapes but lack true definition. A stick figure is an abstract shape depicting a person. Icons are abstract shapes to represent ideas, concepts, or actions.

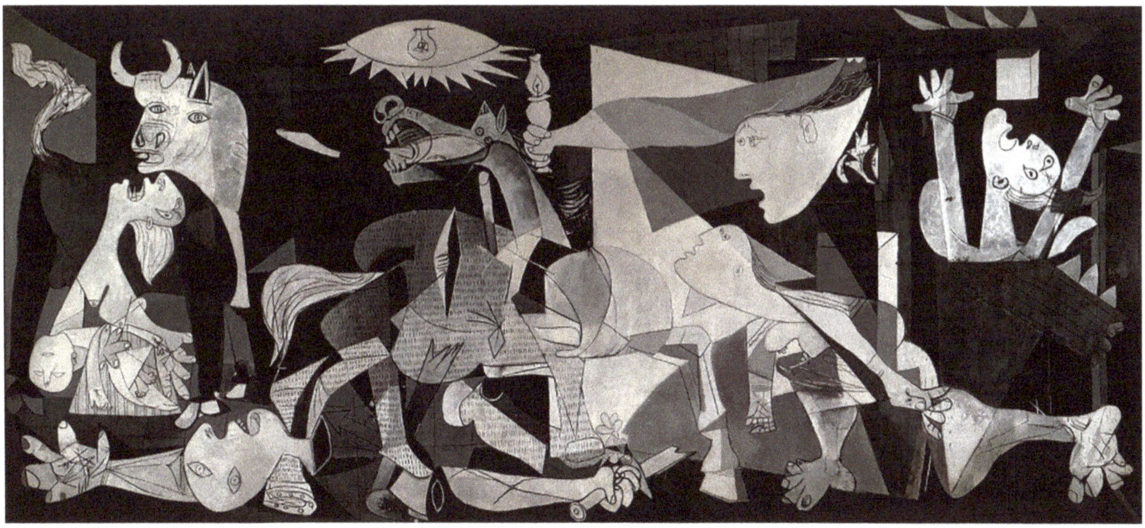

Guernica, 1937, abstract painting by Pablo Picasso.

The Importance of Color

As you learned in *Chapter 3 Color—Psychology of Color*, color has a great influence on our perception of things and how we respond to them. Obviously, combined with the shapes used to create a logo, the two are the essence of its communication along with any type that may be included.

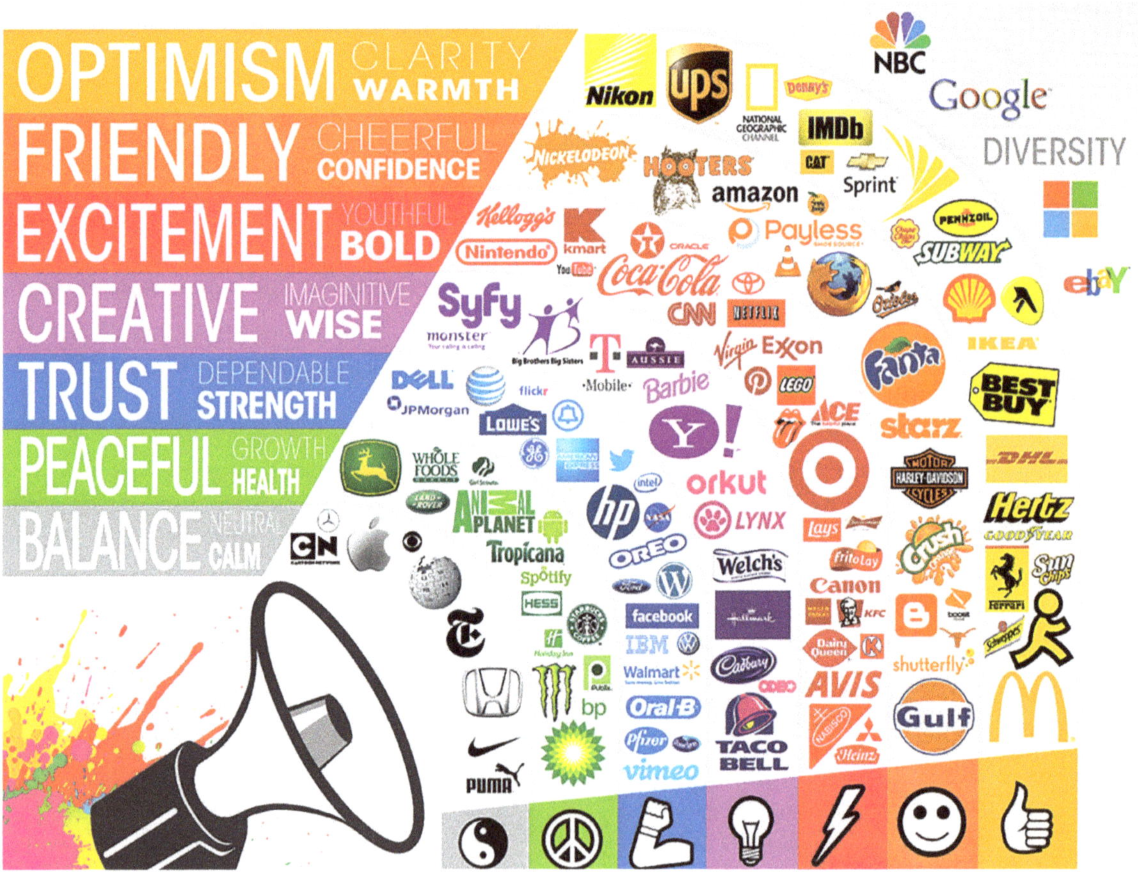

Familiar logos grouped by color with emotions associated with their primary color.

CHAPTER 7

PAPER

"The visionary starts with a clean sheet of paper, and re-imagines the world"
—Malcolm Gladwell

The Importance of Paper

Dr. David Eagleman states, "In humans, touch represents a powerful form of non-verbal communication. Our sense of touch plays a fundamental role in daily life, from learning about objects to communicating with other people."

Neuroscientists, psychologists, and other researchers have looked at how people interact with paper, comparing it to their interactions with other media, in more than one hundred published studies since the early '90s. These studies dominantly show that people read best on paper for three reasons: it makes content more intuitively navigable; it facilitates better mental "mapping" of information; and reading on paper drains fewer of our cognitive resources, making retention a little easier— this according to a presentation paper by E. Wästlund in "Computers in Human Behavior."

Research conducted for Condé Nast revealed that "because paper is 'lighter in its assertion of control,' it draws readers in. [Readers] engage with the content—not just ads but all content—more fully."

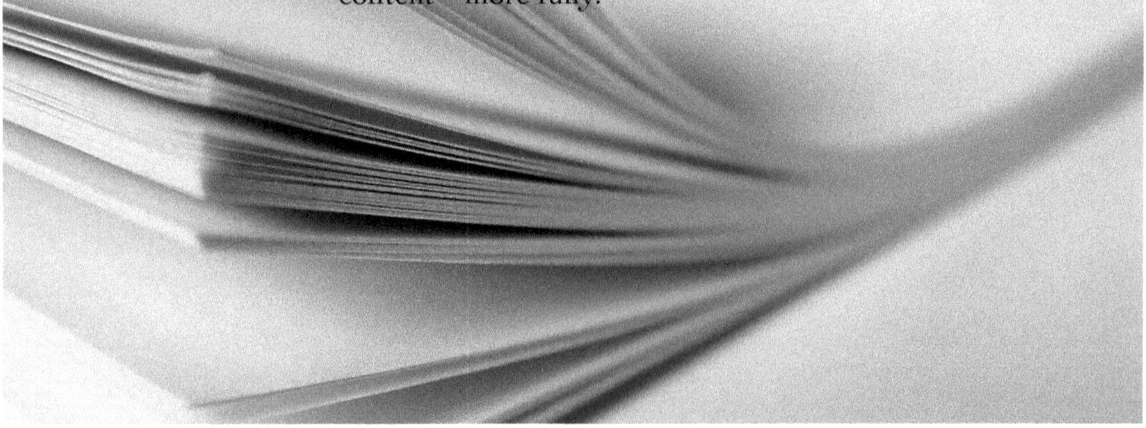

Papermaking

Paper along with ink are the two physical things that make up most printed things aside from specialty printing on fabrics, plastics and other substrates. Following other early forms of "writing materials" such as stone, clay, papyrus, and vellum, its many uses and relative low cost makes it suited to the various printing methods.

A lot of paper is made and consumed. Worldwide, about 400 Million Metric Tons of paper is produced and consumed per year. North Americans alone consume upwards of 500 lbs per person annually according to the Environmental Paper Network. A single tree only makes 16.67 reams of copy paper or 8,333 sheets. How is paper made, and specified?

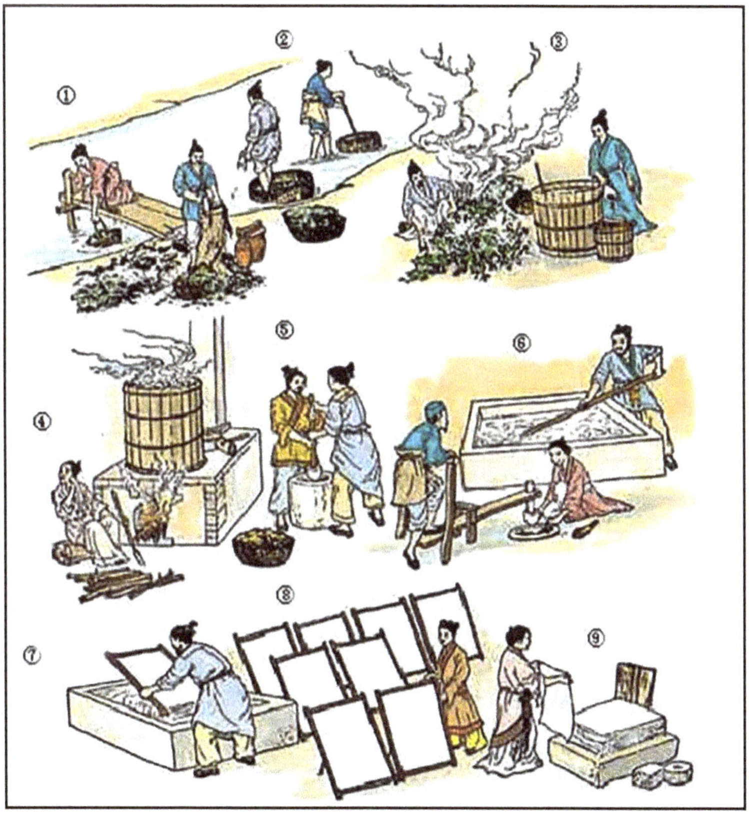

Early Chinese paper appears to have been made from a suspension of hemp waste in water, washed, soaked, and beaten to a pulp with a wooden mallet. A paper mold, probably a sieve of coarsely woven cloth stretched in a four-sided bamboo frame, was used to dip up the fiber slurry from the vat and hold it for drying. Eventually, tree bark, bamboo, and other plant fibers were used in addition to hemp. —Robert C. Williams Museum of Papermaking, Georgia Tech

Commercial papermaking is an extensive process using a great deal of resources including not only wood from natural forests, but from trees grown specifically for papermaking and the associated lumber industry manufacturing waste, such as trimmings and sawdust. It also consumes a great deal of energy in the form of electricity to power the many motors on the huge papermaking equipment and utilizes vast amounts of water.

This diagram depicts the many steps used in the commercial papermaking process. Note that it indicates two sources of raw material (wood) and recycled wastepaper. — Weidenmüller

Most of the water used in the paper production life cycle is used during the manufacturing process, primarily for conveyance of the fibers as they are extracted from logs as wood chips, and through the pulping process. By the same token, most of the energy used in paper-making goes into cooking the

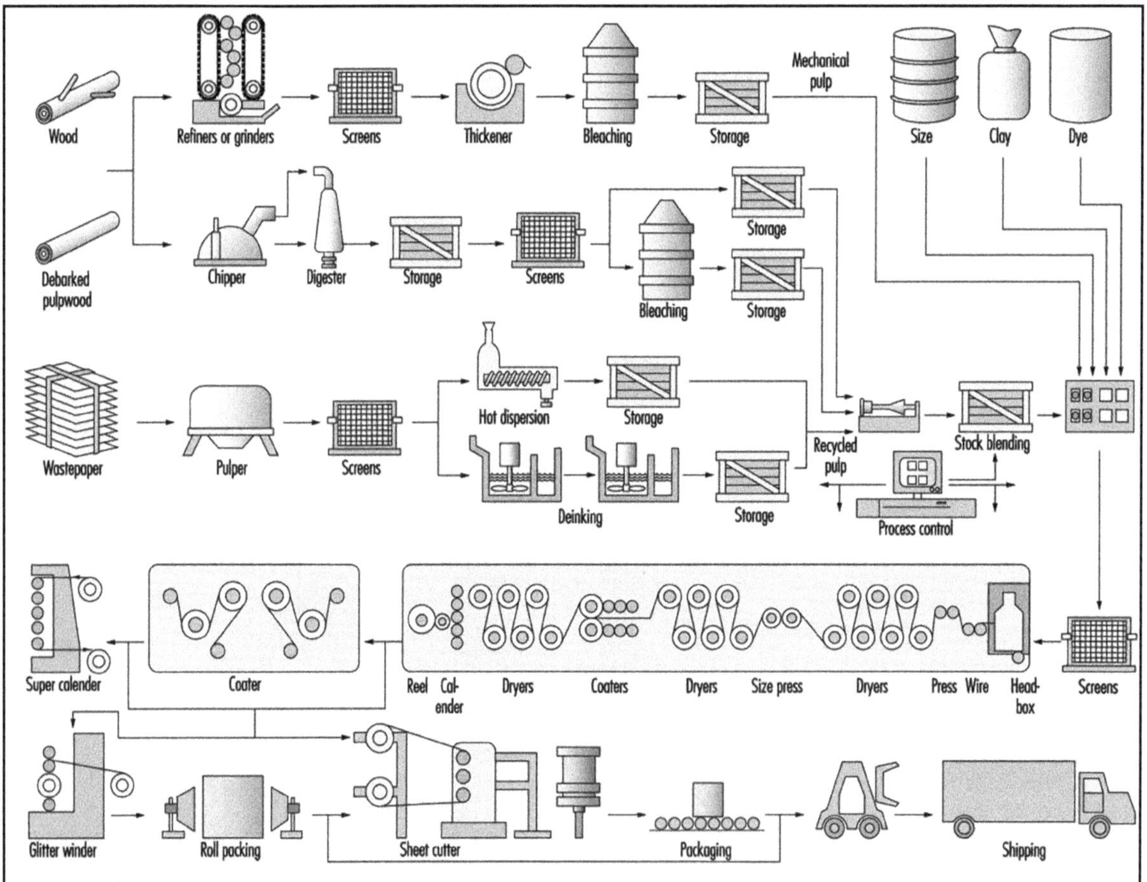

Source: Adapted from Weidenmüller 1984.

pulp, in order to remove the fibers, and drying the wet fibrous mat as it comes out of the paper machine before it is rolled up and ultimately cut into reams or converted into cardboard. According to this Energy Star report, more than $7 billion worth of energy was purchased in 2009 for the manufacture of pulp, paper and paperboard. This is primarily used as boiler fuel for both process-steam and power generation.—"Water and Energy Conservation Opportunities in the Paper Industry,"
—*R.P. Siegel*

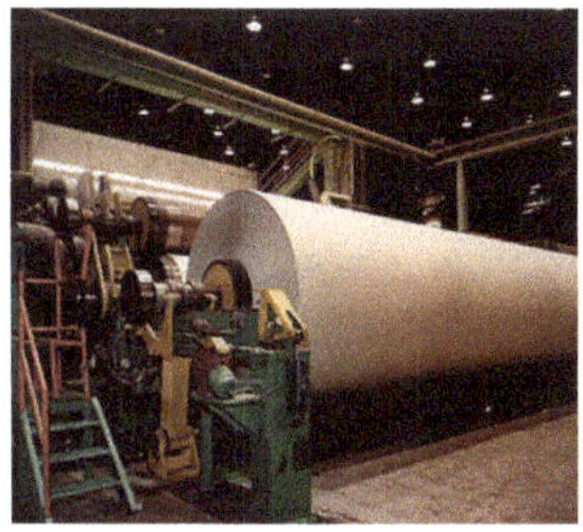

Paper is initially manufactured in huge rolls before being cut down to smaller rolls or sheets.

This consumption, not to mention the use of bleach, dye, and other chemicals are used to create the wide variety of paper produced, not just for printing. At the beginning of the overall process, raw materials enter one of three initial processes where it is pulped. There are three different groups of pulping methods:

Massive equipment and large consumption of resources including not only wood but water, chemicals, and electricity are used in the paper-making process. — Voith Company

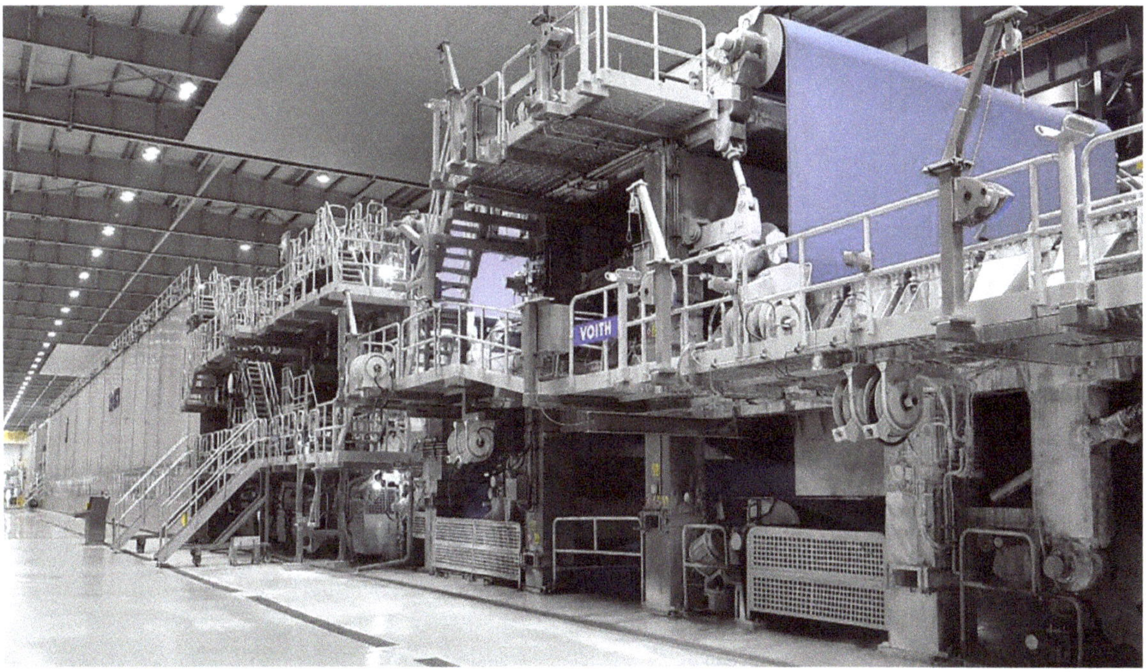

Mechanical Pulping

This method consists of grinding raw material against an abrasive surface to de-fiber the raw material (more generally softwood) without any lignin dissolution. A high yield is obtained by this method, generally more than 95% of the dry-weight of the wood. Some methods use high temperature and pressure to increase the efficiency of the process. Mechanical pulping generates very low polluting effects but is an energy intensive process, as the non-cellulosic wood components are not available (as in chemical pulping) for energy recovery.

Chemical Pulping

This method separates the fibers from the raw material by making soluble all the non-cellulosic components in a cooking liquor at high temperature and pressure. Chemical pulping gives better paper quality, but is potentially the cause of greater environmental pollution. Capital and operating costs are higher than those of mechanical pulping.

Chemi-mechanical Pulping

A wide range of processes combining mechanical and chemical methods are available but they represent a small part of the world-wide paper production. They generally involve a chemical pre-treatment of the raw material, before a mechanical treatment to liberate the fibers. The yields of these processes are situated between those for mechanical and chemical pulping.

This process separates the cellulose fibers from lignin, a natural binding substance in wood and other materials such as cotton. It's the fibers that will make up the bulk of the paper.
—Food and Agriculture Organization of the United Nations

Next bleaching whitens the pulp. Depending upon the paper being made, combinations of pulp may be mixed together and additives, such a sizing, and starch is added which seals the fibers and helps control the degree of ink penetration into the paper. Clay and dyes may be used to provide smooth surfaces and color. Mixed with water the wet mixture, called the **furnish**, now 99% water, is spread on a long wire screen conveyor belt. It is named the **Fourdrinier wire** after the brothers who funded its invention by Nicolas Louis Robert in 1807.

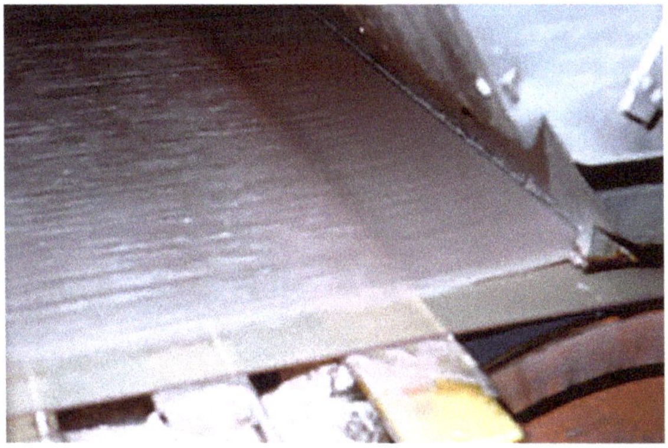

Furnish being applied to the Fourdrinier wire.

This continuously moving wire allows water to drain from the furnish. During this time, the fibers in the pulp align in the direction it is traveling. Then, when there is about 35% water remaining, the furnish may go through an area where it may come into contact with a **dandy roll** which is a wire cylinder with embossed patterns on it. The embossings are transferred to the pulp fibers, compressing and reducing their thickness in that area, thus providing a dark and light image on the finished paper that can be seen easily by holding the paper up to light.

The watermark is a sign of quality. It assures the user that the paper is a fine paper. The watermark generally will identify the manufacturer, the brand name and the amount of cotton fiber, or of a company or organization that is having the paper made.

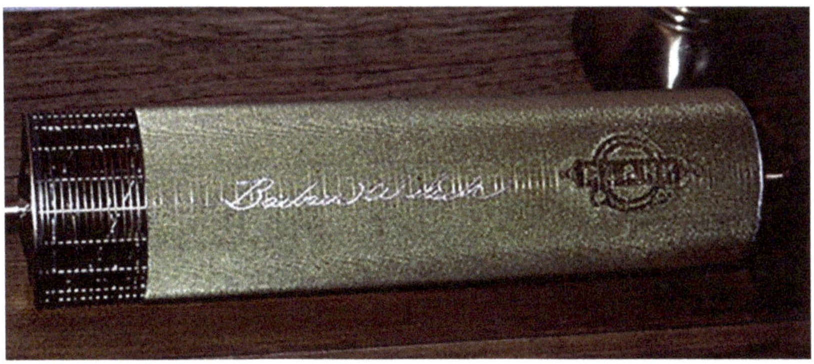

The Dandy Roll is used in the papermaking process to create a watermark.

The "paper" now goes through a series of rollers, called **calender rollers**, and dryers that smoothen, fatten, and dry it. It may get further coatings and then into the super calender at the finishing end. Yes, that is right, calender. The term is derived from Classical Latin *cylindrus*, for cylinder.

The finished roll of paper most likely will be cut into smaller size rolls or sheets depending upon the end use.

Paper is also made from cotton and other plants. Cotton is one of the strongest and most durable natural fibers known to man. Papers manufactured from cotton fiber will last longer and hold up better under repeated handling and various environmental conditions than paper made from wood pulp. Paper made from cotton fiber has an easily identifiable, crisp feel with a snap and rattle to it like no other paper. These quality papers may be as high as 100% cotton, used for legal documents, or as little as 25% for letterhead paper. The United States Department of Printing and Engraving, prints U.S. currency on this kind of paper manufactured under strict guidelines by Crane and Company. The paper is made from a combination of 75% cotton, mostly from the trimmings of jeans from the garment industry, and 25% flax. Watermarks, flecks of color, and a security strip are added during the process.

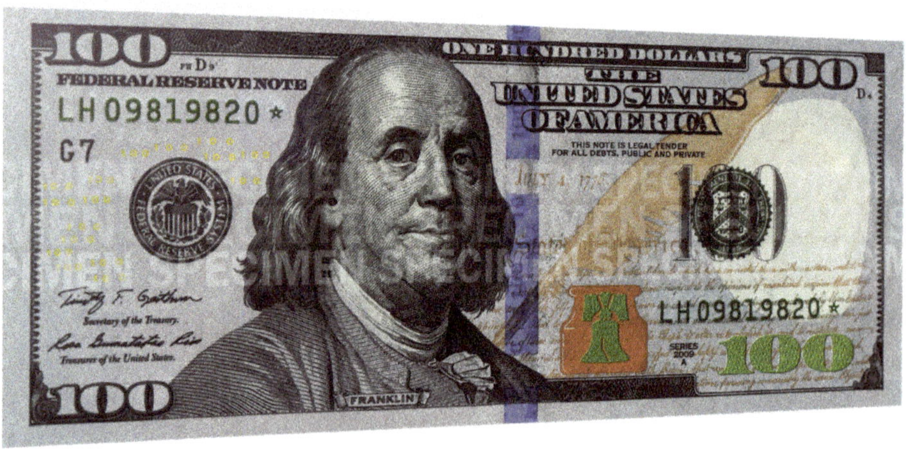

Specifying Paper

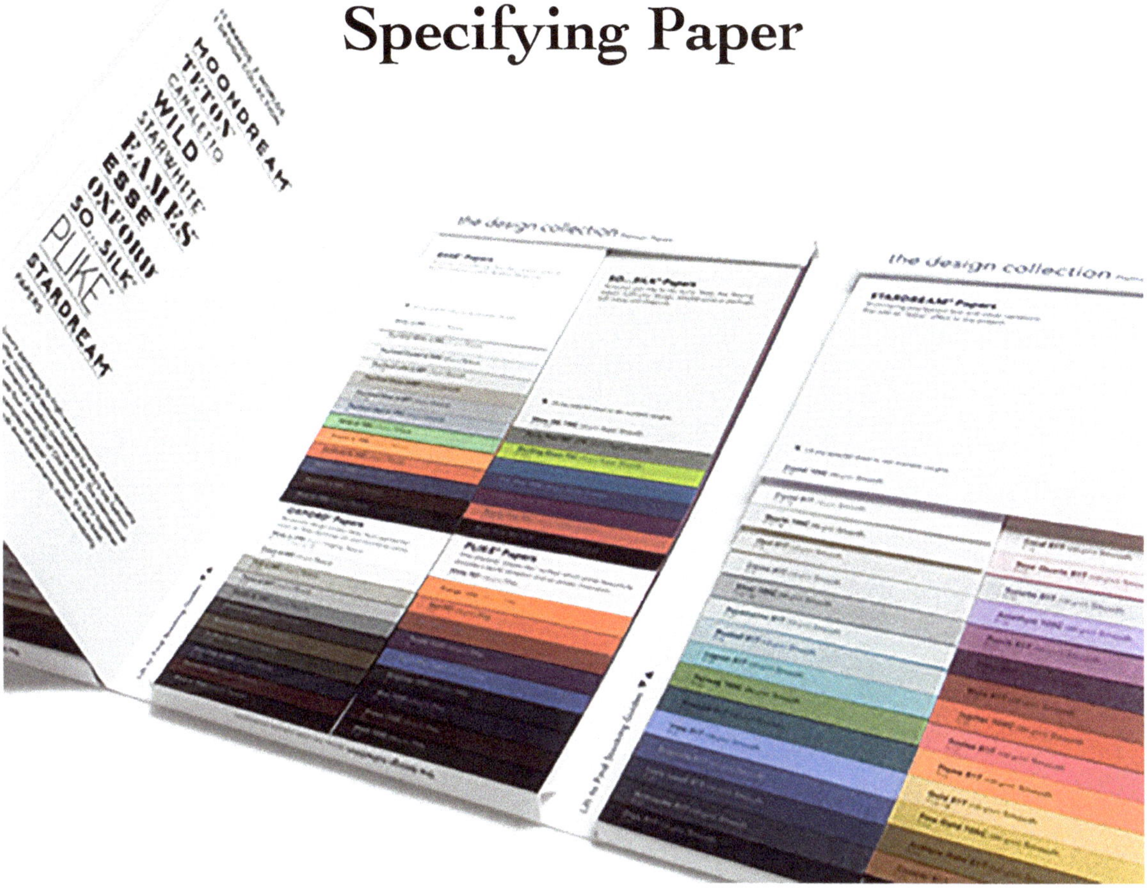

Paper sample book containing Neenah Paper samples. Typically, various colors, grades, and weights of paper are included for a brand of paper, usually of a single finish.

As we saw in the section on papermaking, paper is produced in two basic formats— sheets and rolls. Sheets are cut from the initial roll of paper that exists the papermaking machinery, to common sizes that we'll discuss later. The sheets will be used for various purposes including copying from digital printers to printing from sheet-fed presses. Rolls of paper typically are used for the printing of publications like newspapers and magazines on web presses.

A web press sounds like it has something to do with the Internet, but this is not the case. A web press is an offset printing press that is fed from huge rolls of paper. As the paper unwinds from the roll, it forms a continuous "web" through the press. This web of paper is held taut by a series of rollers, which move the paper through the press. Web presses are also an economical choice for printing books used by some publishers.

Grades

Paper is produced in a wide variety of sizes, colors, finishes, thicknesses and so on. It can however, be classified into a number of categories and distinguished from each other on the basis of their content, appearance, manufacturing history, and/or their end use. Common categories of paper include: Bond or writing (sometimes referred to as script), Book, Cover, Carbonless, Newsprint, and Recycled.

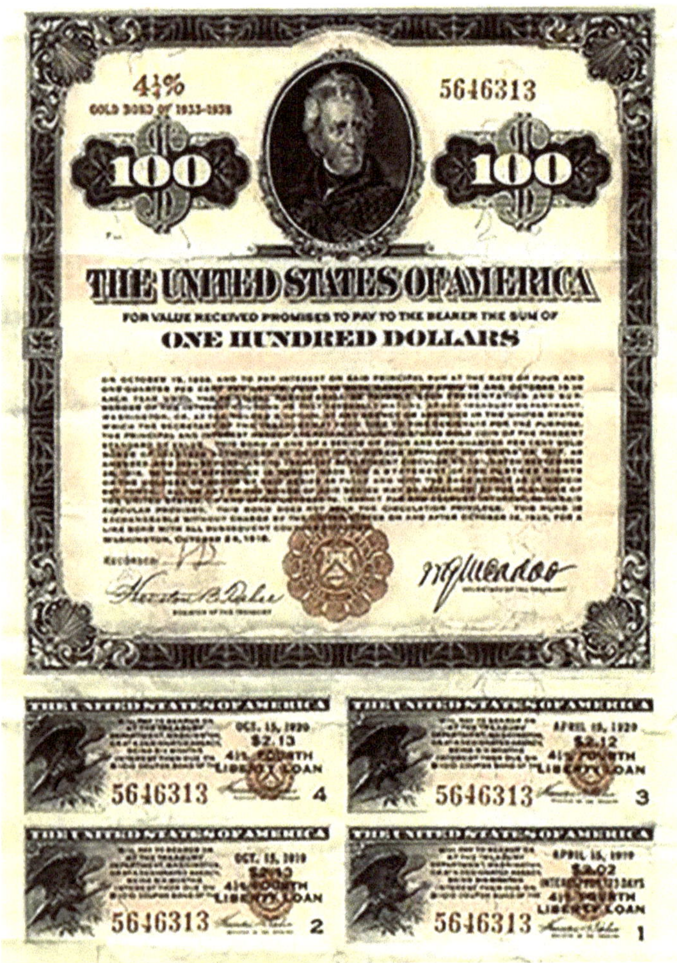

Liberty bonds were first utilized during the first World War to support the allied cause in World War I. Subscribing to the bonds became a symbol of patriotic duty in the United States and introduced the idea of financial securities to many citizens for the first time.

Bond

The term "bond" has no actual meaning in the manufacturing process. The term comes from WW I when war bonds were printed on cotton fiber papers that were extensively watermarked. The extensive watermark was used to protect buyers from bonds sold by counterfeiters (the first safety paper). Following the war, people who wanted a good quality paper would ask for paper like that "bond" paper. Thus, the term has become associated with high quality and generally means the consumer wants to buy a fine paper product. — *Southworth Paper*

Often bond refers to paper that may not have cotton fiber as well. Bond typically is produced in sizes 8 ½" X 11" for stationary and letterheads, 8 ½" X 14" legal, and larger sheets of 17" X 22."

Book

This category of paper is primarily manufactured for the printing of pages of a book, hence its name. Also called Offset paper, the paper is designed specifically for use on offset printing presses. It has good opacity, rapid ink absorption, and permanence. It can be coated or uncoated (discussed later). Offset paper is used for a wide variety of products, such as books, form letters, magazines, manuals, advertising, and common commercial printing.

The paper typically is made from various materials including chemical wood pulp, mechanical wood pulp, and recycled paper. A sub category of book is **text**, an expensive grade that has excellent smoothness to it, making it ideal for halftone reproduction.

Cover

Cover paper is a thick or heavy paper, typically used for the covers of books, catalogs, brochures, manuals, and menus. Sometimes, two layers of cover paper are bonded together to produce double thickness, in which each side may be of a different color paper. This is referred to as duplex cover.

Carbonless

Carbonless paper was first produced in 1954 though a patent was given for the process in 1806! The paper is coated on one side with a layer of a loosely bound polymer-based and dry ink, that when placed between an original document and another sheet of paper, writing on the top sheet "copies" or transfers to the bottom sheet.

Sometimes called NCR paper, which identifies with the company that first produced it, National Cash Register, a carbonless paper used today, has a coating of dye on one side, that when written on transfers to the carbonless paper sheet below it. The paper comes in sets that are of different colors, and coatings. The top sheet is white and has the dye coating on the bottom, the next sheet is yellow and has a clay receptive coating on the top and if there is a third or more sheets, a dye coating on the bottom. The following sheet colors are pink and goldenrod if that many sheets are required for the set.

To produce sets of carbonless or NRC printing, (such as white, yellow, and pink) a stack of printed sheets are "glued" at one edge with a special padding compound (glue) that sticks only to the dye coated side of the paper. Since the top of the top sheet and the bottom of the bottom sheet aren't coated, when fanned apart after dried, they form sets.

Newsprint

Newsprint is a low-cost, non-archival paper produced in rolls primary used to print newspapers. Newsprint papers are produced from 20 to 100% Recycled fiber. A newspaper roll's width is called its web width and is defined by how many front pages it can print. A full roll prints four front pages with four back pages behind it. Most newspapers efficiently print newspapers in multiples of eight pages on a full newsprint roll in two sections of four pages each. The two sections are then cut in half.

Due to economic pressures and at one time a few years ago, a shortage of wood pulp to make paper, the longtime standard 54-inch web (13½ inch front page) has been reduced. Common standard sizes in the U.S. now are 44, 46, and 48-inch webs (11, 11.5, and 12 inch newspaper page widths, respectively).

Recycled Paper

The *Environmental Protection Agency* says Americans recycled nondurable goods made of paper, excluding newspapers, had a recycling rate of 43.1 percent, while newspapers had a recycling rate of 64.8 percent in 2018. According to the *American Forest and Paper Association*, nearly 80 percent of America's paper mills are designed to use paper collected in recycling programs, and they depend on paper recycling to supply the raw materials they need to make new paper.

This resource helps to supplement wood and cotton as materials needed for paper production. Paper is a material that can be recycled up to 10 times to produce new paper.

The bulk of recycled paper is used for packaging. *TechNavio's* analysts forecast the Global Recycled Paper Packaging market to grow at a compound annual growth rate of 8.3 percent over the period 2021-2025.

Paper Dimensions

Paper is produced in a number of standard sizes both as the cut size and basis size following a standard that includes letter, legal, ledger, etc. In Europe and elsewhere, the International Paper size standard, ISO 216 is used.

Cut Sizes

These are common sizes of paper that have been cut and packaged ready for use directly, such as printing a letterhead on letter-size paper, 8 1/2" X 11."

Basis Size

Basis size refers to a standard size for a grade of paper. That size was established historically based upon the paper grades common product use. Bond has a basis size of 17" X 22", which allows for printing of four 8 1/2" X 11" documents.

GRADE	BASIS SIZE	COMMON BASIS WEIGHT (LBS.)
Bond	17" X 22"	20 24 28
Cover	20" X 26"	65 80 100
Book	25" X 38"	50 60 70 80
Index	25 ½" X 30 ½"	90 110 140

Basis Weight

The basis weight of paper is calculated by weighing a ream, or 500 sheets of paper at its basis size. As example, a ream of bond at 17" X 22" would weigh one of the numbers in the above chart. Considering that a standard bond paper used for letterheads, as an example is 8 1/2" X 11," and has a basis weight of 20 lbs. in which a ream would physically weight 5 pounds. That's right, since one can cut four sheets from the basis size sheet—it's one quarter of the 20 pounds.

Paper Descriptions

Grain

The grain of the paper is the direction in which most of the fibers that make up the paper are aligned. This occurs during the papermaking process which is the direction that the Fourdrinier wire moves. This is important when choosing or using paper. The grain direction provides strength in that direction and weakness in the opposite direction. As example, the grain of the paper in a newspaper runs vertically top to bottom. When you hold the paper up to read it, it remains fairly upright. If the grain ran side to side then it would fold over easily and be difficult to read the morning news. Consider a menu for a restaurant. Wouldn't want it in your appetizer would you?

Grain is specified as long or short, equating to the dimension of the paper. On package labels it is indicated as such, or has a line under that dimension. (See Image, next page)

Color

Color certainly varies from paper manufacturer to manufacturer. You will even find sight variations of white such as, solar white, bright white, and natural white.

Finish

The finish is the texture of the paper that is created when it is made. The finish provides that subtle tactile quality of paper that adds another dimension to the overall communication of the product. Remember the Principle of Unity in design? It doesn't just apply to the visual realm. Below are some common finishes described by Southworth Neenah Paper.

Smooth A paper with a smooth finish is one that has no specially manufactured texture. Other terms for paper with a smooth finish include "regular" and "wove." Oftentimes, paper with a smooth finish does not carry a finish designation as was indicated in the package label sample on the next page.

Laid This is a textured finish. Papers made with a laid finish are made to emulate paper as it looked when it was first invented. Laid finish consists of a horizontal textured pattern

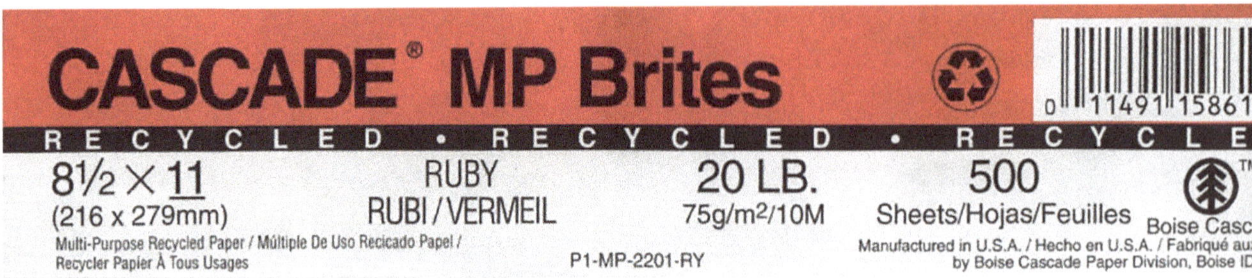

A paper package label indicating various characteristics. Can you find the manufacturer's name, brand name, dimensions, grain, color, basis weight, number of sheets, and grade of this paper? The finish of this paper is not indicated so it's assumed to be smooth.

and a vertical pattern known as "chain lines". The texture is created by using a dandy roll to impress the pattern into the paper along with the watermark at the wet end of the manufacturing process.

Linen

Linen is a textured finish applied to paper by an embossing process done after the paper has been manufactured that has the look and feel of linen fabric. Generally, a linen finish is a very subtle texture that performs well in many laser and **inkjet** printers.

Other

Other less common finishes include Vellum, Parchment, Eggshell, Cockle, and Antique.

Characteristics

Flatness

Flat paper feeds better through a press or digital printer better than one that has curl to it. All paper encountered in normal situations contains some moisture since it is composed of cellulose fibers. This normal moisture content will generally range between 2% and 10% depending on the type of paper, its past moisture history and the atmospheric conditions to which it is exposed. Consider also, that when a paper is printed using the lithographic method it comes in contact with a light film of moisture transferred from the plate to the blanket and there to the paper.

Paper tends to have a slight curl to it because of the nature of the manufacturing process and the residual moisture. When printing both sides of a sheet, the curled side of the paper is placed face down whereby the initial image (and any moisture) is printed on the top side which will cause the paper then to curl up, basically fattening it during the second press run.

Strength

The tensile strength of paper is determined by how well the inner fibers are bonded together, preventing the paper from easily tearing or breaking. Print strength is determined by how well the surface of the paper is bonded together preventing bits of fiber from being lifted off the paper during printing. The bits of fiber then can cause printing quality issues called "hickeys" which are specks that appear on the printed image.

Brightness

Brightness refers to how well light reflects off its surface affecting the contrast of the printed image. Since lithographic inks are transparent, the light is reflected from the paper back through the ink and we see the color. The brighter the paper the stronger the colors.

Opacity

Opacity is the ability of light to pass through a sheet of paper. Poor opacity produces an unwanted result called show-through, when the backside of a sheet, such as an image or text, can be seen through the paper.

Other Characteristics

Rag

The term "rag" is often used interchangeably with "cotton fiber content" and harkens to a period of time when paper was actually made using cotton rags. The more the cotton fiber content, the finer the quality of the paper.

Sulfite

Wood pulp is processed into sulfite, which is then used to manufacture various grades of paper. It is more economical than cotton fiber however, it is also less durable and more acidic than cotton fiber. There are different grades of sulfite, depending upon how much processing has gone into making the pulp. Better quality of sulfite result in higher quality paper.

Acid Content

Paper which has no acid or residual acid-producing chemicals is called "acid free". Papers that are "acid free" will resist yellowing and disintegration longer than sheets that are not acid free. Greater content of wood pulp in the paper will cause high acidity.

CHAPTER 8

Finishing and Binding

"A big leather-bound volume makes an ideal razor strap. A thin book is useful to stick under a table with a broken caster to steady it. A large, flat atlas can be used to cover a window with a broken pane. And a thick, old-fashioned heavy book with a clasp is the finest thing in the world to throw at a noisy cat."
– *Mark Twain*

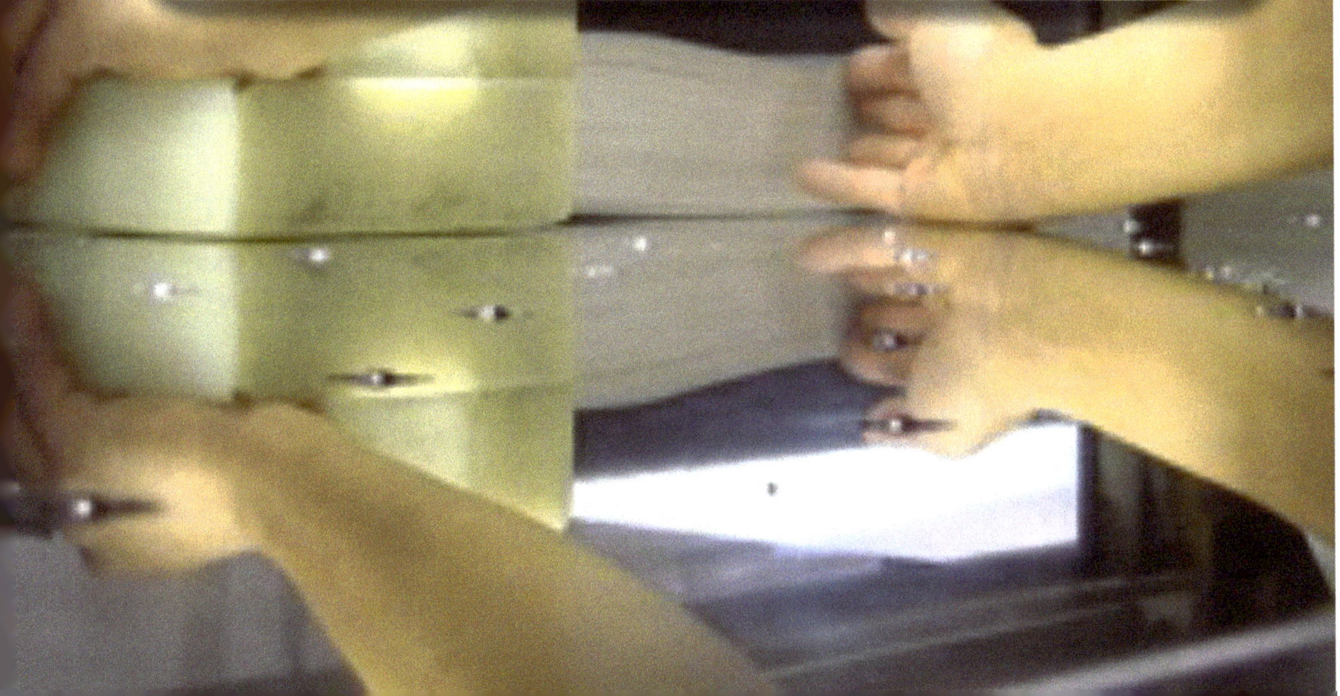

Finishing

An oft overlooked area when designing for print is what can or must be done to a product after it has been printed. This is the post-production area of finishing and binding. The first step often after printing is **trimming** where the printed piece is cut down to its finished size. That might be because of a bleed that required larger sized paper to accommodate it or when several of the same small products like business cards have several printed on each sheet. This is not to be confused with **cutting**, which is cutting large sheets of paper down to size to be used to print.

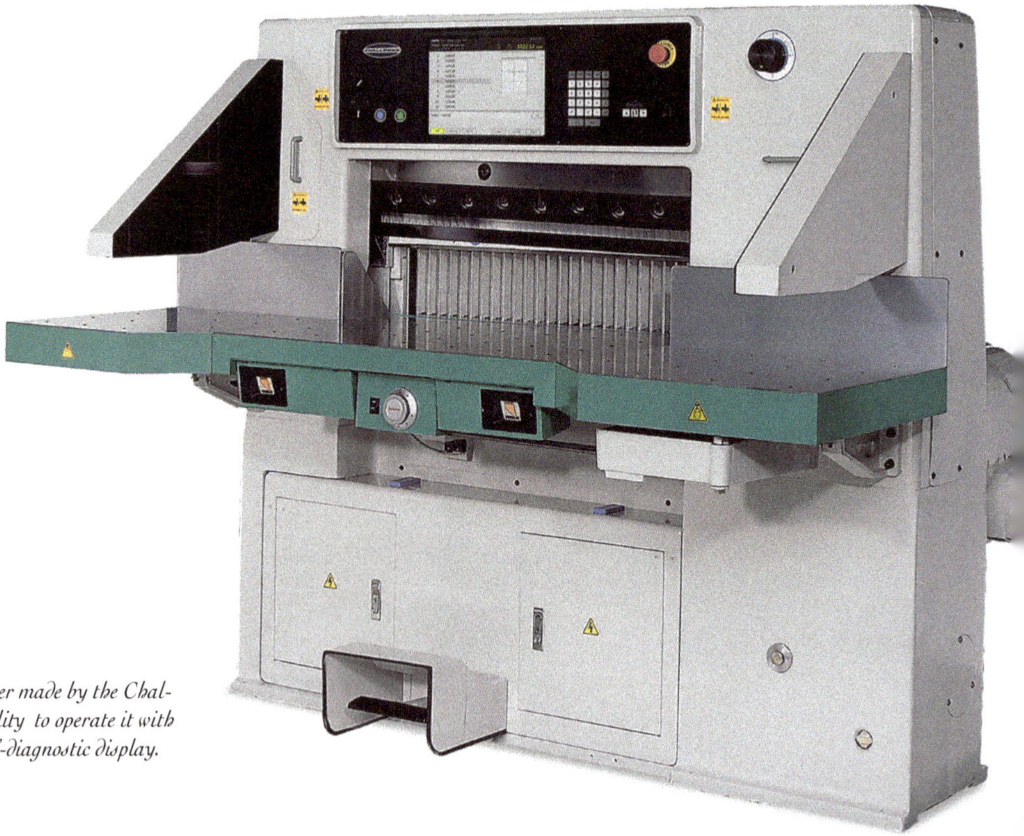

Large commercial paper cutter made by the Challenge Company, features ability to operate it with a touch-screen menu and self-diagnostic display.

Folding

Paper can be folded in a number of ways to produce a finished product like a brochure or as sections of a publication that are assembled to form a book, magazine, or newspaper.

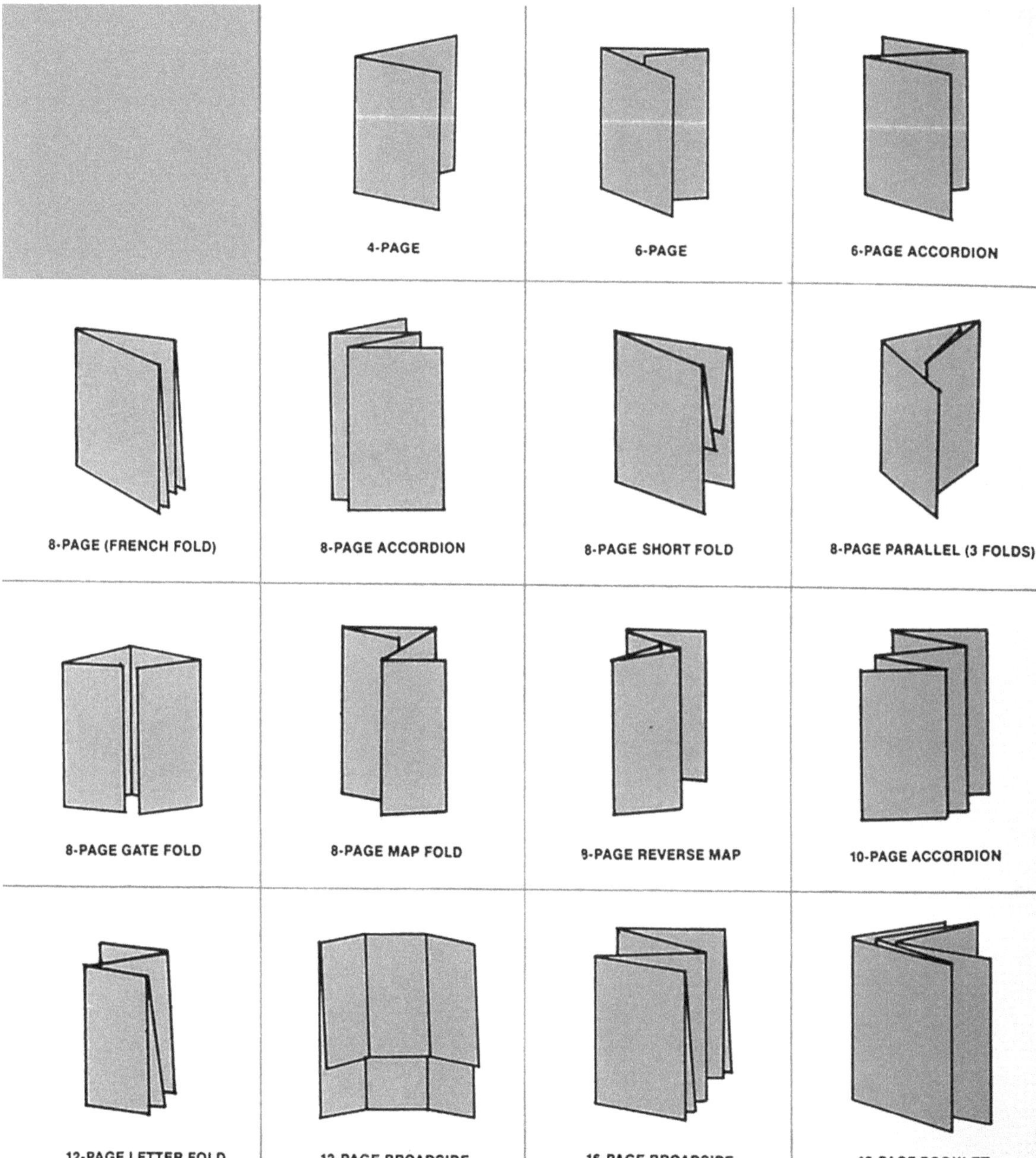

Newspaper presses having a folding section built into the machinery.

Desktop and large floor model folders are used to create inline and right-angle folds. The paper enters the machine and hits a bar, called a buckle, which causes the paper to be pulled into rollers that fold the paper. A number of these folding sections may be arranged and setup on the folding machine to create a variety of folds.

Scoring

Scoring and the following two finishing techniques use a similar process and equipment. A score is a crease put into paper. Typically a specialized rotary creaser on a folding machine is used or more often a letterpress is set up with a creasing rule, basically a flat blunt bar in place of raised type.

Example of a Relief printing die-cutting form. Note the sharpe blades set into a wood base and spongy rubber blocks that help release the paper from the die after the cut has been made.

Scoring the paper compressing the fibers of the paper making it easier to fold. For thick paper this is necessary otherwise the fibers tend to brake as they are folded across the grain. Not a good thing.

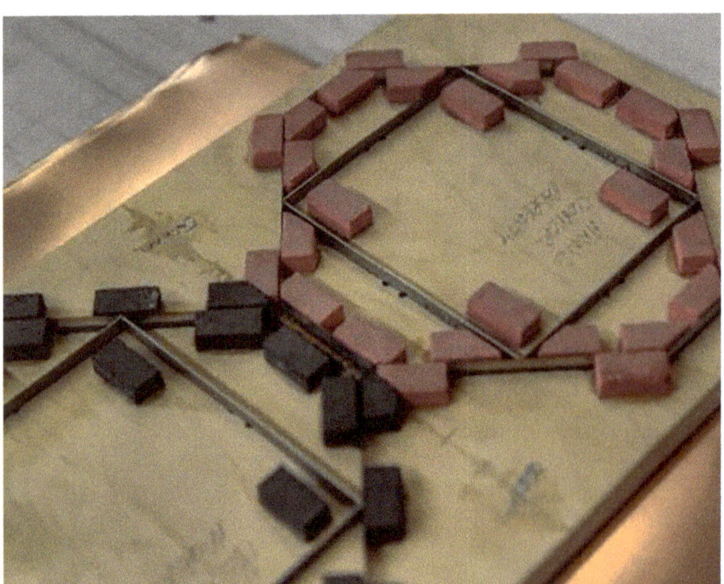

Die-cutting

Also using a letterpress, a die cut which is a sharp metal rule set into a block of wood with sponges surrounding it, cut the paper into a shape much like a cookie cutter. The sponge helps separate the cut portion from the die cut rule. Tags, cards, labels, and boxes are some uses for die-cutting.

Perforation

In essence, this is similar to die-cutting except the sharp edge is serrated and the perforation is straight and not a shape.

Often used for tickets, reply cards, and workbooks, the process can be done with a letterpress or a special attachment placed on a folder.

Embossing

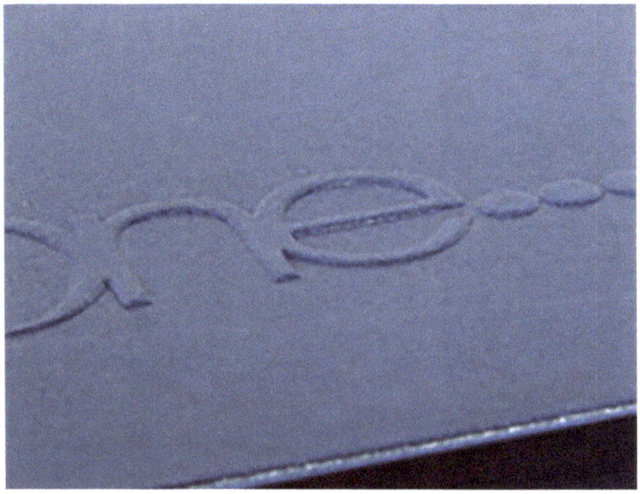

Embossing is the process that creates a raised image on a substrate by pressing it between two dies. One die is in relief (raised), while the other is recessed. When the two are brought together with the stock between them, the clamping force creates a raised image on the paper. Sometimes the paper is printed first and then embossed, **registered embossing**. Other times only the paper is embossed which is called **blind embossing.**

Foil Stamping

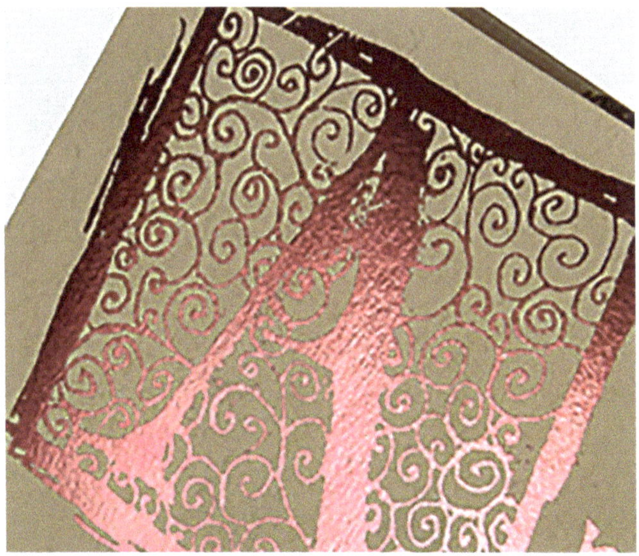

This is a method that transfers a thin layer of metallic tone or color to paper using heat and pressure. Using the letterpress printing equipment and a roll of metallic film, a heated raised metal type or image, stamps and adheres the image to the paper using pressure.

A common product for this finishing

technique are "seals" on certificates.

Numbering

Also using a letterpress, a numbering "machine" by itself or in combination with type, it is locked into the case or frame and put in to the press. When printing, the raised numbers on the machine are inked and print to the paper. At the same time a plunger on the machine, is automatically depressed by the press to ratchet the numbering head to a different figure or digit. The machine can be set to number forward or backwards.

Punching and Drilling

Punching

Punching is done by forcing a metal rod or punch through the paper to produce holes. It is a shearing action with a die placed below the paper. The holes are not necessarily round and often have odd shapes to them, such as for a product card that is to be placed on a hanger. In this case, the designer needs to calculate the weight of the product and its location on the card to identify placement of the hole punch so the product hangs straight.

Drilling

A hollow revolving bit, utilizing special bindery machines, is used to drill holes in paper. A common drilled product is paper for use in ring binders. Binderies that do this type of work would most likely have a drill equipment that has three drilling units to drill three holes into a at one time.

Varnishing

After an image is printed, it may be run back through the press and has a clear varnish"printed" on it. The coating makes the surface resistant to moisture and scratching. For some products like brochures, annual report covers, and

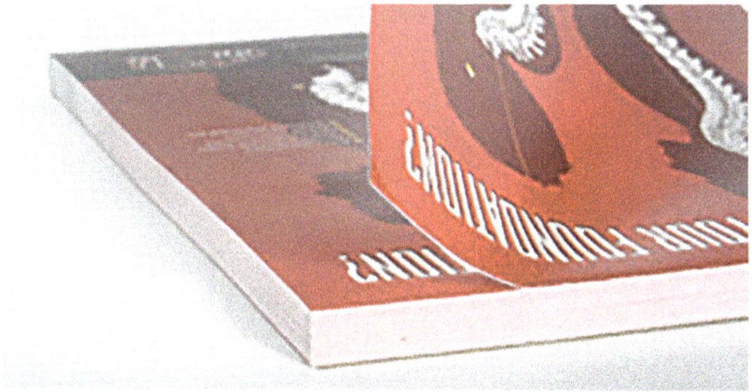

similar items, the entire page may be varnished. Or, it may be that certain images on a page are varnished enhancing the richness of the color. Even a varnish image may be printed by itself, creating a unique printed quality to the design.

Padding

In the chapter on paper, padding of NCR or carbonless paper provided sets to be used was described. Not to be confused with this technique, a different form of padding is the gluing of sheets of paper together to form pads of them. An Elmer's-like glue is painted on one edge of a stack of paper held in a clamp. When dry, they are separated into pads of 50, 100, or so sheets of paper.

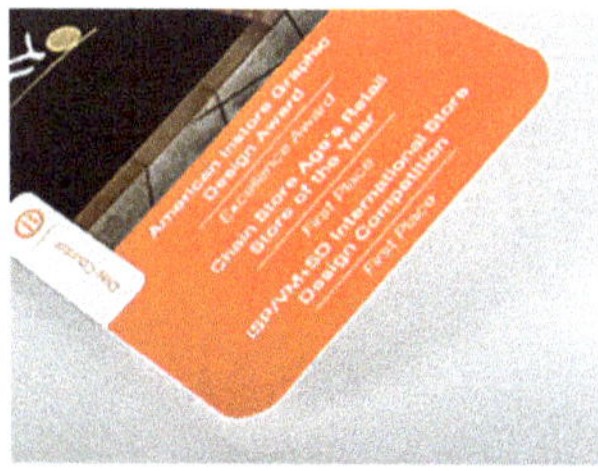

Other Finishing Methods

Round Corener

Creating a round corner using a special machine for the task, is used when the product will have a lot of use, such as a Pantone color book, where the corners will become worn by the continued use.

Spot UV

Spot UV is a post-printing coating technique that adds extra shine and protection to a print job. The technology uses UV light to add the varnish that coats a printed paper. The process can also simulate embossing and fold stamping.

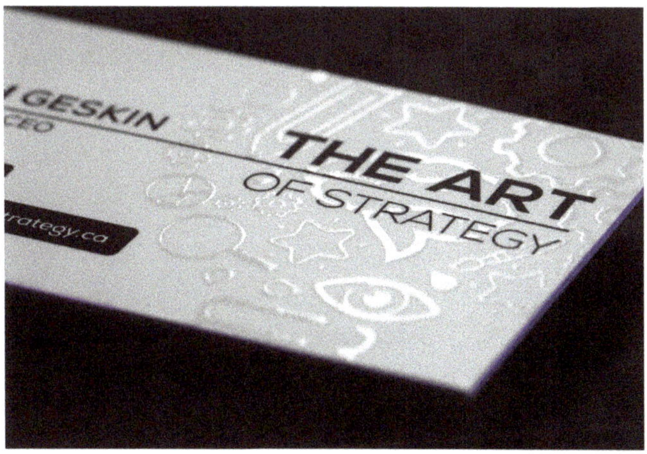

Image courtesy PrintShaQ.

Binding

As we saw in *Chapter 1 - History of Graphic Communications*, the first of what might be considered a "book," were clay tablets that had symbols scribed with a blunt instrument while the clay was moist and then left to dry in the sun and harden.

The First true books, that we would recognize as such, were of oriental origin. They were made from narrow strips of palm leaves or strips of bark. The writing was then scratched on the surface and then filled with lamp black to make the characters stand out. In order to keep the leaves flat it would then be common to place pieces of wood on either side of the pile of the palm leaves. To hold the pieces of wood and palm leaves together, holes would be bored through to the bark and a cord or leather throng woven through. Binding!

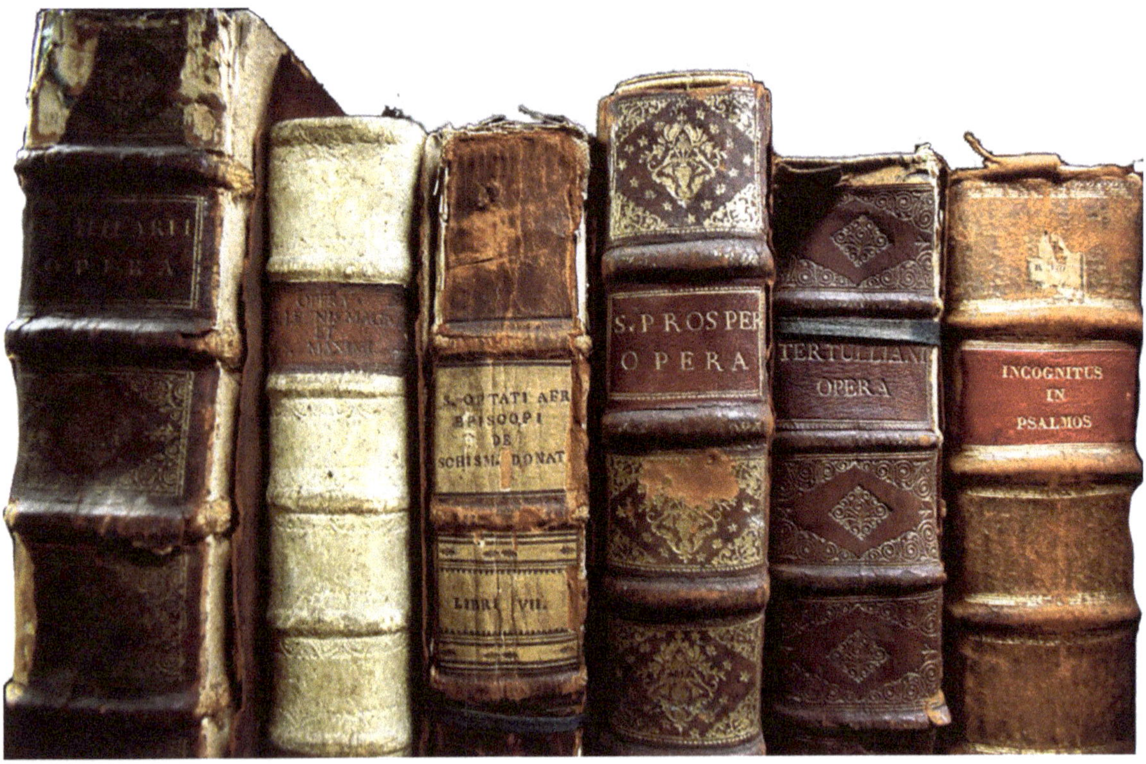

Scrolls were also an early form of a book. The Egyptians used papyrus reeds to fashion their substrate. The hand scribed scrolls were rolled up and stored. It is estimated that the famous library of Alexandria had over 700,000 volumes!

Modern day bookbinding began, about the 6th century with the change from the continuous roll, to books made up of separate sheets usually of vellum. The leaves of these books were held together in the correct order by sewing through the center fold onto flexible bands held at right angles to the back.

With the machine manufacture of paper and printing from movable type came a increase in publishing books. So much so that the occupation of printer and binder became separate.

A number of binding methods have been created since that time and provides options for binding documents

Types of Binding

Saddle Stitch

For this type of binding the signatures of the publications are printed, folded, and gathered together. In a machine called a stitcher, that looks like a giant sewing machine, the signatures are placed one on top of another on an angled plate like a saddle and stitched on the center spine.

Side Stitch

Similar to Saddle Stitch, the signatures are stitched on the side of signatures that lie next to each other.

Case Bound

This is the most complex and permanent form of binding, in which a rigid cover is attached to the signatures of the book by sewing and use of glued end sheets. This is the typical hard bound book we're all familiar with.

Perfect Binding

In this method of binding, the signatures of the book are set side by side in a clamp on a binding machine. The machine cuts off a portion and roughs up the spine. The signatures then are coated with a hot glue compound and are pressed onto a thicker paper cover sheet. The book then has three sides trimmed from it in a cutter resulting in the finished paperback book.

Other Binding Techniques

These techniques are **Plastic Comb**, **Spiral Wire**, and **Post**. All of these utilize some form of mechanical device. Plastic and Post offer the ability to add and remove pages later if desired.

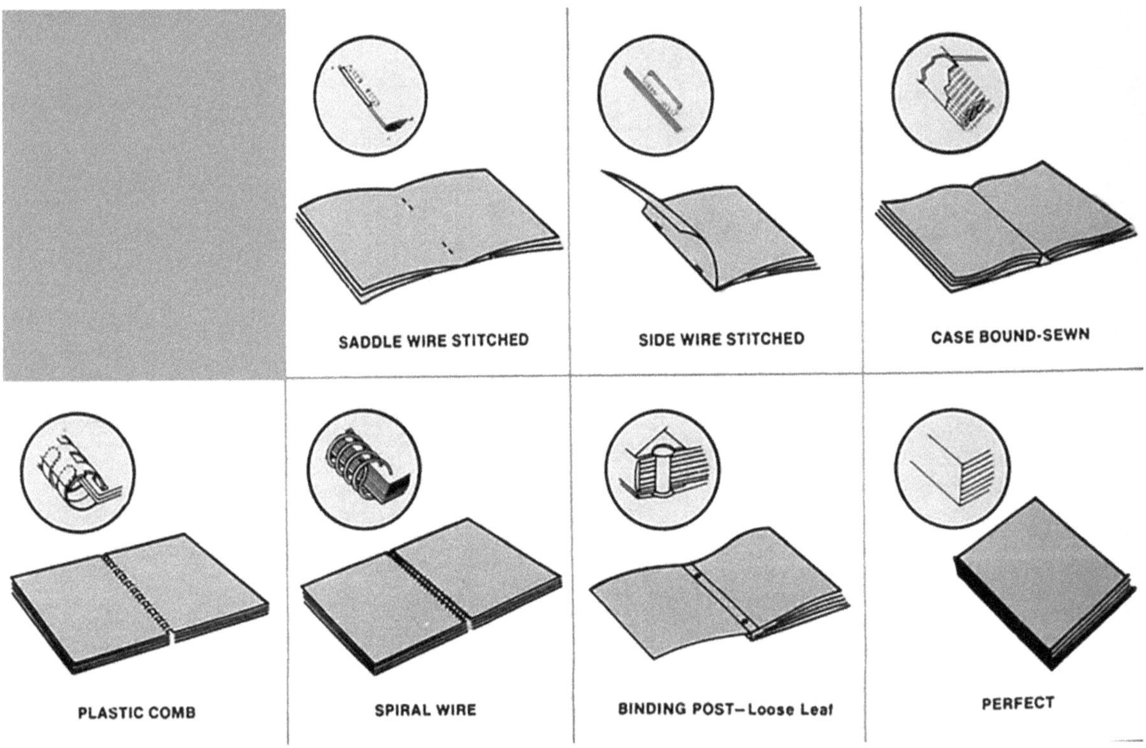

CHAPTER 9

What's Next?

"We must welcome the future, remembering that soon it will be the past; and we must respect the past, remembering that it was once all that was humanly possible."
— George Santayana

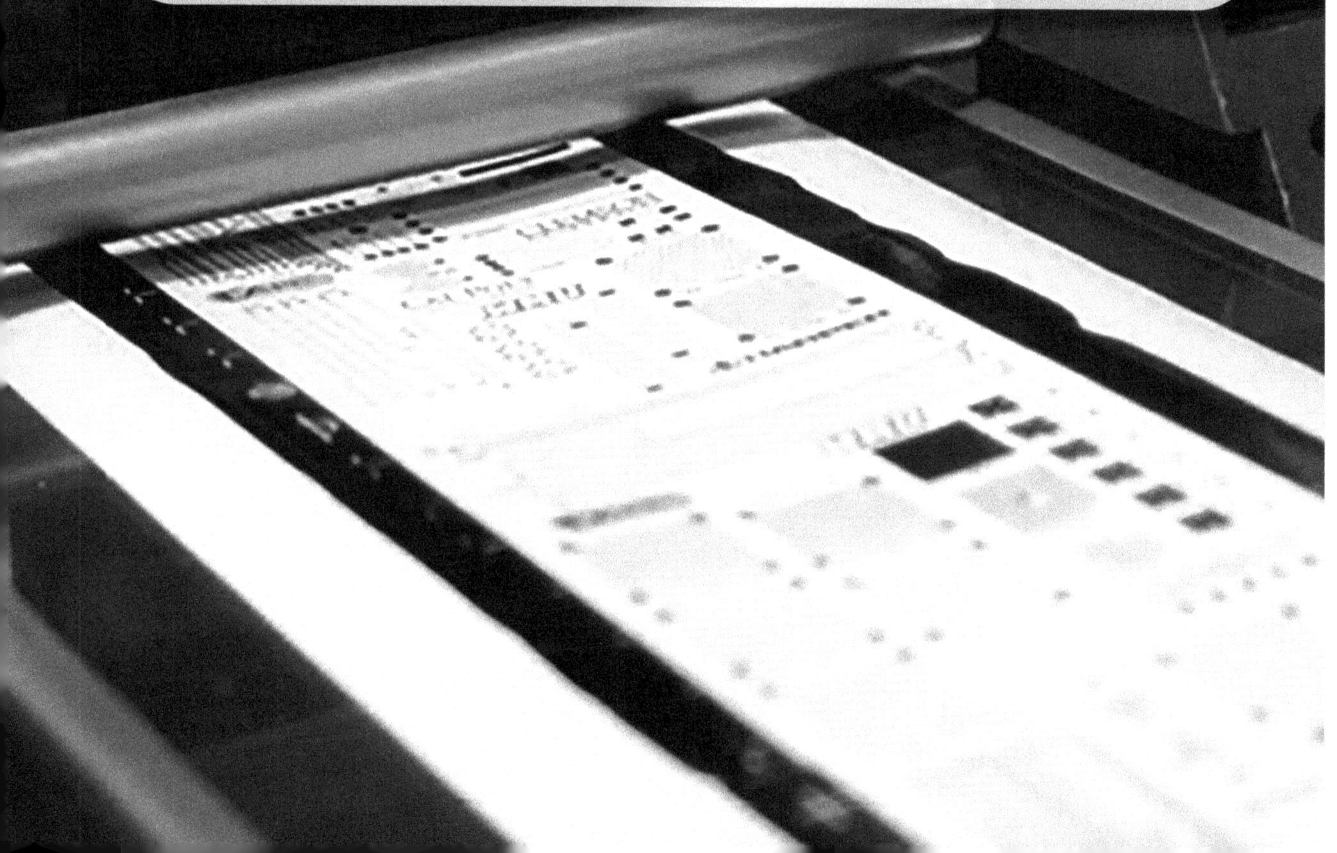

A Change in the Paradigm of Graphic Communications

No longer is the graphic arts an industry solely of paper and ink, nor has it been for quite some time. Following the move from relief or letterpress to lithography during the last century, the industry next change came with the advent of the personal computer, other digital hardware, and the creation of graphics and layout software— in a positive way. Non-professionals began creating layouts and therefore printing and publishing more. Certainly dedicated typesetters and graphic designers were affected adversely, and you can see in the chart below, a steady decrease in the number of printing firms over the past twenty some years.

This chart graphically indicates that by the mid-1990s, the graphic arts (traditional printing) has been in steady decline. An Investigation into Printing Industry Demographics—Frank Romano and David Broudy. © 2010 Printing Industry Center at RIT.

Frank Romano and David Broudy in their book, *"An Investigation into Printing Industry Demographics,"* suggest that the number of printing industry firms has been contracting since 1995, and they project that it will be close to 50 percent of its size in 2015 as compared with 1995. That trend has continued according to IBIS World, "with and annual revenue decline

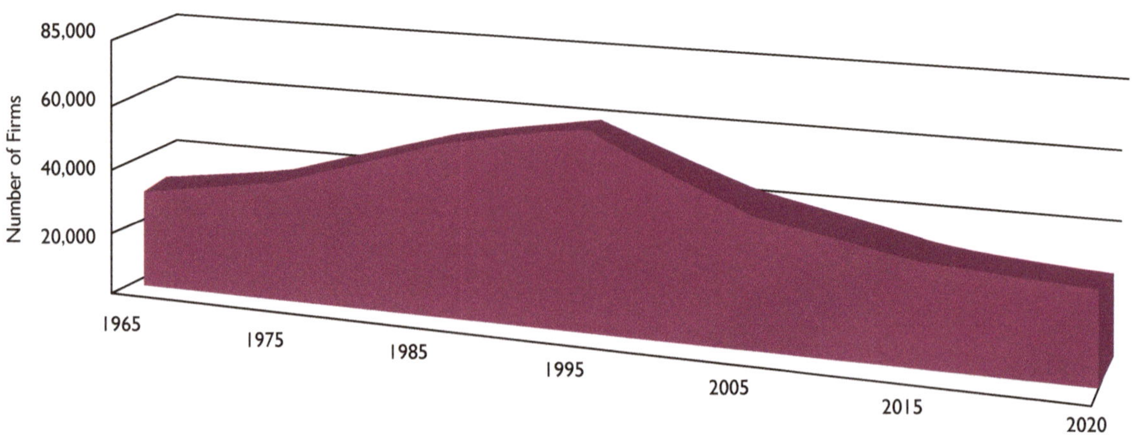

of 2.5% as as digital products and services have increasingly displaced traditional printed materials.The trend is expected to continue over the next five years." What brought on this demise of the industry where U.S. commercial printing shipments went from $141.8 billion in 1995 to $78.2 in 2013, consumer price index adjusted dollars? — Strategies for Management analysis of U.S. Department of Commerce. In addition to the elephant in the room, the Internet, which has grown from an estimated 16 million users in 1996 to 5,168,780,607 as of March 2021 — *internetworldstats.com*, other factors have contributed as well to this downfall.

In *"This Point Forward— The New Start the Marketplace Demands,"* Joseph W. Webb, Ph.D. and Richard M. Romano lists several: broadband increase in capacity and usage, multitude of devices, many mobile(300+ million iPhones and 170+ million iPads), and ease of Internet access. They also indicate the cost of printing increases verses the declining cost of computers and wireless service. Factor in oddly, the steady climb of U.S. Postal rates and one can see why many have turned from print to digital to communicate and receive information. This is direct competition for the product of communication.

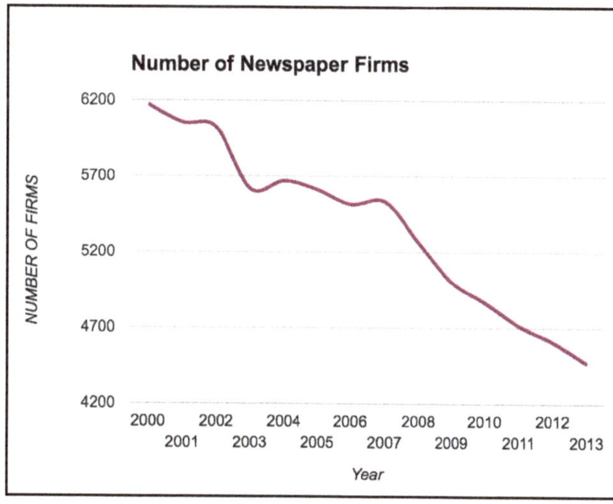

The number of newspaper printers, as an example, are now more than half of what they were in 1995 6,500 to 3,476. Book printers went from 430 to 245 in that same period.

Lastly on this subject, the recent economic woes, have affected the graphics industry like many others, where some went out of business, were consolidated, or their market share was absorbed by other printers. Historically, the printing industry has done well in good and bad times remaining relatively stable. When there is money, people and businesses spend for things that aren't always needed. During poor economic times business tend to spend for marketing, advertising, and promotion. Print is not the only media to do this now, and may even be less effective in many cases.

So what's next? Graphics businesses have been diversifying and providing other services and products to maintain the core business of printing. New or improved technologies are providing other opportunities as well. The increased quality of digital printing, in particular ink jet with better quality inks and even continuous-feed systems, is a current trend. High-speed inkjet presses tend to bring in new business from existing clients and from new customers. In the article in Printing Impressions, *"Inkjet Adoption Fuels Rise of 2014 Inkjet Summit,"* stated, "Inkjet press owners all agreed that being able to eliminate or reduce warehousing costs, print short runs, provide customized or personalized documents and eliminate preprinted forms all resonate with document owners."

Mentioned earlier in *Chapter 8 -Finishing and Binding*", new finishing techniques, such as Spot UV and others such as glitter coating, metalic sheen, and reticulation effect, bring that tactile sense to the printed product, especially packaging, that can't be replicated by digital media.

Addtionally, adaptation of current printing methods and utilization of common graphics software for alternative purposes is happening as we will see in the next section.

Variable Data Printing

Variable Data Printing, or Publishing is similar to mail-merge technique using fields in Microsoft Word or other word-processing software, whereby data from a database is inserted within a document that individualizes it. The resulting letters, envelopes, or other printed document are rather basic in nature.

A rather new VDP process that uses Adobe InDesign and a plug-in, provides great design control, flexibility and high volume customized and individualized printing. Layouts are created using InDesign as normally would be done for traditionally printed products. Where type is to change, a field is inserted much like would be done in Word. The fields are generated in a plug-in panel, such as uCreate Print, developed by XMPie that is added to InDesign.

In addition to text, variable use of images, "descriptions", QR codes, and PURLs may be utilized. QLingo programming allows for if/else statements and more.

A nice feature is the ability to use a Adobe Photoshop image that has a coded layer that will be a variable that XMPie can identify and link to a database to generate a custom image.

An Adobe Photoshop with a text layer that has a layer effect applied to it. Note the layer name has a special coding used in the variable image creation process. In this example, the "first" name changes as the Variable Data Printing takes palce.

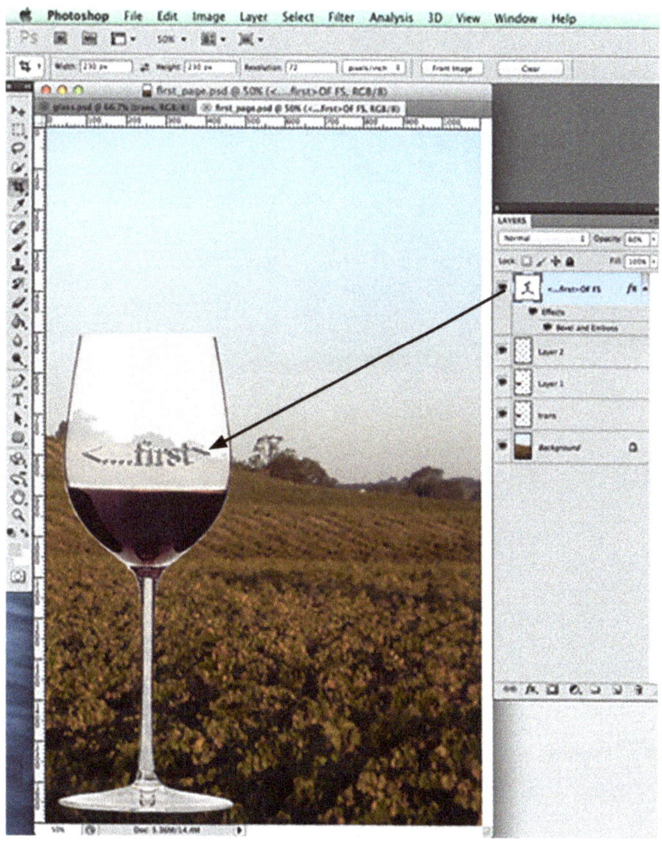

When the document is exported from InDesign, PDF files for each individual document are created and utilized in the digital printing process to produce the final documents.

Below is a prototype for a Wine Club newsletter in which the customer name, address, phone, PURL, and QR change. In addition, since wine clubs typically offer clubs of red, white, or mixed, the names, descriptions, and bottle images change as well based upon the club the customer belongs to. Note also, the person's name on the wine glass.

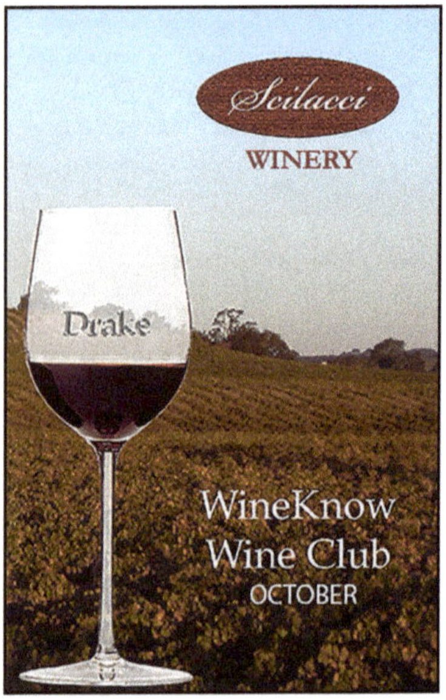

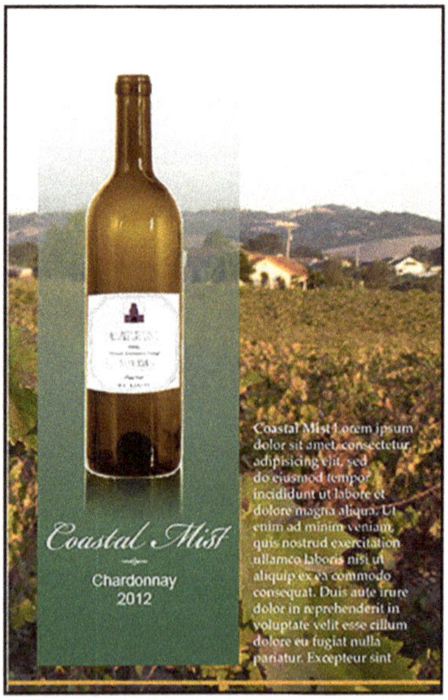

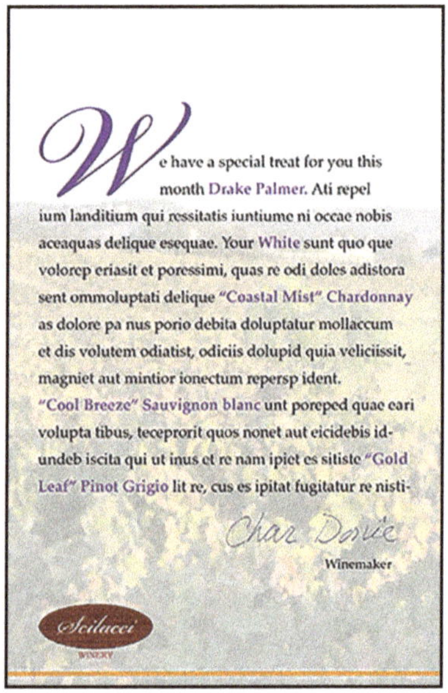

Functional Printing

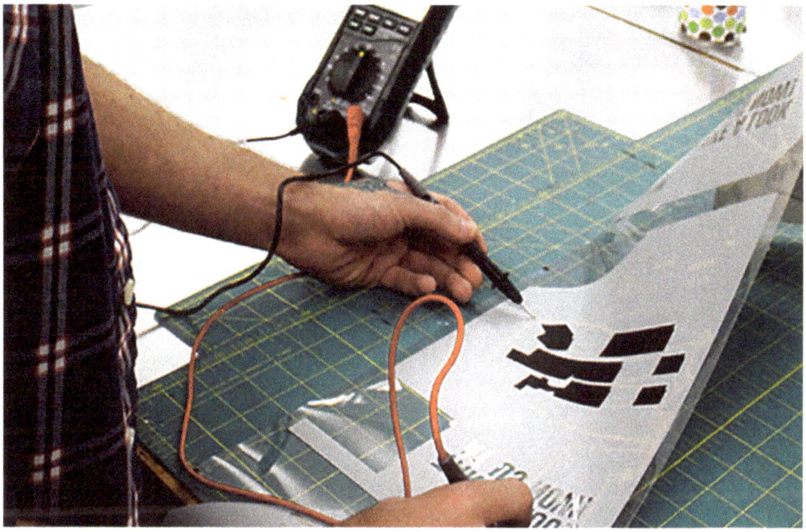

Functional printing, in contrast to graphic printing, focuses on the application of active inks. These active materials may be conductive, insulating, reactive, sensing, optically variable or active in some other way. In printed electronics, conventional or hybrid printing methods are used to deposit conductive and insulating inks to create novel, functional products. It may seem unusual to print electronics when silicon based fabrication is so mature but there are benefits: a) potential for cost benefits; b) additive versus subtractive processing; c) potential for more environmentally friendly materials.

Flexography, gravure, screen-printing, inkjet and several less know method technologies are used for printing electronics. Other products, according to Cal Poly, San Luis Obispo Professor Malcolm Keif, of the Graphic Communication, department and graduate coordinator of the Printed Electronics and Functional Imaging program, are disposable organic

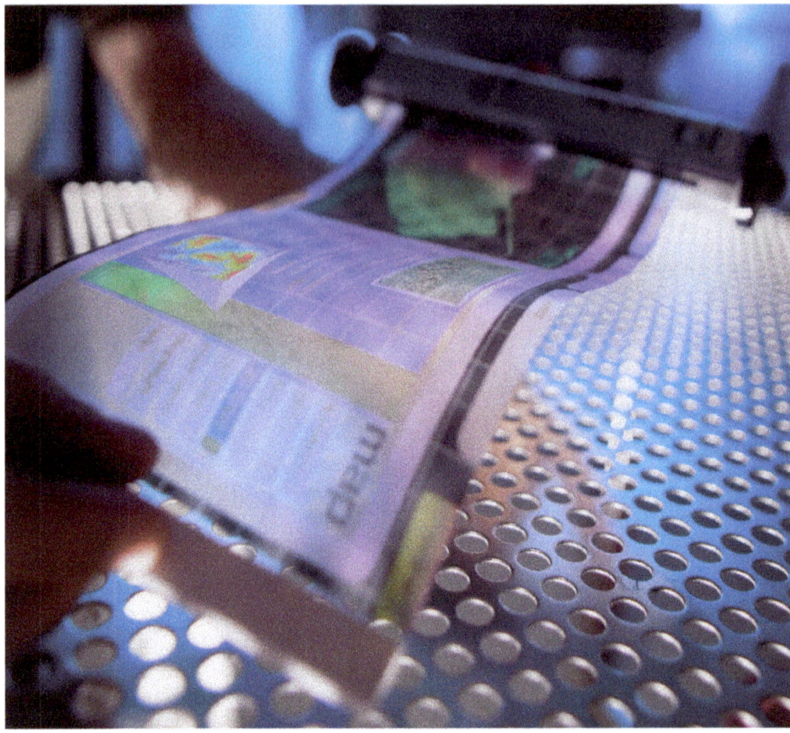

Flexible display technology developed by Arizona State University, as funded by the U.S. Army

photovoltaics (OPVs) or solar cells, sensors and medical uses such as transdermal applications, and electroluminescent (EL) signs and displays— with other undetermined uses.

IDTechEx, in their *"Printed, Organic & Flexible Electronics Forecasts, Players & Opportunities 2014-2024,"* report projects that the total market for printed, flexible and organic electronics will grow from $23.97 billion in 2014 to $70.39 billion in 2024.

Digital Publishing

Digital publishing is the creation of electronic books, commonly referred to as an e-book, and that is simply a printed book in an electronic format. E-books can be produced in numerous formats. Often the books can be partial or entirely re-purposed print layouts. Digital books can be categorized into five types: PDF, Web page, ePubs, interactive digital books, and apps. Each of these with varying degrees of ease of construction and extent of options.

PDF

Portable Document Format or PDF file has been around for a long time. Mainly used for print media, it encapsulates images, fonts, and other information within the document. This helps to solve technical issues common to other methods. More recently the PDF format is viewable in digital format using

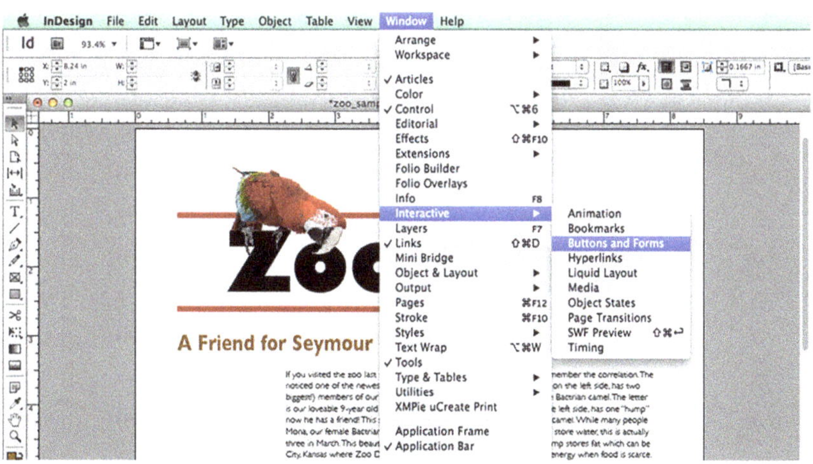

Using the interactive panel, buttons, forms, hyperlinks and more can be added to layouts and exported as interactive PDF files.

a web browser. This type of E-book is typically identical to the printed version, usually downloadable by chapter or with bookmarks for navigation. PDFs can even be interactive having buttons that perform tasks, such as going to the next page with transitions. Audio and video may also be included. These with varying degrees of functionality.

Web Page

One wouldn't think of a web page as an eBook but in reality it is a type of eBook. In its rawest state it is all text, much like novels and other types of books. Web pages use HTML (hypertext Markup Language), a programming method to provide basic formatting such as paragraph and headings. Of course images could be included on the page. But for most books, text is fine and one can easily create a web page eBook by writing the copy or even by downloading public domain original text from such web sites such as *http://www.gutenberg.org/*. Also at this site one can download other eBooks such as ePubs and files for use on the Kindle and other readers. The web page could be created by using an online service like Wordpress or using professional software like Adobe Dreamweaver. One can also "publish online" for Adobe InDesign, in essence creating a Website of pages.

Electronic publication, or ePubs became an official standard of the International Digital Publishing Forum in September 2007. Note that it is fairly basic in layout with a single column with in-line images. However, its advantage over other options is that e-readers are most smartphones, tablets, and computers.

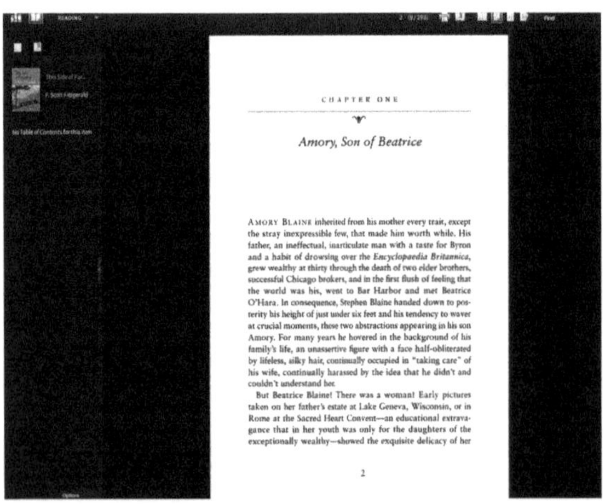

CHAPTER ONE

Amory, Son of Beatrice

AMORY BLAINE inherited from his mother every trait, except the stray inexpressible few, that made him worth while. His father, an ineffectual, inarticulate man with a taste for Byron and a habit of drowsing over the *Encyclopaedia Britannica*, grew wealthy at thirty through the death of two elder brothers, successful Chicago brokers, and in the first flush of feeling that the world was his, went to Bar Harbor and met Beatrice O'Hara. In consequence, Stephen Blaine handed down to posterity his height of just under six feet and his tendency to waver at crucial moments, these two abstractions appearing in his son Amory. For many years he hovered in the background of his family's life, an unassertive figure with a face half-obliterated by lifeless, silky hair, continually occupied in "taking care" of his wife, continually harassed by the idea that he didn't and couldn't understand her.

But Beatrice Blaine! There was a woman! Early pictures taken on her father's estate at Lake Geneva, Wisconsin, or in Rome at the Sacred Heart Convent—an educational extravagance that in her youth was only for the daughters of the exceptionally wealthy—showed the exquisite delicacy of her

2

ePub

This type of format is more like a traditional book that we are accustomed to than the first two examples. ePubs are fairly basic in nature and imitate traditional printed books in that they contain text and a few graphics. Though they have chapters, in essence they are one long continuous document. ePubs have been a around for sometime and can be made using various methods including using Word. The finished ePub is an XML (Extensible Markup Language) file which is a markup language that defines a set of rules for encoding documents in a format that is both human-readable and machine-readable.

More recently Adobe InDesign has been used to create ePubs. At first this required creating a document for each chapter and then combining them into the ePub when exported. Adobe has since streamlined the process with the latest version of the software.

Images are placed in-line and flow with the text. Paragraph styles, in conjunction with a created table of contents, are used to provide navigation and links within the ePub. No page numbers are used.

ePubs can be read on computers using software such as Adobe Digital Editions and Apple iBooks Reader, and on tablets. Some readers have the option of making notes, looking up words, turn pages etc. Since ePubs are created in many ways other than by using InDesign, such as those produced by Amazon (for the Kindle) and Barnes and Noble Nook, there are often Digital Restrictions Management (DRM) systems that can make them proprietary to the type of tablet used.

eBooks

This format is more like a digital book that we would think of that is interactive and can contain multimedia. Apple iBooks Author is an application that has been used recently to create eBooks however, Apple has phased out the app in favor of Pages which contains many of iBooks Author's features. Some options such as including "quizzes" are not

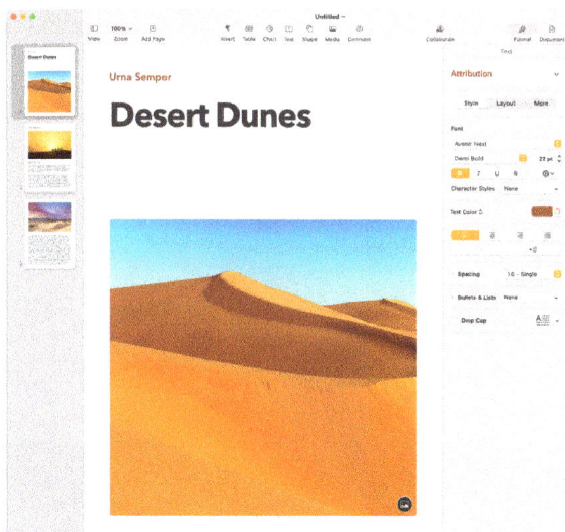

Apple's Pages has taken over the duties of the phased out iBooks Author.

currently part of the app. Though the focus is on creating books, there is plenty of room to create other types of layouts including reports and newsletters.

Apps

The last type of digital books is a stand-alone application, such as ones created for an iPad. With features like those described in an eBook, these apps can also have motion, transitions, user interaction, and much more.

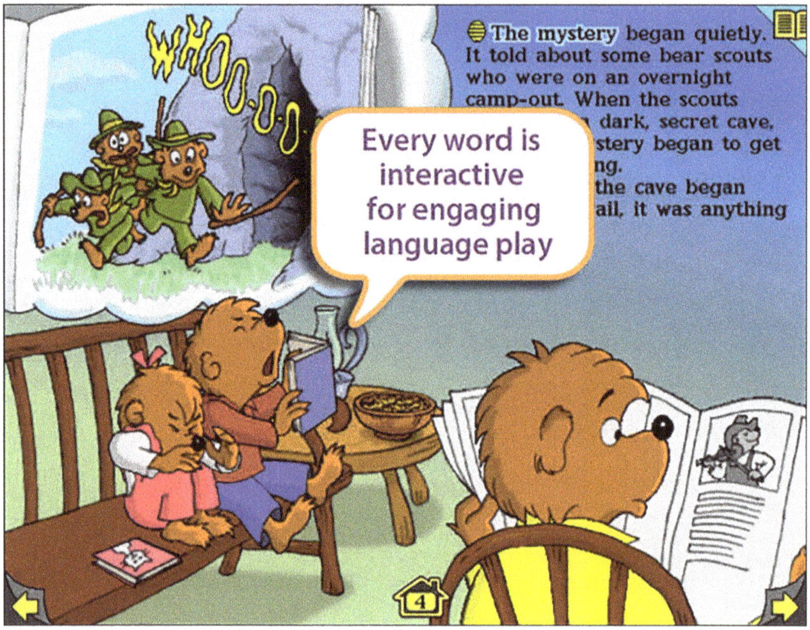

A children's interactive book, "Berenstain Bears in the Dark," by Wanderful, Inc.

CHAPTER 10

Conclusion

"Right and wrong do not exist in graphic design. There is only effective and non-effective communication."
— Peter Bilak

In the end, how does one design and create something that is attractive, contemporary, and provides communication? It's not the new technology, it's not the new software that does this, rather it's the person that has insightful perception, has an understanding of basic design concepts, pays attention to detail, and knows a trick or two that does.

So go forth and follow the processes outlined in this book. Using good perception, identify the design problem and the desired message to be communicated. Select appropriate colors, typography, materials, and reproduction methods. Utilize principles of design to produce graphics and layouts, using suitable technology, that when reproduced in print or digital form, will effectively and efficiently provide communication.

Glossary

Accordion Fold

Bindery term for two or more parallel folds which open like an accordion.

Analogous Colors

An analogous color scheme consists of 3-5 hues that are adjacent to each other on color wheel.

Basis Weight

Weight in pounds of a ream of paper cut to the basic size for its grade.

Bind

To fasten together sheets or signatures and attach covers with glue, wire, thread, or by other means.

Bindery

Print shop department or separate business that does trimming, folding, binding and other finishing tasks.

Blanket

In offset printing, its the thick rubber sheet (on a roller) that transfers ink from the plate to paper.

Bleed

Printing that goes off the edge of a sheet after trimming.

Blind Embossing

A bas-relief emboss without ink or foil.

Bond Paper

Grade of strong, durable paper generally used for letterheads, envelops, etc.

Book Paper

Grade of coated or uncoated paper suitable for books, magazines, and general printing.

Byte

A byte is a unit of digital information that most often consists of eight bits.

Case Bind

To bind by gluing signatures together to a case made of binder's board covered with fabric, plastic, or leather. The type of binding used in hard bound books.

Cast Coated

Coated paper with a high gloss finish.

Coated paper

Clay coated paper with a smooth finish.

Collate

Bindery term for the gathering of sheets or signatures.

Color Bar

Strip of colors printed at the edge of a press sheet used to evaluate ink density by the press operator.

Color Correction

Methods of improving color to be more realistic.

Color Matching System

A system of numbered ink swatches used to communicate color. A good example is the Pantone Matching System or PMS color.

Color Separation

The process of separating color originals into the four primary printing colors, cyan, magenta, yellow, and black. For photographic images, this means creating four halftone separations.

Comb Binding

To bind by inserting teeth of flexible plastic comb into holes punched into a stack of paper.

Continuous-tone
All photographs and images that contain gradient tones from black to white.

Complimentary Colors
A complementary color scheme consists of two hues on opposite sides of the color wheel.

Copy
All furnished materials (type, pictures, artwork, etc.) to be used in the production of printing or digital products.

Cover Paper
Papers used for covers of catalogs, brochures, booklets or similar products.

Crop Marks
Lines on an image showing the portion to be eliminated.

Crossover
An image that extends from one page of a publication across the gutter to the opposite page.

Dandy Roll
Wire cylinder containing embossed images that create watermarks during the papermaking process.

Densitometer
A device used to measure and control the density of color during the printing process.

Desktop Publishing
Begun in the mid-1980s, personal computers such as IBM and Macintosh, used new WYSIWYG software programs, such a Aldus PageMaker to create layouts on a computer. The term is attributed to Paul Brained of Aldus. Up until this time cut and paste using rubber cement or hot wax was used to create layout that then would be photographed and made into negatives which were used to make lithographic printing plates.

Die-cutting
The process of using a sharp steel rule to cut special shapes for labels, boxes or containers from printed sheets.

Dot Gain or Spread

Dots printing larger on paper than intended. Typically occurs in uncoated paper such as newsprint.

Dummy

Yes, a real graphic's term. A preliminarily layout showing position of illustrations and text as they will be in the final printed piece. May also be blank sheets of paper that are numbered to indicate the imposition of pages in a publication for design purposes or production.

Duotone

Photographic image printed using two different halftones and colors, often, black and light color like yellow or light blue.

Electrostatic

A process for printing or copying in which electrostatic forces are used to form the image in powder or ink directly on the surface to be printed.

Emboss

To press an image into paper so that it creates a relief image.

Engraving

A method of cutting or incising a design into a material, usually metal, with a sharp tool called a graver. One of the intaglio methods of making prints, in engraving, a print can be made by inking such an incised (engraved) surface. It may also refer to a print produced in this way. Most contemporary engraving is done in the production of currency, certificates, etc.

Etching

An intaglio printing process in which an etching needle is used to draw into a wax ground applied over a metal plate. Sometimes, rosin is sprinkled on the surface of the plate, and heated. The technique provides a tonal image area. The plate is then submerged in a series of acid baths, each biting into the metal surface only where unprotected by the ground. The ground is removed, ink is forced into the etched depressions, the un-etched surfaces wiped, and an impression is printed. Also, both the design etched on a plate and an impression made from an etched plate. Too often confused with engraving.

Foil Emboss

To foil stamp and emboss an image.

Foil Stamping

Letterpress printing method using a thin metallic or pigmented film and a die.

4-Color Process

Printing technique using the four process colors of ink (cyan, magenta, yellow, and black), to simulate color photographs or illustrations. Also known as a subtractive process or full-color printing.

Flexography

Flexography is a form of relief printing that utilizes flexible rubber, nylon, or plastic plates or cylinders, and fluid inks or dyes for printing on fabrics and impervious materials such as plastics, as well as on paper. Packaging products are commonly produced by this method.

French Fold

Two folds at right angles to each other.

Grain

In paper, it is the direction in which most of the fibers lie.

Gravure

Sometimes referred to as Rotogravure because of the cylinders that the images are on, is a type of intaglio printing process, which involves engraving the image onto an image carrier. In gravure printing, the image is engraved onto a cylinder because, like offset printing and flexography, it uses a rotary printing press. Once a staple of newspaper photo features, the rotogravure process is still used for commercial printing of magazines, postcards, and corrugated (cardboard) product packaging.

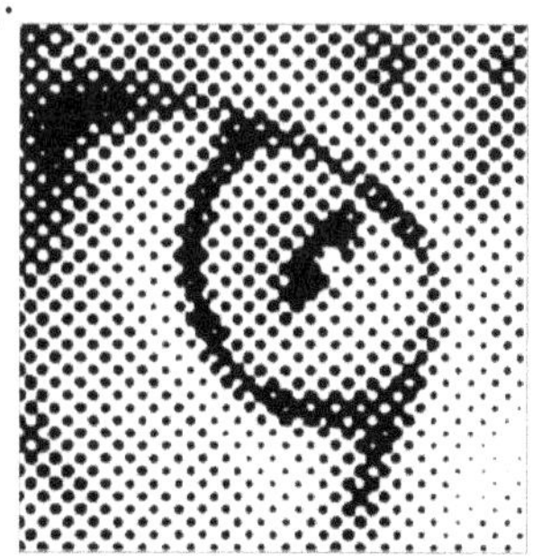

Halftones

A halftone is a technique used to simulate continuous tone imagery in printing using variable size dots.

Hickey

I put this one in just for grins. Yes, like *dummy*, it is a real printing term. It refers to a donut-shaped spot or imperfection in printing, most visible in areas of heavy ink coverage. Any spots or specks due to dirt on the press, dried ink, paper particles, etc.

Highlight

The lightest areas in a photograph or halftone.

Hue

Hue is the same as most would call color. It is the inherent color referred to by name, such as yellow or pink.

Hypertext Markup Language (HTML)

Hypertext Markup Language or HTML is the foundational structure of a Web page. Using "tags," it tells a Web browser how to display a Web page's words and images for the user.

Imposition

Arrangement of pages for printing of a publications, such that the front and back of each sheet printed, a signature, contains the correct page relationship.

Impressions

The number of copies being printed.

Inkjet

Inkjet printing is a type of computer printing that creates a digital image by propelling droplets of ink onto paper, plastic, or other substrates.

Intaglio

Intaglio printing is printing from a recessed or sunken image area. Three forms of Intaglio printing include: engraving, etching, and Gravure.

Laid Finish

Parallel lines on paper which simulate the surface of handmade paper.

Letterpress

Common industry term for relief printing. Letterpress was the primary printing method in use until the mid-1950s. It's main uses today are for specialty printing and finishing techniques such as embossing and foil stamping.

Lines per Inch

The number of lines or rows of dots per inch in a halftone.

Lithography

Lithography is printing from a flat surface in which the image has been created photographically (or digitally) and reproduction based upon the theory that water and oil do not mix. Invented by Alois Senefelder, 1798.

Makeready

In printing, it is all the activities required to set up a press before printing, which typically includes printing a few copies.

Monochromatic Color

A monochromatic color scheme consists of one hue, varying values (lightness, darkness).

Munsell Color System

A three-dimensional color system that describes color that uses 100 steps for hue, starting with five main colors and five additional colors, and adopts an ordering system with 10 units of value and an open scale called chroma (similar to saturation).

Morie

Undesirable pattern in a halftone or screen tints, made when screens are improperly aligned. Also occurs when a printed halftone is halftoned.

Offset Lithography

This printing techniques is a combination of a method- Lithography, and an additional process called "offset." It is called offset since the image doesn't go directly from the plates to the paper, but is offset or transferred to a "blanket" cylinder and then printed to paper.

Opacity

The property of paper which minimizes "showthrough" of printing from the backside or next sheet. Could also be associated with the transparency of computer created images.

Pantone Matching System (PMS)

A color matching system commonly used by designers and printers, that consists of color swatches and formulas. Most graphics software provide for the specification of these colors as well.

Perfect Bound

Binding of a book in which the cover is hot glued to interior pages, and then trimmed.

Pica

Unit of measurement used in typesetting to measure line length. One pica = 1/6 of an inch or is equal to 12 points.

Point

Unit of measurement for type used for measuring type size and line spacing (leading). Equal to 1/72 inch.

Pressureless Printing

Different than electrostatic (Xerox) printing, pressureless printing or ink jet printing has droplets of tightly controlled ink sprayed onto paper or other substrates.

Primary Colors (Traditional)

These are colors that cannot be created through the mixing of other colors. The the colors in a traditional color wheel- three primary colors of red, yellow, and blue.

Ragged Left (Flush Right)

Typesetting format in which type is justified on the right edge. Common typesetting format that has a casual feel with little hyphenation.

Ragged Right (Flush Left)

Typesetting format in which type is justified on the left edge. Not commonly used, except as a caption on a image on the left side of the image.

Ream

Five hundred sheets of paper.

Recto

Right hand page of an open publication.

Register

Positioning and aligning of images when printing.

Registration Marks

Printed lines or "targets on a layout used by printers for positioning and alignment of colors.

Relief Printing

Printing from a raised or relief inked surface. Early beginnings in China with fired clay "characters." Later, Johann Gutenberg further developed the method (unknowingly) using movable individual type and printing press.

Saddle Stitch

To bind by stapling sheets together where they fold at the spine.

Saturation

When referring to color, it is component of color that is the amount or intenseness of a hue (color).

Score

To compress paper along a line, typically done with a letterpress, so it will fold more easily preventing the fibers in the paper from breaking.

Screen Printing

Printing by forcing ink through an open image area. Silk or more likely a synthetic fabric stretched on a frame has a stencil placed on it that blocks the non-image area, and allows ink to be forced through the porous fabric using a squeegee.

Secondary Colors (Traditional)

Secondary colors are created by combining two primary colors such as yellow and red to form orange. The other two secondary colors are violet and green.

Shadow

The darkest areas in a photograph or halftone.

Side Stitch

To bind by stapling through sheets along one edge.

Signature

A sheet of printed pages which, when folded, become part of a publication.

Spine

Binding edge of a signature or publication.

Spoilage

Paper wasted during makeready, during printing, and bindery operations.

Substrate

Any material on which printing is done.

Subtractive Colors

A color separation system in which primary color filters red, green, and blue are used to "subtract out" secondary colors of cyan, magenta, and yellow respectfully. A fourth color black is obtained by using all filters. This process is used to reproduced continuous tone color images which is known as process color, four-color, or full-color printing.

Tints

Various even tone areas of a solid color. 20% blue as example.

Tertiary Colors (Traditional)

A tertiary color is a color made by mixing either one primary color with one secondary color, or two secondary colors.

Trapping

The use of chokes and spreads of to different ink colors to provide a slight overlap to aid in printing registration.

Trim Size

Size of the printed product after the last trim is made.

Value

Value refers to the lightness or darkness of something. As a component of color it is the lighter or darker version of a hue. Adobe Photoshop calls value, brightness.

Variable Data Printing or Variable Data Publishing (VDP)

VDP is a type of on-demand printing process in which text and graphics is altered in-process to create individualized printing and publication.

Verso

Left-hand page of an open publication.

Watermark

Distinctive design created during manufacturing using a *dandy roll.*

Web Press

A press, such as a newspaper press, which prints from rolls (or webs) of paper.

Woodblock Printing

An early form of relief printing text, images or patterns used widely throughout East Asia and first developed in China circa 200 AD. The non-image area is carved from a block of wood leaving a raised imaged that is inked and used to print from.

www.ingramcontent.com/pod-product-compliance
Lightning Source LLC
LaVergne TN
LVHW070853210926
848482LV00016B/922